THE
1920s

John F. Wukovits, *Book Editor*

David L. Bender, *Publisher*
Bruno Leone, *Executive Editor*
Bonnie Szumski, *Series Editor*
David M. Haugen, *Managing Editor*

Greenhaven Press, Inc., San Diego, California

AMERICA'S DECADES

Every effort has been made to trace the owners of copyrighted material. The articles in this volume may have been edited for content, length, and/or reading level. The titles have been changed to enhance the editorial purpose.

No part of this book may be reproduced or used in any form or by any means, electrical, mechanical, or otherwise, including, but not limited to, photocopy, recording, or any information storage and retrieval system, without prior written permission from the publisher.

Library of Congress Cataloging-in-Publication Data

The 1920s / John F. Wukovits, book editor.
    p.   cm. — (America's decades)
    Includes bibliographical references and index.
    ISBN 0-7377-0297-4 (pbk. : alk. paper) —
    ISBN 0-7377-0298-2 (lib. : alk. paper)
    1. United States—Civilization—1918–1945. 2. Nineteen twenties. I. Title: Nineteen twenties. II. Wukovits, John F., 1944–   . III. Series

E169.1 .A1128 2000
973.91'5—dc21   99-087874
                                                            CIP

©2000 by Greenhaven Press, Inc.
P.O. Box 289009, San Diego, CA 92198-9009

Printed in the U.S.A.

Contents

Foreword   7

Introduction: A Decade of Prosperity and Turmoil   9

Chapter 1: Politics

1. Stock Market Madness *by Cabell Phillips*   21
Many people wanted to forget the suffering and devastation of World War I and return to a normal life. Part of that desire manifested itself in people buying stocks to get rich quick.

2. Unfit for the Job: The Presidency of Warren G. Harding *by Edmund Stillman*   29
Warren G. Harding showed that even a person of limited capabilities could rise to the top office. Unfortunately, the nation suffered as a result.

3. "Keep Cool with Coolidge"—the Hands-Off Approach of President Calvin Coolidge
by Paul Sann   42
Calvin Coolidge succeeded Warren Harding, but he made little impact on the nation. Instead of firm leadership, he allowed the nation to drift without direction.

4. The Great Crash Ends an Era of Prosperity
by Edwin P. Hoyt   47
For ten years residents of the United States enjoyed unparalleled prosperity and good times. That collapsed in 1929, when the Great Crash ushered in a decade of suffering.

Chapter 2: Intolerance in the 1920s

1. The Ku Klux Klan Strengthens Its Hand
by Arnold S. Rice   58
Intolerance experienced a rebirth in the 1920s. One organization that preached hatred and bigotry, the Ku Klux Klan, found new support in northern states.

2. Segregation in Housing: A Case Study
by John F. Wukovits   69
One black family hoped to live in a white neighborhood. When one town's reaction led to a killing, famed
attorney Clarence Darrow argued on the family's behalf.

3. A Jailed Teacher: John Scopes and the
Antievolution Law *by Don Nardo*   82
Intolerance reached into the nation's classrooms to
produce one of the decade's most compelling courtroom cases. Teacher John Scopes's challenge to a law
banning the teaching of evolution carried implications
for all instruction.

4. Sacco Guilty, Vanzetti Innocent? *by Francis Russell*   97
Another trial captured headlines throughout the
decade. Even today, the controversy remains over
the innocence and guilt of two immigrants.

Chapter 3: Prohibition

1. Prohibition Dries Up a Thirsty Nation
by Page Smith   111
One of the most unique experiments of the 1920s was
the nation's attempt to expunge alcohol from daily life.
After an arduous political battle, the law took effect,
and the nation was never the same.

2. An Amazing Pair of Prohibition Agents
by Herbert Asbury   118
To battle the efforts of organized crime, the U.S.
government hired hundreds of agents. Two of the
most talented at capturing their quarries were the
men called Izzy and Moe.

3. America Ignores the Law *by Edward Behr*   131
As meticulous as Izzy and Moe and other federal agents
were, most people in the nation were determined to
enjoy alcohol. They sometimes had to create ingenious
methods.

Chapter 4: Culture and Entertainment

1. **Women Enjoy a New Morality**
   by Frederick Lewis Allen   141
   Fewer restrictions inhibited women in the 1920s. They
   reacted in ways that challenged established procedures
   and created new ones.

2. **The Growth of Black Pride** *by Geoffrey Perrett*   153
   Black artists and writers spurred a cultural renaissance,
   while other African Americans packed their belongings
   and moved to the northern states. Their actions produced ripples that changed American society.

3. **Film Comedy Comes of Age in the 1920s**
   by Gerald Mast and Bruce F. Kawin   164
   The infant Hollywood film industry turned to comedy
   in the decade. Consequently, famous stars like Charlie
   Chaplin drew millions of paying customers to the
   theaters each week.

4. **An Epic Feat: Gertrude Ederle Swims the Channel**
   by Susan Ware   178
   The decade produced sports champions who are
   revered eighty years later. One proved that a female
   could achieve notable results in the athletic arena.

Chapter 5: Science and Invention

1. **A Musical Explosion** *by Page Smith*   191
   The 1920s produced a wide variety of music. Romantic
   ballads vied with a flurry of jazz and blues for listeners.

2. **Automobiles Fuel the Transportation Revolution**
   by Fon W. Boardman Jr.   197
   Advances occurred in many areas of transportation in
   the 1920s. Chief among them was the automobile.

3. **Charles Lindbergh Crosses an Ocean**
   by Walter S. Ross   206
   An epic milestone happened in 1927 when a shy
   aviator flew his small aircraft across the Atlantic Ocean
   to France. His feat united two continents and produced
   one of the nation's most acclaimed heroes.

Chapter 6: Legacy

1. The Nation Plummets into the Abyss of Depression *by Robert Goldston*   222

The good times and fun of the 1920s ended when the 1929 stock market crash heralded the Great Depression of the 1930s. President Herbert Hoover did what he could to alleviate the economic disaster, but he came up short.

2. A Merciful End to a Failed Experiment
by Herbert Asbury   233

Prohibition stumbled along throughout the decade. In the face of widespread opposition to and flaunting of the law, its proponents gradually realized its time had passed.

Chronology   244

For Further Reading   247

Index   249

Foreword

In his book *The American Century*, historian Harold Evans maintains that the history of the twentieth century has been dominated by the rise of the United States as a global power: "The British dominated the nineteenth century, and the Chinese may cast a long shadow on the twenty-first, but the twentieth century belongs to the United States." In a 1998 interview he summarized his sweeping hypothesis this way: "At the beginning of the century the number of free democratic nations in the world was very limited. Now, at the end of the century, democracy is ascendant around the globe, and America has played the major part in making that happen."

As the new century dawns, historians are eager to appraise the past one hundred years. Evans's book is just one of many attempts to assess the historical impact that the United States has had in the past century. Although not all historians agree with Evans's characterization of the twentieth century as "America's century," no one disputes his basic observation that "in only the second century of its existence the United States became the world's leading economic, military and cultural power." For most of the twentieth century the United States has played an increasingly larger role in shaping world events. The Greenhaven Press America's Decades series is designed to help readers develop a better understanding of America and Americans during this important time.

Each volume in the ten-volume series provides an in-depth examination of the time period. In compiling each volume, editors have striven to cover not only the defining events of the decade—in both the domestic and international arenas—but also the cultural, intellectual, and technological trends that affected people's everyday lives.

Essays in the America's Decades series have been chosen for their concise, accessible, and engaging presentation of the facts. Each selection is preceded by a summary of the article's content. A comprehensive index and an annotated table of contents also aid readers in quickly locating material of interest. Each volume begins with an introductory essay that presents the broader themes of each decade. Several research aids are also present, including an extensive bibliography and a timeline that provides an at-a-glance overview of each decade.

Each volume in the Greenhaven Press America's Decades series serves as an informative introduction to a specific period in U.S. history. Together, the volumes comprise a detailed overview of twentieth century American history and serve as a valuable resource for students conducting research on this fascinating time period.

Introduction: A Decade of Prosperity and Turmoil

Few decades in U.S. history are as identifiable and carry as many associations as the Roaring Twenties. The decade produces images of flappers, gangsters, and bathtub gin. It is also marked by two easily remembered, defining events. The period opened with a national desire to forgo serious world affairs in favor of fun, fads, and fashion, and it ended with the crash of 1929 that dissolved into the Great Depression of the thirties. In between, Americans partied, introduced to the world fantastic technological advances, cheered an array of legendary sports figures, accumulated dizzying profits in the heady stock market, and flaunted the law by openly violating Prohibition. Gangsters, especially Chicago's Al Capone, vied for newspaper headlines with heroes such as Charles Lindbergh; women's fashion overshadowed reformers; and Hollywood became as famous as Wall Street.

A Robust Economy

For practically the entire decade, the nation reveled in a robust economy. Wages steadily grew to the point where a skilled laborer possessed 50 percent more buying power with his money in 1927 than he held in 1913. In eight years, from 1921 to 1929, the gross national product rose from $74 billion to $104 billion.

Realizing that the nation was weary of sacrifice, businesses expanded their operations and offered customers a broader variety of products. Chain operations, able to pass on savings to customers because they purchased products in such enormous volume, dotted the landscape from ocean to ocean. J.C. Penney opened 1,395 stores by 1929, the F.W. Woolworth Company managed 1,825, and the Atlantic & Pacific Tea Co. (A & P) dwarfed its competition by operating more than 15,000 stores nationwide by 1929.

To lure more customers, stores created the installment method of purchasing, or buying on time. If someone wished to buy a product but lacked the necessary money, stores arranged for them to pay a small amount at the time of purchase, then pay the balance in equal payments, or installments. Since the economy seemed strong, no one worried about making future payments.

The economy so dominated the 1920s that President Warren Harding's successor, Calvin Coolidge, muttered in 1925 that "the business of America is business."[1] Products poured out of factories, and storeowners enjoyed record sales.

Especially inviting was the stock market, which made money-making look easy. All an investor needed to do was invest money in the stock market, then sit back and wait for the stocks' prices to increase. Investors did not even have to hand over the entire value of the stock. They could buy on margin—purchase shares for as little as 10 percent of their value, with the promise to pay the remainder once the value of the stock rose. Since the price of stocks spiraled throughout the decade, few worried about where the money would come from for that, either.

Prohibition

Along with the booming legal economy, Prohibition allowed for a flourishing black-market economy. Prohibition, which became the Eighteenth Amendment on January 16, 1920, prohibited the manufacture, sale, and transportation of alcoholic beverages, and its implementation instituted a decade-long struggle between government law enforcement agencies attempting to administer the law and those portions of American society intent on breaking the law.

For years various reform groups had led drives to make alcohol illegal. Organizations such as the Anti-Saloon League argued that liquor led to many of society's ills and contended that an alcohol-free nation would see a decline of crime and the restoration of family values.

On the other side, many Americans believed that they possessed an inherent right to drink, and the era of Prohibition failed almost before it began. Men and women patronized the local speakeasy, where they could freely purchase their favorite beverage, or they bought alcohol from a neighborhood bootlegger, so named because smugglers frequently hid illegal alcohol in the legs of boots. Local police departments, faced with an almost impossible task, frequently turned a blind eye to the illegal actions or accepted outright bribes. Disregard for the law became so rampant that the nation's leading political humorist, Will Rogers, stated that "Prohibition is better than no liquor at all."[2]

Where there is a demand for a product, someone is certain to fill the need, and Prohibition allowed for a huge black market dominated by criminal groups. Each big city had its local crime syndicate, but the one that surpassed the others in efficiency, organization, and ruthlessness was headed by Al Capone in Chicago. Capone supplied most of the alcohol to the Chicago area, and he ran the town as though it were his own little kingdom. He enjoyed a free hand because most city officials and police agencies worked for him. Rivals gradually disappeared in a wave of violent gang slayings, leaving the illegal bootlegging industry wide open for Capone. At the peak of his tenure, Capone earned $60 million a year.

Law enforcement agencies faced an insurmountable task. With thousands of miles of unguarded border between Canada and the United States, smugglers had little difficulty bringing liquor across from Canada. For instance, a flotilla of rowboats and speedboats supplied liquor across the Detroit River from Windsor, Canada, to the Detroit, Michigan, region, and hundreds of ships anchored off the Atlantic Coast and set up shop as floating taverns. Understaffed federal agencies could only mount a few well-publicized raids or make hit-and-miss stops at speakeasies to arrest the patrons. Since by the middle of the decade less than 20 percent of the nation supported the law, most agencies realized that they could do little to halt the flow of the beverage.

Thus, rather than reducing crime, as proponents of the

law had argued, Prohibition actually contributed to an increase. Ordinary citizens who would rarely have thought of breaking a law felt no inhibitions in purchasing alcohol, and even President Harding kept a ready supply on hand in the White House for his card-playing buddies. An estimated one hundred thousand speakeasies operated in New York City, and hardware stores sold instructions on how to make bathtub gin or set up portable stills.

Eventually, the nation turned against Prohibition, and the failed experiment came to an end. The Twenty-first Amendment, passed in 1933, repealed the Eighteenth Amendment.

The public's devil-may-care attitude toward Prohibition was prevalent in other areas of life. Much of the cynicism was a reaction against the privations of World War I, the event that dominated the previous decade. Thousands of the nation's young men had died on European battlefields from 1917–1918 and many more had been wounded. Consequently, people grew weary of the costs and demands imposed by warfare. Once the war ended, the nation's mothers and fathers demanded the speedy return of their sons from what they saw as nothing more than a futile endeavor to help European nations solve problems that had little to do with the United States.

An ever-expanding number of citizens urged politicians to concern themselves only with issues that directly affected the nation. Gigantic oceans separated the United States from Europe and Asia, and these isolationists argued that it benefited the country to take refuge behind these barriers. Adherents to this view claimed that neither military adventurism in far parts of the world nor economic crises in Europe required America's attention. As a result, a succession of agreements limited the nation's role in world affairs. The 1921 Washington Naval Conference drastically limited the amount of money appropriated for the U.S. Navy, while the Kellogg-Briand Pact of 1928 pledged sixty-four nations to denounce war as an instrument of national policy.

Isolationism affected Americans' attitudes toward international entanglements as well as immigrants and minority political groups, such as American Communists.

Intolerance

The tone for the decade was set in 1919 with "the Red Scare." Stunned by the speedy Communist takeover in Russia, government officials and the American public feared that the American Communist Party would attempt a similar seizure in the United States. To forestall such a move, Attorney General A. Mitchell Palmer instigated a series of raids against suspected political radicals. While many Communists fell into the government's net, thousands of civilians with no connection to communism, mainly recent immigrants, were apprehended without benefit of an attorney and thrown in jail.

The police burst into private homes and union halls to pick up suspected Communists. In one city authorities handcuffed and chained together the people they arrested, then marched them through the local streets. Three hundred suspected Communists were falsely rounded up in Detroit and held in jail for one week before the charges were dismissed in court.

The issue occupied center stage in the Sacco-Vanzetti murder case, in which two Italian immigrants were accused of murdering a factory paymaster and his guard. The trial divided the nation into two camps, especially when the two were convicted on the basis of suspicious evidence. Despite emotional protests around the nation from people who advocated the men's release, Nicola Sacco and Bartolomeo Vanzetti were executed in 1927.

The fight against immigrants and minorities was led by the hooded, white-robed members of the Ku Klux Klan, an organization devoted to maintaining white supremacy. The Klan enjoyed newfound popularity as Americans vented their dislike for foreigners and minorities. Mixing hatred of African Americans, Catholics, and Jews with an emphasis on what the organization called sound traditional American values, the Ku Klux Klan expanded to more than 4 million members by the middle of the decade. Showing surprising popularity in northern states such as Indiana, the Klan even marched through the streets of Washington, D.C., in an impressive, and unsettling, display of power.

Blacks and Women Make Progress in the Face of Prejudice

Although not completely successful in gaining equality with whites, African Americans fought against prejudices and gained some ground in the area of civil rights. Two groups that were founded in the 1920s and made significant contributions toward eradicating bigotry were the National Association for the Advancement of Colored People (NAACP) and Marcus Garvey's Universal Negro Improvement Association (UNIA). The organizations strove to bring equality in the workplace, to apply pressure in the political realm, and to instill pride and value in black Americans.

On the cultural front, blacks contributed a burst of creative efforts in a movement that became known as the Harlem Renaissance, an explosion of literary and musical talent centering around a New York City neighborhood on Manhattan Island. Writers and poets such as Langston Hughes and Countee Cullen wrote searing diatribes about being black in a white-dominated world. Singer Paul Robeson electrified audiences in New York and London with his powerful stage persona and moving voice. Duke Ellington and Louis Armstrong popularized jazz, and Bessie Smith brought blues to segments of society that had never heard it before.

American women also made great strides toward equality in the decade, spurred on in large measure by receiving the right to vote in 1920. Since men were needed to serve in the military during World War I, many women took jobs on the home front that would have traditionally been held by men. Instead of being confined to teaching, social service work, nursing, and secretarial work as in the past, women entered publishing, managed shops and restaurants, and took sales positions in department stores.

Employment, along with more relaxed attitudes toward gender roles and sexuality, gave women a greater sense of freedom. They abandoned the restrictive dress and social mores that dictated the 1910s and attended parties on their own, smoked cigarettes in public, and drank whiskey. For role models, they looked to Hollywood idols such as Theda

Society's change in attitude toward sexuality and gender roles during the 1920s gave women a greater sense of freedom. Women began to dress and act in ways that before had been considered improper.

Bara, Joan Crawford, Mary Pickford, and the "It" girl, Clara Bow, who popularized the flapper image.

Movies

Such actresses were only a few of the many that fueled Americans' love for movies. Hollywood continued to expand its domination of the infant film industry. By 1925 filmmaking had become the country's fourth-largest industry. Comical characters such as Charlie Chaplin or the Keystone Kops, as well as matinee idols such as Rudolph Valentino and Douglas Fairbanks, were the headline stars of the decade.

Two gigantic steps in filmmaking occurred at decade's end. In 1927 singer Al Jolson starred in *The Jazz Singer*, the first film in which sound was used. From then on, silent films made a speedy exit from the American scene, replaced with hundreds of sound films that poured out of studios. The following year a young businessman named Walt Disney introduced Mickey Mouse in the first Hollywood cartoon to feature sound, *Steamboat Willie*.

Sports

Besides movies, Americans' favorite form of entertainment was sports. The twenties were so heavily populated with sports heroes that it has been labeled "the Golden Age of Sports." Memorable personalities and epic-making events from a wide variety of sports dominated those years.

In baseball the immortal Babe Ruth swatted home runs by the dozen. In the process he not only led the Yankees to World Series championships but also restored honor to a game that had been tarnished by the infamous Black Sox scandal of 1919, when some members of the Chicago White Sox accepted bribes to lose the World Series. Record crowds flocked to stadiums to see Babe Ruth and his teammates battle with opponents.

Football grew popular in the decade as well. After an outstanding collegiate career at the University of Illinois, in which he gained more than thirty-six hundred yards in three years, Red Grange popularized the professional version of the game. At the University of Notre Dame, fabled coach Knute Rockne guided his team to five undefeated seasons, and the running backs known as "the Four Horsemen" galloped into sporting legend.

Bobby Jones elevated golf to the sports pages with his triumphs in the United States and overseas, and Bill Tilden and Helen Willis dominated tennis. Jack Dempsey reigned as boxing champion, and Gertrude Ederle gave women around the world something to cheer about when she successfully swam the English Channel.

Technology and Transportation

Another area that experienced phenomenal growth in the 1920s was technology, particularly as exemplified in radio, transportation, and flight. The decade opened in 1920 with the nation's first radio broadcast when Pittsburgh's KDKA announced the results of the 1920 presidential election between James Cox and Warren Harding. Before long, radio challenged newspapers and magazines in bringing information to the American people, who were fascinated with the fact that they could actually hear the voices of important people.

By 1926 the country's first radio network had been established, the National Broadcasting Corporation, and stations around the nation offered a steady diet of music programs, news, and sports. By decade's end more than six hundred radio stations operated throughout the United States.

The growth of the automobile industry also had a dramatic impact on Americans' lives. Henry Ford's mass production techniques enabled most Americans to afford a car, and more people could travel about the country and explore new places. This led to a demand for improved roads, more restaurants, and good motels.

Travel by air became more important in the decade as well. No longer did air travel remain in the domain of military strategists or daredevils. Ordinary citizens utilized it as a quicker method of moving about the nation.

Two men in particular advanced aviation in dramatically different ways. Billy Mitchell worked tirelessly to promote air power as the military weapon of the future. Against stiff opposition from within and without the military, Mitchell argued that the nation had to construct a powerful air division or face defeat in future wars. Even though he demonstrated air power's utility by sinking a battleship in 1921 in a practice aerial bombing attack, he failed to convince his military superiors. After being court-martialed for accusing his superiors of negligence, Mitchell resigned from the army.

Charles Lindbergh faced no such disgrace. He electrified the world with his famous 1927 crossing of the Atlantic Ocean in his aircraft *The Spirit of St. Louis*. Air travel became more commonplace, and just as the automobile made the nation more accessible to Americans, air travel opened the world to more people.

The Stock Market Crash

The decade wound down in the fall of 1929 with the stock market collapse. After ten years of soaring values, Wall Street commodities plunged to frighteningly low depths on Black Tuesday, October 29, 1929. The stock market collapsed in a frenzy of selling in which a record 16 million shares were dumped. Over the coming months investors lost millions and unemployment skyrocketed. Almost seven hundred banks closed in 1929, and eighty-five thousand businesses went bankrupt between 1929 and 1932.

President Herbert Hoover tried to stem the economic chaos, but he was not a believer in intruding the government into every aspect of American life. Secretary of Treasury Andrew Mellon even advised Hoover to allow the economic downturn to take its natural course because "it will purge the rottenness out of the system,"[3] but Hoover was not willing to go that far. He thought that the government should play a limited role in helping the economy, mainly acting as an intermediary to develop cooperation among society's different interest groups.

Hoover stood firmly against the use of government as a welfare organization. He argued that government handouts weakened the nation's moral strength and contributed to developing a class of citizens that would become dependent on government for its survival. Instead, he relied on "rugged individualism"—the belief that people would correct their ills through their own efforts. Instead of the federal government stepping in, Hoover encouraged local charities, business organizations, and individuals to assist the needy of their areas.

Hoover did take a few definite steps. He tried to reassure Americans that the economy was sound and that they should go about their business as usual. He requested that employers not reduce their workforces or lower wages, and he asked labor leaders to refrain from strikes. Hoover pushed through massive public works programs to provide jobs for unemployed workers. He helped establish the Federal Farm Board to assist farmers, the Federal Home Loan Bank Act to provide money for home purchases, and the Reconstruction Finance Corporation to provide financing for large businesses.

However well meaning his actions were, Hoover's measures did little to stem the economic devastation. Unemployment spiraled as the twenties ended, and companies folded in record numbers. It would take a new leader with a revolutionary vision—Franklin D. Roosevelt and his New Deal—in the 1930s to make any impact on the nation.

Though it did not cause the Great Depression of the 1930s by itself, the stock market collapse was a major factor in ushering in the troubles that followed. For ten years the nation had enjoyed prosperity; it would now face turmoil. It would take another world war, in another decade, to fully revitalize American industry.

1. Quoted in Time-Life Books, *This Fabulous Century: 1920–1930*, p. 96.

2. Quoted in Edward Behr, *Prohibition: Thirteen Years that Changed America.* New York: Arcade Publishing, 1996, p. 172.

3. Quoted in Danzer et al., *The Americans: Reconstruction Through the 20th Century.* Evanston, IL: McDougal Littell, 1999, p. 495.

CHAPTER 1

Politics

AMERICA'S DECADES

Stock Market Madness

Cabell Phillips

Following the misery and death involved in World War I, Americans focused on fun, fads, and comforts. One of the areas people turned to was Wall Street in New York City, where the center of the stock market stood. Investors in the 1920s purchased large volumes of stocks, usually by borrowing money with the intent of paying back the loan from the profits earned on the stock purchased. For much of the decade, since the value of stocks rose to dizzying proportions, Americans made money.

Cabell Phillips, veteran news reporter and historian of the United States in the 1900s, explains the stock market frenzy that grabbed the 1920s in his account of America in the 1920s and 1930s.

If millions upon millions of Americans were desperate, frightened, and even rebellious, they had good cause to be. The Great Depression was the most pervasive, the most persistent, and the most destructive economic crisis the nation had ever faced. If, in perspective, scholars today minimize the threat of this crisis to the fundamental institutions of American life—the capitalist free-enterprise doctrine in particular—few were so sanguine at the time. When that desolate winter of 1932–33 settled in, most people believed, with a sort of fatalistic despair, that the world they

---

had known was dead and that the world ahead was un-knowable. And some said, "Good riddance."

Poverty in the Midst of Prosperity

How had we reached this fearful dilemma?

The roots of the Great Depression can be traced back to the world war of 1914–18 and even beyond. Some author-ities describe it as the ultimate collapse of the industrial revolution, with the machine devouring man. It is, indeed, a fact that technology made enormous strides during the first two decades of the century and then took another giant step forward under the impetus of the war. The auto-mobile came into its own, the production line replaced the craftsman's bench in thousands of factories and shops, the radio was developed and flourished like a weed in the sun, machines dug coal five times faster than miners with picks and shovels, food processing revolutionized the grocery business and the dinner table, electrical energy multiplied human energy a hundred times over and in hundreds of dif-ferent ways, and families by the tens of thousands fled the drudgery and loneliness of the farms for the drudgery and loneliness of the cities. Between 1920 and 1930 economists ceased pondering the question of "America's capacity to produce," which had preoccupied them for fifty years, and turned belatedly to "America's capacity to consume," about which they had much to learn.

It is a pity they didn't turn to it sooner, because their classic postulate about the automatic balancing of supply and demand had begun to fall apart before their eyes. For in that same decade, while productivity per man-hour in manufacturing went up 43 percent (two and one-half times as fast as the population), factory wages went up less than 20 percent. The profits of a hugely productive industry went not into higher wages or lower prices but into divi-dends, into more machines and factories—and into specu-lation. The money didn't go where the people could use it to buy the things they had produced.

Income distribution was further restricted by the rapid

growth of monopoly in a dozen fields. There were more than a thousand mergers of local utility companies in 1926 alone, and by 1930 one-half of the total electrical output in the country was controlled by *three* huge holding companies. A study made in 1930 indicated that nearly one-half of the nonbanking corporate wealth in the country was held by the 200 largest corporations, which in turn were under the interlocking control of some 2,000 individual executives and financiers. In the corporate society that mushroomed during the twenties the worth of the individual as a free agent and master of his economic destiny took a nose dive in the marketplace. Laissez-faire [belief that government should not interfere with commerce] was an incompatible bedmate for an Economy of Abundance.

Meanwhile the whole farm sector of the economy was allowed to stagnate and even to fall backward during this dizzying decade. No one except the farmers seemed to care, least of all President [Calvin] Coolidge (a farm boy himself), who proclaimed, "The business of government is business," and acted accordingly in countless official decisions. While net farm income remained static at about $9 billion during all the years that corporate and speculative profits were zooming off the charts, the value of farm lands decreased from $80 billion to around $55 billion, and the rate of farm bankruptcies multiplied six times over. Farmers were the first victims of the Great Depression. They fled their sterile acres in droves, at the rate of 600,000 annually during the closing years of the twenties, and crowded into the towns and cities, where, before long, they would fall under another kind of blight—namely, unemployment.

Although the tinder that fueled the Depression had been gathering undetected for a decade, the spark that set it off was struck in a single week in October, 1929, when the stock market crashed. This is a chronological oversimplification, of course, because the ultimate crash itself, like the climax of a Greek tragedy, was preceded by an inexorable and prophetic chain of events extending over many weeks. But that was when the roof finally fell in. The New Economic Era, so devoutly extolled by a whole generation of statesmen, savants, and moneymen, disappeared forever in the debris. In the popular mind at least, and in the minds of some experts as well, the Great Depression dates from the Great Crash.

The Nation Jumps on the Stock Train

The psychological virus that set off the orgy of speculation in the last half of the decade of the twenties has never been isolated. There is, of course, a strong susceptibility to the fast buck in the American bloodstream, and it had broken out in epidemic proportions before, as in the Crédit Mobilier scandal of the nineteenth century and the "panic" of 1907. What triggered this speculative madness in about the year 1926 is uncertain, but this time the seizure was to be of heroic proportions.

The focus of the infection was the New York Stock Exchange, and a few facts about that institution will help to set up the picture.

The volume of trading on the Exchange (the total number of shares bought and sold) rose by a series of unprecedented leaps from 451 million in 1926 to over 1.1 billion in 1929. In these same four years the daily average top price for twenty-five leading industrials rose from $186.03 to $469.49 per share. That meant a "paper profit" of about 250 percent, or a real profit of the same pleasing amount if one had bought at the low and sold at the high levels.

A large proportion of the trading, possibly a third or more, was done on margin. A broker required only about a 10 or 20 percent down payment by the customer on a block of stock and in effect loaned the customer the remaining portion of the purchase price. This easy-payment plan (it wasn't so easy if the value of your stock went down and you had to put up more margin) naturally excited the gambling instinct not only of unwary amateurs but of professional speculators as well. Buying on margin was established practice, but under the feverish scramble to "get into the market" the volume of these loans rose prodigiously, from $3.2 billion in September 1926 to $8.5 billion in September 1929. This was equal to about one-half the entire public debt of the United States Government, which stood that year at $16.9 billion. So intense was the demand for this Wall Street "call money," for which the brokers were willing to pay as much as 15 percent interest (charging their margin customers four or five points more), that many banks and corporations across the country sent their surplus funds to Wall Street to cash in on the bonanza.

By the beginning of 1928 speculating in the stock market had become almost a national mania. It was not true that "everybody" was "in the market," as was commonly said at the time; it just seemed that way. Actually, only about a million persons owned stocks on margin in September 1929—chiefly the amateur and professional speculators—and about two million owned shares outright. But the mania, like the national obsession with a seven-game World Series, had made most of the citizenry vicarious speculators. Next to crime, the most engrossing news on any day's front page was likely to be what had happened on the market: Radio up another $6\frac{3}{8}$; bears rout bulls in raid on Anaconda; Cleveland's Van Sweringen brothers reported buying heavily to extend their rail empire; an unknown newcomer, Frisbee Consolidated, startles the analysts with a meteoric rise, and so on. Nearly everyone could translate the esoteric language of the financial specialists into the patois of Main Street. Your barber or streetcar conductor was as emphatic in his expertise as your banker or lawyer. Enough people whom you knew, or knew of, were dabbling in the market to give verisimilitude to the impression that everybody was doing it: a spinster aunt, a school principal, the clerk at the post office, the taxi driver, the typist in the office pool. Everyone was prepared to believe such stories as that of the banker's chauffeur who had held on to his fifty shares of something-or-other after the banker had dumped his, and cleaned up a cool $1,500. Exploits such as these were the talk of the town—any town—the stuff of exciting folklore.

To satisfy this urge for fast riches, brokerage offices pro-liferated across the country, in cities, suburbs, and small towns, like recruiting stations in wartime. Most branch of-fices had direct wire connections with New York or other big city establishments, and bore the outward marks, at least, of respectability. Others consisted of no more than a battery of rented telephones installed in a vacant store or hotel suite, manned by a squad of confidence men who kept their packed suitcases handily by their sides. These "bucket shops" and "boiler factories," dealing in the shards of un-listed, unknown, and even nonexistent securities, differed from the starched-collar establishments mainly in that they offered their victims a faster, closer shearing.

Investment Trusts Spur the Stock Market Frenzy

To accommodate the timid and the skeptical, there was a sharp revival of the investment trust in the late twenties. An investment trust was a company that owned nothing but the stock of other companies. An investor with as little as ten dollars could buy a share in the trust in the expectation that he would profit proportionately as the trust reaped divi-dends from its portfolio. He was assured of the additional advantage over the freelance speculator that the trust's op-erations were guided by Wall Street experts of great wis-dom; there was usually an impressive roster of bankers, cor-poration executives, and financiers on the letterhead.

There were fewer than a hundred investment trusts in existence in 1926; by the summer of 1929 there were more than 500, with more than $3 billion worth of shares held by an unnumbered legion of principally small investors. It was usual practice for the organizers to cut themselves and their friends in for sizeable blocks of the new stock at less than the opening price. If the trust had prominent backing, as many of them did, an almost instantaneous rise in price was assured. Thus, in January 1929 J.P. Morgan and Com-pany, the most impeccable name in high finance, launched an investment trust called United Corporation. The part-ners and their friends bought in at $75 a share in advance

26

of the public offering. When the shares went on sale the price was $92; before the first week was out they had been bid up to $100.

Inevitably, many of these trusts were tacked together on the shakiest of foundations, but it seemed not to matter. The public demand for their stock was insatiable. In many instances the value of the shares offered exceeded by two or three times the total value of the stocks and other assets on which they were based.

New investment trusts were spawned by a process of in-breeding that almost guaranteed a sterile offspring. In the summer of 1929, for example, the New York financial house of Goldman, Sachs and Company floated the Shenandoah Corporation, a third of whose assets was stock in another investment trust, the Goldman Sachs Trading Corporation. Within a few weeks, the same company announced the creation of still another and larger trust, the Blue Ridge Corporation, 80 percent of whose capital consisted of stock in the Shenandoah Corporation. Thus one investment trust could be built atop another, and the people who bought nearly $250 million worth of stock in Shenandoah and Blue Ridge owned virtually nothing that represented real wealth: no factories, no airlines, no oil wells, nothing but a ticket in a lottery. There were few laws in 1929 about how the sucker trap could be baited.

Nobody Wants to Listen

The dazzling pace of the investment splurge was not without its Cassandras [predictors of doom]. "It is perfectly well recognized by 'insiders,'" the *Journal of Commerce* observed late in 1928, "that a market of the kind that has been going on cannot last indefinitely but must undergo a readjustment." Possibly the "insiders" did know it, but few of them, even those in positions of responsibility in government, wanted the unpleasant task of saying so. Secretary of the Treasury Andrew W. Mellon was no man to spread the alarm; he and his family had profited handsomely in the great bull market. President [Herbert] Hoover could not bring himself to rock the boat, although he confessed years later in his published *Memoirs* that he realized it was sailing in perilous waters. When the Federal Reserve Board issued a cautious and ambiguous warning that speculation was approaching the danger point, Arthur Brisbane, the widely read Hearst columnist, reproached it scornfully: "If buying and selling stocks is wrong, the government should close the Stock Exchange. If not, the Federal Reserve should mind its own business."

Up and up the market soared, gaining speed and spinning off miracles as it went. Between 1928 and 1929 the value of new capital issues offered jumped from $9.9 to $11.6 billion. Between June and the end of August of the latter year there was a gain of an unprecedented 110 registered on *The New York Times* average of 25 industrials, reaching an all-time high of 449 on September 3. To better illustrate what this meant, here are the gains made by a few blue-chip issues in the eighteen months between March 3, 1928, when many thought mistakenly the peak had been reached, and September 3, 1929, when the peak actually was reached: American Can, 77 to 181⅞; American Telephone and Telegraph, 179½ to 335⅝; General Electric, 128¾ to 396¼; Montgomery Ward, 132¾ to 466½; Radio Corporation of America, 94½ to 505; United States Steel, 138⅛ to 279⅛; Electric Bond and Share, 89¾ to 203⅝.

Unfit for the Job: The Presidency of Warren G. Harding

Edmund Stillman

To be a capable president, a leader must possess sufficient dynamism to stir the nation, political talent to mold alliances, and an intellectual capacity to grasp what actions might be effective in the prevailing mood of the times. George Washington exhibited such qualities in the aftermath of the American Revolution, as did Abraham Lincoln in the Civil War, and Theodore Roosevelt in the early 1900s. Unfortunately, the 1920s suffered through three undistinguished leaders. Warren G. Harding, the first of the three, failed every measure by which a successful president is evaluated. He was a man of limited abilities who was sadly out of place in the White House. Historian Edmund Stillman describes Harding's hectic years.

I nauguration Day, March 4, 1921. The contrast could not have been more glaring when the two men, the old President and the new, rode together in the open Pierce-Arrow cabriolet under a sunny, cloudless sky to Capitol Hill. The crowds that lined the way saw on the one hand Woodrow Wilson, shrunken, white, tense hands gripping his invalid's cane, and on the other Warren Gamaliel Harding, of leonine head, plump, affable, the prophet of the return to "normalcy," the neologism he had coined during his stag-

Excerpted from *The American Heritage History of the Twenties and Thirties*, by Edmund Stillman. Reprinted by permission of *American Heritage Magazine*, a division of Forbes, Inc. Copyright © Forbes, Inc.

geringly successful campaign, in which he appealed to the longings of an American people exhausted by the strain of three years of world war and its aftermath and impatient to try to return to the pleasant prewar life.

Wilson had been the autocrat, the dogmatic schoolmaster, forever dragooning the American people to work for a cause, whipping them down the unpleasant road of international responsibility. Harding asked nothing of them. Easygoing, kindly, totally devoid of intellectual qualities, he was the abstraction come to life of the average sensual man.

Harding's Rocky Start

And he was that with a vengeance, had the nation only suspected. The man they had chosen over colorless Governor James M. Cox of Ohio by a landslide was a small-town sport and womanizer. If he was not truly a hick, he was as close to being the embodiment of the back-country politico, the practitioner of courthouse intrigue and of statehouse trafficking in shady contracts, as the American Presidency has ever known.

Warren Harding's origins were humble, a fact he made no effort to disguise, thereby endearing himself to the plain men of the nation. They identified with him, seeing him as the incarnation of the banal American dream that every mother's son, similarly devoid of qualities, might aspire to the most high. For Harding, the son of a small-town schoolteacher turned doctor, had only a mediocre schooling (he had acquired a Bachelor of Science degree in 1882 at Ohio Central College, a now-defunct freshwater academy of higher learning whose faculty totaled three). Harding had moved to Marion, Ohio, before the turn of the century and there, at the age of eighteen, with a friend, took charge of a bankrupt newspaper, the *Star*, in which his father had purchased a half interest. The job seemed to fit him.

But fate would single out this all-too-common man for greatness, or at least a kind of notoriety that has set him down in history as perhaps the worst President the United States has known, surpassing in fatuity even such presidential ciphers as James Buchanan and John Tyler and rivaling in indifference or insensitivity to rampant corruption the administration of Ulysses S. Grant. In the end fate would also prove unkind, for in Marion, Warren Harding, then scarcely twenty-five years old, met a girl, one Florence Kling, five years his senior, a divorcee, the unalluring daughter of one of the great powers of back-country Ohio. Her money, connections, and most importantly her driving ambition would propel the passive young man into politics, into the White House, and eventually into disaster. . . .

At the close of his term in 1905, Harding retired from politics until 1910, when he ran for governor of Ohio and was soundly thrashed. But two years later the uncertain Harding was persuaded to make another try—this time for a vacant senatorial seat in Washington. By a quirk of fate, the man of small endowments won.

Thus far, except for minor setbacks, the story would seem to be one of unqualified successes. Harding, however, was shadowed, in his youth and to the day of his death, by the persistent story that he was tainted by Negro blood, that he was, in short, a "bad nigger" trying to pass. Florence Harding's father, Amos Kling, who apparently believed the story, threatened Harding in the street, and when his daughter defied him and married the young man, refused to speak to her for seven years. . . .

Harding Lands the Nomination

It was Florence Harding's ambition that would, in the end, bring him down. Joining with Harry Daugherty, a minor statehouse politician whose personal political ambitions had long since been blasted—Daugherty was compared by the contemporary *The New York Times* to a stumble-bum who wisely decides to manage others—she pushed Harding relentlessly on. In 1912 Harding introduced the name of William Howard Taft in nomination for the Presidency at the Republican convention, and four years later he served as chairman of the convention. He began to catch the eye of the party's national leadership, and the careful maneu-

Cartoon on the Teapot Dome Scandal

Bribery and graft plagued Warren Harding and the Republican Party in the 1920s. Particularly damaging was the Teapot Dome scandal. The following cartoon expresses how the Democratic Party benefited from the embarrassment the scandal caused the Republican Party.

© *N. Y. "Tribune."*

The First Good Laugh They've Had in Years.

Mark Sullivan, *Our Times: The United States, 1900–1925.* New York: Charles Scribner's Sons, 1935.

vering behind the scenes by Florence and Daugherty bore fruit at the war's end.

For the Republicans victory was in the air in 1920. The country longed to repudiate the adventurous policies of the Wilsonians so that winning the Republican nomination would be tantamount to national victory. But there were obstacles standing in Harding's way. There was no shortage of able or famous Republicans to run, among them [Army] General Leonard Wood, Governor Frank Lowden of Illinois, Senator Hiram Johnson of California, Charles Evans Hughes, only narrowly defeated by Wilson in 1912, Senator William Borah of Idaho, and even that dark horse Herbert Hoover. But the leading figures were deadlocked. After four ballots it became clear that a compromise candidate would have to be found. Harding, running fifth in the balloting, was that man.

Summoned at two o'clock in the morning before a dozen or more party politicos in a "smoke-filled room," where the destiny of the nation was being hammered out, Harding was told of his probable nomination the following day. Were there any impediments to his running for the Presidency? he was asked.

Harding asked for time to ponder. Since his political career had to date been a cipher, the party politicos could only have been alluding to the persistent racial slurs and to his sexual irregularities. Young Nan Britton, whom Harding had established in New York and met regularly in third-rate hotels, was even then in Chicago with Harding's daughter of less than a year.

But after consulting his conscience for ten minutes, Harding found it good. The next day he was nominated on the tenth ballot with Governor Calvin Coolidge, famed for his handling of the Boston police strike, as his running mate. In November the nation went on to elect Harding by a plurality of seven million votes over Cox.

Harding's Cronies

"We're in the Big League now," a gleeful Harding told his associates on being elected to the Presidency, but Harding was plainly out of his league and out of his depth. In the end the responsibilities of the office he assumed would destroy him precisely because Harding, with his limited horizons, did not understand that the political morality appropriate to the courthouse in Marion, or even to the statehouse in Columbus, did not equip him to discharge his awesome duties as the President of the United States. . . .

Harding was not unaware of the looming problems of the peace treaties with Germany, Austria, Hungary, and Turkey, of the tariff, of the naval arms race, and of mass unemployment. It can be fairly said, then, that Harding saw his administration as something larger than a reflection of small-town provincialism.

There was, for one thing, his pledge to the country to appoint to his Cabinet the "best minds," men who would implicitly make up for the intellectual deficiencies of the chief. In this respect Harding, to a remarkable degree, kept his pledge. In Charles Evans Hughes, his Secretary of State, and Herbert Hoover, his Secretary of Commerce, he appointed men touched by a certain greatness. In Andrew Mellon, his Secretary of the Treasury, and the elder Henry Wallace, his Secretary of Agriculture, he named men of unquestionable competence.

But it was not to the best minds that Harding would in fact turn for advice. He asked visitors to pray for him; he begged a neighbor to "talk to God about me every day by name and ask Him somehow to give me strength for my great task. . . ." Uncomfortable in the presence of excellence, or even competence, he staffed most of his Cabinet and administration with affable nonentities—or worse. This was his "Poker Cabinet" and thus he was to come to ruin.

Who were these men around him?

Item: Harry M. Daugherty, Attorney General of the United States, former courthouse politician and trafficker in liquor permits and immunities from prosecution, who, later evidence was to reveal, had come to Washington in 1920 fully twenty-seven thousand dollars in the red and who, within less than three years, deposited seventy-five thousand dollars in his brother's Ohio bank. Furthermore, in his possession was found forty thousand dollars' worth of bonds, traced by the courts to a bribe, and two thousand shares in an aircraft subsidiary that during the war had bilked the United States government out of three million five hundred thousand dollars in overcharges and had never been indicted.

Daugherty ran the "Little House on H Street," where Warren Harding slipped away of evenings for all-night poker, dirty stories, and, so it was rumored, available girls. Daugherty would boast in after years that nothing had ever been proved against him, that he had escaped court conviction on every charge. But that he did escape, he invariably neglected to add, was solely attributable to the protective umbrella of the Fifth Amendment.

Item: Albert B. Fall, Secretary of the Interior, a man whom Harding had first considered for the Secretaryship of State in preference to the judicious Charles Evans Hughes. A former senator from New Mexico, he had come to his post in 1921 near bankruptcy, the taxes on his Southwest ranch holding nine years overdue. Within two years he had stocked it with blooded cattle and bought adjoining lands to round off his spread at a cost of one hundred and twenty-five thousand dollars—on an official salary of twelve thousand dollars per year. Later exposed as the archmanipulator of the Elk Hills and Teapot Dome [land-leasing] scandals, Fall, unlike the luckier Daugherty, would spend a brief time in jail.

Item: Jess Smith, ex-officio member of the Department of Justice and the "man to see" in that aptly named Department of Easy Virtue, the Attorney General's roommate at the Little House on H Street (where both lived rent free at a scale of fifty thousand dollars per year), hanger-on, small-time sport, slack of lip, invariably greeting callers at his unofficial office with the cry "Whaddaya know?" At last, when the first hints of the corruption in the Harding administration began to come to light, Smith shot himself. Conveniently, most of his and Daugherty's papers had been burned.

Item: Charles Forbes, director of the Veterans' Bureau, onetime Army deserter, professional good fellow, a man whom Harding had picked up one day while on a senatorial junket and had never bothered to investigate. Forbes presided over a department that dispensed five hundred million dollars yearly in pensions, hospital supplies, and construction contracts. In time investigation would bring to light that Forbes in late 1922 had declared surplus several million dollars' worth of government-owned hospital supplies. These were sold, without benefit of competitive bidding, to a Boston firm for about six hundred thousand dollars. One million towels, for example, bought by the government for thirty-four cents each were sold at three cents. Forbes, too, would serve a short time in jail. His chief assistant, Charles F. Cramer, legal counsel to the Veterans' Bureau, would also take his own life.

Item: Thomas W. Miller, alien property custodian, a man who had control over more than thirty thousand active trusts seized as enemy property during World War I. In one instance involving the German Metallgesellschaft and Metall Bank, whose confiscated stock was worth seven million dollars by September, 1921, Miller was brought into contact with the German owners by Jess Smith, acting as intermediary. Effecting the return of the firm's assets within a matter of days, Miller pocketed for his trouble $50,000 out of a total fee of $391,000 in bonds and $50,000 in cash, a sum paid by the German principals, who were apparently more than satisfied that value had been rendered. The rest of the huge fee went to men as varied as Attorney General Daugherty, Jess Smith, and Republican National Committeeman John T. King. Miller, too, would be exposed and go to jail. . . .

The Inadequate President

Initially, to be sure, the duties were not too stiff, and if Harding had enjoyed his status as senator, how much more did he revel in the pageantry of the Presidency. He was oppressed, however, by a sense of inadequacy. Witness his despairing confidence to a golfing companion, "Judge, I don't think I'm big enough for the Presidency." To David Lawrence, then a young newsman, he admitted, "Oftentimes, as I sit here, I don't seem to grasp that I am President. . . ."

But he could not conjure away the urgent problems, the crowding events of an era of defiant normalcy: the tax issues, the tariff issues, growing unemployment. A note of desperation began to creep into Harding's voice. William Allen White recalled a talk at the White House with the President's assistant Judson C. Welliver, who quoted the unhappy Harding as crying out: "I can't make a damn thing out of this tax problem. I listen to one side and they seem right, and then—God!—I talk to the other side and they seem just as right, and here I am where I started. I know somewhere there is a book that will give me the truth, but hell! I couldn't read the book."

Nor did he know much more about foreign affairs. America had intervened in a vast European struggle, helping to convert a dynastic and commercial conflict into an ideological crusade that had overturned the established order of things. In the aftermath of that war America's responsibilities were legion. But Harding confided to a visitor: "I don't know anything about this European stuff." Fending off questions, he advised: "You and Jud get together and he can tell me later; he handles these matters for me."

That is to say, Judson Welliver, together with the stately Charles Evans Hughes, one of the few able men in the Harding administration, made the foreign policy decisions for the President. . . .

The Scandals Mount

It was "Doc" Charles Sawyer who first brought an intimation that something might not be quite right in the Veterans' Bureau. Hospital administrators and others, disturbed by the way Forbes was selling hospital supplies to a private firm at a fraction of their cost to the federal government, had voiced their misgivings to Sawyer. The doctor spoke to the President, and Harding, perturbed, ordered the sale of surplus hospital supplies temporarily halted. He was soon visited by Forbes, who assured him expansively that everything was in order and that the Veterans' Bureau was being honestly and efficiently operated.

Forbes attempted to lay public suspicions by arranging for a superficial investigation by a War Department official, who, of course, found nothing amiss. At this Harding, gullible to the last, allowed sales to resume, and Forbes was soon doing business again. By this time, though, the hounds were closing in, and Forbes found it wise to go abroad in January, 1923. When Cramer found that there was to be a Senate investigation, he, in March of 1923, shot himself in the head in the house on Wyoming Avenue he had bought from Harding two years before. Before ending his life, Cramer took the trouble to pen a letter to the President, presumably detailing all. This letter a Department of Justice man duly delivered, only to have it refused by the despondent President, who, rather mysteriously, seems to have been aware that Cramer was dead although he had been roused from bed to receive the message. Baffled, the agent turned it over to Harry Daugherty, who arranged for it to disappear. Shortly thereafter Forbes resigned.

Nor was the Forbes scandal all. In May, 1923, Jess Smith put a bullet in *his* brain. Even Harding at last was beginning to realize the dimensions of the corruption. The President, behind closed doors, was heard to whimper to himself, "What's a fellow to do when his own friends double-cross him?"

Thus Harding by the spring of 1923 was a man distraught. He could not bear the duties of the Presidency, and he could not, amiable spirit, truly comprehend the massive venality and faithlessness of those he had put in a position to wield great power in the land.

Harding determined on a trip, a cleansing voyage of the soul. He would go to Alaska. The trip was initially conceived as one more poker-booze-and-girls junket, but as the shadows thickened over the administration, the plans were revised: the journey to Alaska would be a pilgrimage of duty. He would take the Duchess [his wife, Florence] along with him; he would take outstanding men.

And simultaneously in this harrowing spring and summer he sought to pull himself together, to make of himself what he had never been: a self-denying man. If he could not (fatal flaw) quite bring himself to dismiss old friends, he would at least regenerate his own life. The tearful Nan Britton herself proposed that she make a trip to Europe, the all-night poker ended, the booze stopped. Unbelievably, in the Era of Prohibition the nation's White House at last went bone dry, or nearly so. Warren Gamaliel Harding went on the wagon. . . .

The trip was not a success. How could it have been? Incessantly the President played bridge, dragooning the men of his entourage into marathon sessions that lasted without appreciable break for ten or twelve hours or more. Oftentimes the President would merely sit and stare out the windows of the train, lost in thought. He was visibly depressed.

And in the end, quite simply, he died. On the way back from Alaska he suffered a coronary thrombosis, which, by a supreme irony, was incorrectly diagnosed as acute indigestion by Doc Sawyer, who was, like all the other venal or merely incompetent cronies, as Harding repeatedly asserted, "good enough for me."

The nation mourned Warren Gamaliel Harding as a good man, a giant that day fallen in Israel. The funeral cortege, as the train crossed the land to Washington and thence to the final resting place back home in Marion, Ohio, was hailed at every crossroads by doleful crowds. It was only as the 1920's drew to their close that the true dimensions of the disaster that had been the Harding administration became known. Charlie Cramer had put a bullet in his head; Jess Smith had put a bullet in his head. Forbes went to jail in 1925. Harry Daugherty resigned as Attorney General of the United States in 1924; his records had already been burned and he took the Fifth when he was brought to trial in 1926. But all that was trivial compared to the great Teapot Dome scandal, which shook the nation.

The origins of the case were simple enough. For years the United States Navy, then shifting from a coal to a petroleum navy, had feared for the sufficiency of its oil reserves in the event of war. Over the years, three great oil fields had therefore been set aside: Naval Reserve No. 1 at Elk Hills, California; Naval Reserve No. 2 at Buena Vista Hills, California; Naval Reserve No. 3 at Teapot Dome, Wyoming. These reserve lands, however, had not solved the Navy's problem. Though the government had, by and large, resisted pressure by private operators to lease lands within the reserves, the oil fields were threatened with depletion, for drilling on adjacent privately owned oil lands threatened constantly to drain the oil pools under government control.

How to meet the challenge of oil depletion had vexed preceding administrations ever since 1909. The obvious choices were to drill what was known as offset wells on the government land to match the drainage of the adjacent private wells or to lease the lands to private speculators, who would pay royalties to the Navy either in money or in kind.

The first alternative had been the decision of the Wilson administration, but the Harding administration, true to the Republican doctrines of *laissez faire*, preferred the second one. And very conveniently the second alternative had the advantage of benefiting the oil interests that had backed Warren Harding (more than half a million dollars of oil money had alleged to have been spent in 1920 to elect Harding). The oil interests also liked Albert Fall, who was a good friend to the great oil buccaneers Harry Sinclair and Edward Doheny. They soon had much more reasons to like Fall.

Fall's stratagem was a simple one. The oil reserves were under the jurisdiction of the Secretary of the Navy, an amiable cipher named Edwin Denby. The problem of jurisdiction offered no insuperable obstacles. Less than three months after becoming Secretary of the Interior, Fall induced the trusting President to transfer jurisdiction to the Department of the Interior. A year later, without benefit of competitive bidding, Fall leased Teapot Dome to Harry Sinclair's Mammoth Oil Company. In two separate contracts that same year, 1922, he leased Naval Reserve No. 1 at Elk Hills to Edward L. Doheny's Pan-American Petroleum and Transport Company. The Navy was to receive a moderate royalty, and the two beneficiary companies undertook to build oil storage tanks for the government.

Fall always argued that he had aided the Navy, which, had it received moneys, would have been forced to turn them over to the federal government rather than use them for needed storage construction. No doubt Fall, not to say Sinclair and Doheny, clothed the deal in the raiment of national interest.

But the sordid facts remain: when the scandal broke, Fall was revealed to have received one hundred thousand dollars in cash from Doheny and a cool two hundred and sixty thousand dollars in Liberty bonds from Sinclair. Fall went to jail for accepting a bribe, but by a quirk of justice neither Sinclair nor Doheny was convicted of offering that bribe (". . . the law," as Mr. Bumble puts it in *Oliver Twist,* "is a ass, a idiot"). But Sinclair at least was to serve two terms in prison: three months for contempt of the Senate for refusing evidence and six months for contempt of court for attempted coercion and bribery of his jurors.

Thus the sorry record: suicides, jailings, disgrace. In after years a minor bagman of the Harding administration would spread the story that the President had been murdered by a despairing Duchess, who had put the vexed and troubled man to sleep out of the compassionate desire to spare him disgrace and the concomitant desire to revenge herself for his petty amours. Others speculated that Harding, like Cramer and Smith, had committed suicide.

The soberer verdict will probably stand: Warren Gamaliel Harding may be said to have died of a broken heart in the real sense of the expression.

"Keep Cool with Coolidge"—the Hands-Off Approach of President Calvin Coolidge

Paul Sann

Americans did not notice much improvement in presidential leadership when Calvin Coolidge took office following Harding's death. Called "Silent Cal" because he spoke so infrequently, Coolidge believed that the best government was the one that governed the least, especially in regards to regulating businesses. In this atmosphere, American industry flourished while simultaneously drawing nearer to the calamity of the stock market crash.

A former executive editor of the *New York Post* newspaper, Paul Sann compiled a lively account of the 1920s. In this selection, he describes the presidency of Calvin Coolidge.

T here was one very sour note for the Republicans in the 1924 Presidential campaign. The unfolding Teapot Dome scandal had begun to demonstrate that the Ohio Gang's [President Warren G. Harding and his advisers] two-year-and-five-month visit in Washington very likely had set an all-time record for thievery and corruption in the national government. This was the story:

Three months after taking office President Harding signed an executive order turning over to his Interior Department the custody of the government oil fields at Elk

Hills and Buena Vista, California, and Teapot Dome, Wyoming. The reserves since 1909 had reposed under the Navy's jurisdiction as a gigantic defense store. Harding's Secretary of the Interior, Albert M. Fall, had many dear friends among the private oil interests and in 1922 he leased the Teapot Dome Reserve to Harry F. Sinclair's Mammoth Oil Company and the Elks Hills Reserve to Edward F. Doheny's Pan-American Company. The leases were made in secret. Capitol Hill never knew the war reserves were in private hands until a Wyoming oilman wrote to his congressman and wanted to know how come Harry Sinclair had been able to lease Teapot Dome without competitive bidding. The resulting senatorial inquiry, under the tireless Tom Walsh of Montana, produced astonishing revelations.

It turned out that Fall had received $260,000 in Liberty bonds as "loans" from Sinclair and $100,000 in cash from Doheny. The immensely wealthy Doheny told the investigators that he had sent his son over with the money, nesting in a little black satchel, because his old friend Fall wanted to buy a new ranch in New Mexico and needed a stake. He said it was "a mere bagatelle" to him and he saw nothing improper in lending money to the Secretary of the Interior who was about to lease the nation's oil reserves to him for his personal profit.

In the eventual trials, Fall drew a year's jail sentence for accepting a bribe from Doheny but Doheny, in a separate trial, was found not guilty of paying any bribe to Fall. Sinclair beat the case against him but was jailed years later on two counts: contempt of the Senate and contempt of court for having a Burns detective shadow the jury in one of his trials.

There was an embarrassing sidelight in the oil scandal having to do with Sinclair's financial relations with the Republican National Committee. It turned out that the promoter had helped pay off the costs of the Harding campaign with a gift of $75,000 and a "loan" of $185,000 for which he had taken only $100,000 in repayment. The Republican chairman at the time happened to be Will Hays, later borrowed by Hollywood as the ideal man to police movie morals.

On another front, in 1927, the long arm of scandal fell heavily on Harry Daugherty. The former Attorney General had to stand trial after the Harding Administration's Alien Property Custodian, Thomas W. Miller, was sent to jail because $50,000 stuck to his hands in a curious transaction in which the American Metal Company—originally deemed to be owned by a German bank—managed to recover $6,000,000 in war-seized assets. The company paid out a total of $441,000 for various services in the process of getting its money back, and another party who picked up $50,000 was Jess Smith, Daugherty's roommate and lifetime buddy. Smith took his own life long before this item came out, but Daugherty was hauled into court because circumstantial evidence placed him somewhere in the lush Metal Company deal; however, a jury acquitted him after deliberating for 66 hours.

Coolidge Wins the Election

In the 1924 campaign, as it happened, the Republicans had an antidote for such of the Harding scandals as were already in the public record. Their candidate was Calvin Coolidge and he himself had ushered out of the Cabinet not only Albert Fall, but also Secretary of the Navy Edwin L. Denby, in bad repute for maintaining too much silence when the nation's oil reserves were wrested from his hands and handed over to Fall. So the candidate's own halo of primitive Yankee honesty was secure; it would never tilt. Indeed, if anyone were needed to clean up the oil-smeared Potomac reservation, the man from Vermont fitted the role perfectly. There would be no fast-buck guys around the White House while he had the key. Beyond this happy circumstance, there appeared to be enough prosperity in the happy air to override Teapot Dome and any disclosures to come.

And, better still, Senator Robert M. LaFollette had entered the presidential sweepstakes on the Progressive ticket. His vote figured to dissipate whatever long-shot chance the badly split Democrats might have had with their compromise candidate, John W. Davis, picked on a record one-hundred-third ballot only after the long deadlock between Alfred E. Smith and William G. McAdoo and the blistering July heat in New York had wilted the convention delegates.

Thus, as the campaign proceeded, *Time* magazine was able to report week after week that while Davis rolled through the whistle-stops "Cal Coolidge sat tight and kept his peace." Why not? The Republican slogan was "Keep Cool With Coolidge"; why get into needless debates on the issues? Why debate the Harding record? He was dead. Why debate the recurrent Davis cry that the Republicans were the party of Big Business and wouldn't do anything for the little man? "This is a business country," Coolidge said in his one radio speech, with the United States Chamber of Commerce as his host, "it wants a business government." He must have been right. He drew 15,725,016 votes against 8,386,503 for Davis (third in thirteen states) and 4,822,856 for LaFollette.

A Hands-Off Approach

In the next four years Coolidge demonstrated, if nothing else, that he was the most relaxed Chief Executive the nation ever had. Irwin (Ike) Hoover, the White House's Chief Usher, said the President usually found time for a two- to four-hour afternoon nap. When he didn't, he might rock on the porch for a while, watching the Model T's going by on Pennsylvania Avenue, feasting on the good expanse of lawn, or perhaps dwelling idly on the great abundance that lay over the land. Will Rogers asked him how he kept fit, and he said, "By avoiding the big problems."

Coolidge avoided all manner of problems, big and little. He steered clear of the Prohibition mess, simply issuing an occasional manifesto saying the law really should be obeyed; unlike his predecessor, he could honestly claim that he for one wasn't helping the bootleggers by using their stuff. He didn't get too deep into foreign affairs, letting far-away Europe sweat out its own reconstruction problems. On the broader domestic scene, he kept an eye peeled to see that no new-fangled ideas crept into government; things were all right the way they were. He put the lid on suggestions that Washington do something about the frenzied speculation in Wall Street; the financial community knew what it was doing.

Years later, when the notion was put forth that Coolidge had spurned another term because he foresaw the depression, H.L. Mencken entered a strong dissent in the *Baltimore Sun.* "He showed not the slightest sign that he smelt black clouds ahead," Mencken said. "On the contrary, he talked and lived only sunshine. There was a volcano boiling under him, but he did not know it . . . Here, indeed, was his one really notable talent. He slept more than any other President, whether by day or night. Nero fiddled, but Coolidge only snored." Irving Stone, in an essay called "A Study in Inertia," noted that the passive country squire in the White House "believed that the least government was the best government; he aspired to become the least President the country ever had; he attained his desire." The Beards were more genteel in their judgment of New England's favorite son. "Never in all his career," said the historians, "had he shocked his neighbors by advocating strange things prematurely; neither had he been the last of the faithful to appear on the scene in appropriate armor. Conciliation and prudence had been his watchwords; patience and simplicity his symbols of life."

The man himself made no large claims about his horizons. "There is only one form of political strategy in which I have any confidence," his autobiography said, "and that is to try to do the right thing and sometimes succeed." The Yankee President did succeed. He managed five years and seven months in the White House without getting into any kind of trouble. He went out of office—"I do not choose to run for President in 1928," he said—wearing all kinds of garlands, and there would be no surgical examination of his reign until after the Great Crash of 1929. Not till then would the post mortems cast some doubt on the record and much-heralded wisdom of Calvin Coolidge.

The Great Crash Ends an Era of Prosperity

Edwin P. Hoyt

Americans enjoyed a thriving economy for much of the decade. A large portion of the prosperous times rested upon a foundation of buying stocks, a foundation that most realized too late was fraught with risks. Since stock values spiraled at a dizzying pace in the 1920s, prominent businessmen as well as ordinary citizens repeatedly borrowed money to purchase more stocks with the intention of paying back the loan from the profits of the stock they bought. In 1929 the entire structure collapsed and helped usher in the Great Depression. Historian Edwin P. Hoyt captures the catastrophic Wall Street collapse in this selection from one of his many books.

On October 21, 1929, when the New York Stock Exchange opened trading on the last stroke of ten o'clock, the financial world rested confident and serene. During the previous week the market had dropped, causing some men who were given to comparisons to recall the "rich men's panic" of 1903. In that year "undigested" new securities carried on brokers' credit had suddenly flooded the market to the point of depression. But the comparison was generally regarded as useless since in 1903 the financial community had not been protected by requirements for brokers' loan reports and regular financial statements of brokers who dealt with the public on margin (as the public seemed surely protected in 1929). In September, 1929, the output of new securities was the highest of the year, but that happy statistic was regarded as just another reflection of continued and unbridled prosperity.

The Crisis Approaches

The Monday morning edition of the *Wall Street Journal* noted that the professionals in Wall Street were as "bearish" as they had been at any time in the year, but "bearishness" did not extend to many amateurs. Later that Monday stocks slumped sharply in the heaviest trading day on record. Nearly 6,100,000 shares changed hands. On the New York Stock Exchange the trading was so intense that the stock ticker fell behind at the end of the first ten minutes and the end of the day saw the ticker one hundred minutes behind the market. This lapse did not paralyze the brokers on the floor of the exchange since they could move readily from one trading point to another to keep abreast of price changes, but the delay in reports caused consternation in the markets of Denver, St. Louis, and San Francisco, which relied on telegraphic reports to keep posted on movements in Wall Street.

Some stocks broke sharply. Commercial Solvents, for one, dropped 145 points that day, and there was noticeable "distress selling" on the Curb Exchange, which meant brokers were unloading stocks held on narrow margins when their margin calls had gone unanswered by customers over the weekend.

By nightfall the professionals had recovered their aplomb. None of them were seriously worried, although they expressed sympathy to the losers among their customers. It was easy to find plausible reasons for the decline, from announced suspicion that a "bear" pool of wealthy investors had combined forces to drive down the price of stocks, to presumed worry by stockholders who had amassed large paper profits and were willing to lose part of those profits to protect the remainder and get out of the market for a few days. There was no real concern on Wall Street, except by a few Cassandras like [investor] Roger Babson.

One reason for broker serenity was the recovery of U.S. Steel that day. Steel had opened at 212, dropped to 205½, but by the end of the day had picked up to 210½, and since Steel was regarded as the bellwether of the market the brokers went home to dinner in good humor on Monday evening. . . .

On Tuesday the . . . market rallied. U.S. Steel went to 216½, although it closed lower at 212⅛. Roger Babson frantically advised his followers to sell their stocks and buy good bonds, but Charles Mitchell of the National City Bank said he saw nothing to worry about. . . .

Mitchell was not worried. Neither was Richard Whitney, presiding over the Stock Exchange in the absence of President Simmons on his honeymoon. Whitney did not even feel impelled to make a statement on the condition of the market on that Tuesday.

Wednesday, October 23, was an evil day on stock markets all over America and the end of the day was notable for significant changes in tone of the statements made by business leaders. Literally thousands of small investors were wiped out when they failed to supply cash to back their stocks and replace their share of the four billion dollars in paper losses suffered that day. Official Washington expressed surprise that the market remained so negative. Professor Fisher [of Yale University], speaking before the District of Columbia Bankers' Association, noted that the stock slump was surely "temporary." Bankers and brokers began discussing "support" of a market that had not seemed to need any support twenty-four hours earlier.

Support could come in several ways: by heavy investment in stocks by large investment trusts, which were reported to have cash reserves of at least a billion dollars, by a lowering of the rediscount rate on loans—an action by which the Federal Reserve Bank could make money easier to borrow, or by outright banker support, which meant the banks themselves would buy stocks in quantity.

In Chicago that Tuesday night Alexander Legge, chairman of the Federal Farm Board, warned the national convention of meat packers that the condition of American farmers was becoming serious. Mr. Legge said he was concerned because farmers must realize that four bushels of grain sold at $1.50 a bushel was a better investment for the farmer than five bushels sold at $1. Mr. Legge's comparison caught the eye of the nation because on the Chicago grain market wheat futures fell to $1.24⅞, a thirty-three cent drop in price in less than three months. . . .

Stock Values Plummet

After another poor day, on Wednesday night the atmosphere in Wall Street changed markedly. On Thursday morning when the big clock on the west wall above the floor of the New York Stock Exchange struck ten and Superintendent William B. Crawford struck the gong to announce the opening of trading, brokers surged to the trading stations, clutching handfuls of orders from customers—orders to sell. These were not usual "sell" orders. Kennecott Copper opened with a lot of 20,000 shares, General Motors the same; with such volume the ticker fell behind immediately. This was "dumping." As the extent of dumping became known the sell orders multiplied, along with rumors. The worst hour came between eleven fifteen and twelve fifteen, as investors across the country panicked and ordered their brokers to "sell at the market"—sell as quickly as possible before prices dropped further.

Prices were dropping five, ten, even fifteen points a minute. Auburn Motors plunged from 260 to 190, Montgomery Ward from 84 to 50. Usually, 750 or 800 brokers occupied the floor during a day's trading, but this day 1,100 brokers and a thousand assistants crowded around the trading stations, shouting and gesticulating to catch the eyes of the trading specialists.

The public gallery, seldom crowded, was jammed to overflowing. Winston Churchill, former British Chancellor of the Exchequer, dropped in for a few moments to view the confusion on the floor, then went on his way uptown to prepare for an important speech he was to make that evening. Other watchers stayed on, fascinated by the roar of the excited market place. It was the worst crash in history, so severe that by twelve thirty, Acting President Richard Whitney ordered the exchange's visitors' gallery closed to cut down the noise and help end the unceasing flow of rumors which said, erroneously, that the Chicago and Buffalo stock exchanges had been forced to close their doors in the flood of selling.

By noon that day a crowd had gathered on the steps of the U.S. sub-treasury building, eyes fixed on the entrance to the J.P. Morgan bank. A platoon of reporters and photographers stood there, waiting impatiently for developments. Inside the building, five of the most important bankers in the United States discussed the week's events. Outside, the crowd continued to wait for a report of the meeting.

The bankers conferred for twenty minutes, then four of them walked outside dolefully, leaving Thomas W. Lamont, senior partner of J.P. Morgan and Company to speak to the press. J.P. Morgan was in Europe, so Lamont was the spokesman for the Morgan bank. Five minutes later Lamont came out to hold an impromptu press conference at the entrance.

"There has been a little distress selling on the Stock Exchange," the banker began, in what eventually may be adjudged the financial understatement of the century. That was the closest Lamont came to recognizing the existence of panic. He went on to say that no financial houses were in trouble, that brokers reported margins were being maintained satisfactorily, and that the little bit of distress was caused by a "technical condition" which none but the professionals could be expected to understand. At that moment, [reporter] Burton Rascoe later wrote, every bank in the country was probably technically insolvent because of the plunge in value of stocks that secure outstanding loans.

An Attempt to Restore Investor Confidence

Skimpy and unrealistic as Lamont's statement was, it caused an immediate revival of optimism on the floor of the

New York Stock Exchange, not because of what Lamont had said, but because it was known that the most important bankers of all had met together. Brokers, investors, and speculators forced themselves to believe that the bankers had agreed to support the market. In fact the bankers had done so and the proof of it came an hour later when Richard Whitney appeared on the floor of the exchange, walked over to post No. 12, the station where U.S. Steel was traded, and began buying steel, with an initial bid of 205. The stock had slumped during the morning to 193½.

Here was a master stroke, both in timing and in selection of the man to do the buying, a man known as a "Morgan broker," a dignified, imposing figure in his own right, who exuded an air of confidence and well-being. Whitney did not stop to explain what he was doing. He walked purposefully from one trading station to another, ordering stocks in lots of ten and twenty thousand shares, not ostentatiously, not jumping the price above the last quotation, but buying at the last previous quotation.

In half an hour, Whitney had ordered two hundred thousand shares of various stocks, representing more than twenty million dollars worth of purchases. Richard Whitney did not have to comment, it was apparent to Wall Street that a bankers' pool had come to the rescue of the market.

Wall Street hoped, that afternoon, that the Federal Reserve Board would come to the assistance of the financial community by lowering the rediscount rate on loans, and in Washington the board met twice, the second time with Treasury Secretary Andrew Mellon. By the time the board held its second meeting, the action of the New York bankers was known. The board members decided the market was under control so no action was taken. The board was true to its principle: interfere with business only when there seemed to be no other course.

On the floor of the stock exchange there were some indications of rallying. Some stocks moved upward during the last hour of trading but others moved down. It was late in the day and there was no sense to be made of the pattern, and at three o'clock, when Superintendent Crawford gavelled the gong three times to announce the end of the trading day, the sweating brokers, collars torn open, hands full of orders that would have to wait, breathed a collective gasp of relief and began to file back to their offices for a night of work.

On Thursday night fifty thousand Wall Street employees worked late, sending out calls to customers for more margin to cover losses, entering records of sales and purchases, assessing the positions of the brokerage houses at the end of a day in which nearly thirteen million shares of stock had changed hands on the New York Stock Exchange. Nearly half as many shares had been sold on the smaller Curb Exchange that day. Thousands of accounts, most of them in the $1,000 to $10,000 range (which represented amateur investors) were closed out, and hundreds of thousands of shares of stock were earmarked for sale the following day when calls for margin remained unanswered by stunned speculators around the country. . . .

Later on that night of Black Thursday, October 24, the brokerage and banking houses registered cautious optimism, once again sure that the worst was over and that the market would begin to rise. On the demand of Charles Merrill, who had removed himself from the market, Merrill Lynch and Company advised its customers to keep their margins high without formal request, but also noted that it was a good time for investors with ready cash to buy stocks outright. Thirty-five of the largest brokerage houses on the New York Stock Exchange (who did 70 per cent of all the business on the exchange) wired clients all over the country predicting quick recovery of the market. The house of Hornblower and Weeks prepared advertisements which would run in eighty-five newspapers recommending purchase of "sound securities."

Mistaken Optimism

The next day, Friday, U.S. Steel opened at 207, and the big bankers said everything was under control. There was an implicit promise that they would not allow affairs to get out of control again. The original group in the bank coalition was reinforced. Altogether the bankers represented pledges of more than a quarter of a billion dollars to support the market. President Hoover issued a reassuring statement to the effect that fundamentally business was on a sound and prosperous basis. Banker Lamont, in a telling slip, had asked reporters on Thursday if they knew of the failure of any financial houses. This next day he had taken pains to reassure himself that "the street" was sound.

The street—Wall Street—was anything but sound. It was undergoing the most spectacular disaster of all time—but no one could call the turn from one day to the next. So long had the financial world steeped itself in optimism that no one appeared to be able to recognize the earmarks of disaster. Governor Franklin D. Roosevelt, who might have stepped in to regulate the New York stock exchanges, criticized speculators in general but expressed his confidence in the improvement of business and political morality. [General Motors president] Alfred P. Sloan, returning from Europe, remarked that the slump was "healthy" for the business world. Senator Carter Glass of Virginia, a conservative who frowned on speculation, argued on the floor of the Senate in favor of a 5 per cent tax on stock held less than sixty days. Senator Glass was trying to combat speculation, which Senator King of Utah characterized as a "national disease." Senator King proposed an investigation of the Federal Reserve System to discover why the Treasury had not caught the downward trend and had not stopped it in time to save millions of dollars in losses.

These were all indications of the national feeling that the worst was over, a belief that persisted through the weekend of October 26 and October 27. The stricken speculators cried themselves to sleep or drowned their woes in bathtub gin or, like Arthur Bathein, an officer of the Northern Pacific Finance Company of Seattle, shot themselves to death in the privacy of offices that no longer meant wealth or position, but ruin. Some continued to be listed among the missing, among them [investor] Abraham Germansky.

The worst had not yet come. On Monday, October 28, stock prices plunged another fourteen billion dollars, and stocks which had resisted the earlier disaster fell hard and fast. Eastman Kodak dropped 40 points. General Motors went down only 6¾ points, but so large was the volume of General Motors stock sold that this spread meant a loss in values of nearly $350,000,000.

In this second week the disaster took a new turn: those who had been wiped out in the market began to withdraw their savings from the banks. The stock of New York's First National Bank dropped $500 a share that day. The banker coalition, surprisingly, did nothing. The Federal Reserve Board met again in Washington, but took no action.

Total Collapse

On Tuesday, October 29, the market collapsed in a splash of trading which involved sixteen and a half million shares, and while several industrial giants announced extra dividends to be paid on their stocks in an effort to stimulate confidence, the confidence was gone. Bank stocks began to fall off. The value of New York's First National Bank dropped from $6,800 a share to $5,200 and the first broker's failure was announced: John J. Bell Company of the Curb Exchange suspended activity, wiped out. There was only one bright spot in the entire dismal picture, if one could call it that. The state of New York, which levied a stock transfer tax of two cents per $100 on stocks, had collected $1,500,000 from six days of stock market trading.

The bankers had shown their inability to understand what was happening or to stop it. So had the United States Treasury Department. So had Governor Roosevelt in Albany. New York City Mayor James Walker displayed his understanding of high finance when he spoke to the group of motion-picture exhibitors at the Astor Hotel and advised them to refrain from showing newsreels which pictured the run on the market.

On the American side of the Atlantic Ocean, there was

no understanding of either the course of events or of the portents for the future. The American philosophy made no provision for the collapse of the nation's economic system. Americans from President Hoover to Roger Babson predicted that a turning point was just around the corner.

In the city of London, however, financial men were far enough removed from events and from the fatal optimism of New York to realize what was happening in America. The first cries of "I told you so" gave way at the end of the first week of collapse to sober consideration of the effects of the American disaster on the rest of the world. "We are watching the complete disorganization of a complex market by an assault upon it of a leaderless and panic-stricken mob," said the London *Daily Mail*'s financial editor, who looked on from afar in awe.

CHAPTER 2

Intolerance
in the 1920s

The Ku Klux Klan Strengthens Its Hand

Arnold S. Rice

Though the Ku Klux Klan first organized in the years following the Civil War, by the early 1900s it had experienced peaks and valleys in an attempt to recruit new members. Spreading a message of hate is not always simple, but Klan supporters continued their efforts. In the 1920s they enjoyed a rebirth, particularly in some northern states that had previously never been home to Klan sympathizers.

In this excerpt, professor Arnold S. Rice, an expert on the organization, examines the growth of the Klan in the 1920s.

It is a serious mistake to think that the Ku Klux Klan of the 1920's was a powerful force only in the Deep South. To be sure, the order was founded in Georgia, and then spread rather quickly to the neighboring states of Alabama and Florida. However, the Klan reached its first peak of success, after the Congressional investigation in October, 1921, in the vast area to the west of the lower Mississippi River, in Texas, Oklahoma, and Arkansas. Then the organization took firm root on the Pacific coast, first in California and later in Oregon. And by 1924 the fraternity reached extraordinary success in the Middle West generally and fantastic success in the states of Indiana and Ohio particularly.

One of the most astute of the many contemporary students of the Klan, Stanley Frost, calculated that the order at its height of activity had about 4,000,000 members distributed as follows: Indiana, 500,000; Ohio, 450,000; Texas, 415,000; California, New York, Oklahoma, Oregon 200,000 each; Alabama, Arkansas, Florida, Georgia, Illinois, Kansas, Kentucky, Louisiana, Maryland, Michigan, Mississippi, Missouri, New Jersey, Tennessee, Washington, and West Virginia, between 50,000 and 200,000 each.

Who Joined the Klan?

One might wonder at the large number of Klansmen in states having so few Negroes, Catholics, Jews, or foreign-born—states lacking, therefore, in all those things against which the Klan railed and upon which it thrived. The secret is that in the 1920's the bulk of the people in the states of the western reaches of the lower Mississippi Valley, the Pacific coast, and the Middle West were the descendants—both physical and spiritual—of that old American stock from which the anti-Catholic and nativistic movements of the preceding century drew their chief support.

The Klan was in the main a village and small town phenomenon. Neither the city, as a potpourri of many racial, religious, and ethnic groups, nor the country, as an isolated area with far-spread inhabitants, lent itself to the effective launching and developing of a local chapter. The appreciable Klan following in many of the large cities and much of the countryside all over the United States during the 1920's must not be discounted. But the secret fraternity drew its millions primarily from the villages and small towns which had been left rather undisturbed by the immigration, industrialization, and liberal thought of modern America.

Eligible for membership in the Invisible Empire, Knights of the Ku Klux Klan was any white, native-born, Christian, American male, who (in order to debar Catholics) owed "no allegiance of any nature or degree to any foreign government, nation, institution, sect, ruler, person. . . ."

Among those millions of individuals who could, and did, join the order, one contemporary observer, Robert L. Duffus, found six classes: (1) the organizers and promoters; (2) businessmen; (3) politicians; (4) preachers and pious laymen; (5) incorrigible "joiners" and lovers of "horseplay"; and (6) bootleggers who joined for protection. Using this classification as the basis for a discussion of the caliber of men who associated themselves with the Klan—and this classification will have to serve for lack of another by a contemporary more knowledgeable and objective—it becomes immediately apparent that Klansmen belonged to a variety of socio-economic classes.

Not always, but sometimes, the leaders of a community would join the local Klan chapter. In each new territory that the Kleagle [local Klan leader] "worked," he made a practice, for obvious reasons, of approaching the prominent citizens first. Imperial Kligrapp [national Klan leader] H.K. Ramsey, writing of the Klan's Second Klonvokation, held in Kansas City, Missouri, in September, 1924, declared that "Ministers of the Gospel, Attorneys (some representing our common judiciary), Educators, business men (a number of them millionaires and capitalists) . . . all sat together."

After the Kleagles had flattered and persuaded as many of the leading citizens of the community into joining the secret fraternity as they could, they then turned their attention to enlisting the middle class. The remark of Ramsey, as a member of the Klan's hierarchy, might well be taken with the proverbial grain of salt. Nevertheless, it is most important to note that practically all anti-Klan writers described the vast majority of Klansmen as members of America's respectable middle class. One journalist, for example, wrote that most Klansmen were "solid, respectable citizens, kind and loving husbands and fathers, conscientious members of their churches"; another penned that most of the persons who joined the order were "good, solid, middle-class citizens, the 'backbone of the Nation'."

After the Kleagles had enlisted as many of the middle class as they were able, they then directed their sales talk to the less desirable elements. Hustling agents "sought out the poor, the romantic, the short-witted, the bored, the vindictive, the bigoted, and the ambitious, and sold them their heart's desire." Stanley Frost, in his reportorial study of the Klan for *The Outlook,* commented that he had not learned of a single case in which a Kleagle refused an individual membership in the secret fraternity—"no matter how vicious or dangerous he might be"—if he had the necessary $10. Henry Peck Fry, who resigned from the Klan as a disillusioned Kleagle, branded his former colleagues for "selling memberships as they would sell insurance or stock.". . .

Rise of the Klan

There was something about the United States of the 1920's that influenced a surprisingly large number of Americans in their decision to join the order. The spirit of the times demands analysis.

The decade 1920–1930 was what it was largely because of the effects of World War I. During the armed struggle America mistrusted and mistreated aliens, deprived itself of food and fuel, and poured its money into the Liberty Loan campaigns. But the war was over too quickly for the nation to spend fully its ultra-patriotic psychological feelings. In the decade following, America permitted itself to reject the League of Nations, to curtail immigration, to deport aliens wholesale, and to accept the Klan with its motto of "one hundred per cent Americanism."

Another result of the war was the intensifying of racial antipathies. The bearing of arms and the freedom of contact with whites in France by Negro servicemen and the receiving of high wages by many Negroes of the South who moved to northern cities in order to work for war industries made the colored people of the nation feel a human dignity they had never before experienced. During the 1920's this served to increase hostility on the part of whites and to decrease the endurance of such hostility on the part of Negroes. The Klan was quick to capitalize on the feeling of those whites who believed they saw everywhere Negro "uppitiness."

A third effect of World War I was the violent death of the

old American way of life—evangelical, didactic, prudish—and the sudden birth of a new. (No event serves as a nation's cultural watershed better than a war.) The 1920's meant "modernism." And "modernism," among other things, meant the waning of church influence, particularly over the younger people; the breaking down of parental control; the discarding of the old-fashioned absolute moral code in favor of a freer or "looser" personal one, which manifested itself in such activities as purchasing and drinking contraband liquor, participating in ultra-frank conversations between the sexes, wearing skirts close to the knees, engaging in various extreme forms of dancing in smoke-filled road houses, and petting in parked cars. A host of Americans were unwilling, or unable, to adapt themselves to this post-war culture. In the Klan they saw a bulwark against the hated "modernism," an opportunity to salvage some of the customs and traditions of the old religio-moralistic order. . . .

That the bigoted of the nation found "truth" in the Klan is self-evident. It must be emphasized that the secret order was most shrewd in the way it varied its appeal from one section of the country to the other to suit the paramount prejudice of the area. The Klan's plank was chameleonic: on the Pacific coast it was anti-Japanese; in the Southwest, anti-Mexican; in the Middle West, anti-Catholic; in the Deep South, anti-Negro; in New England, anti-French Canadian; in the large cities of the Northeast, anti-alien-born; on the Atlantic coast, anti-Semitic.

Many ruffians took the sacred oath of allegiance to the Invisible Empire. The Klan as a bulwark against "modernism" conveyed to the simple and sincere members of the order nothing more than a crusade to reform the wayward of their community. Translated into practical application such a crusade meant teaching someone a "lesson"—perhaps an adulterous neighbor, the town drunkard, a merchant who habitually short-changed and short-weighted, or a corrupt official. Taking punitive measures against a wrongdoer without benefit of the regularly established police and court systems leads more often than not to injustice and cruelty. While appearing to be acting selflessly in behalf of the Klan, hoodlums saw a wonderful opportunity to get their fill of sadistic orgies. Taking refuge under the hood and robe, rowdies on a "night-riding" mission could wield with abandon the tar bucket and bag of feathers, whip, branding iron, acid bottle, or pocket knife. . . .

Then there was the costume. The robe of the rank and file of the secret order was of white cotton, girdled with a sash of the same color and material, and with a white cross upon a red background stitched below the left shoulder. The headdress was a white cotton peaked hood from which a red tassel hung. The entire outfit cost $5. The costume of an officer was more resplendent and more expensive, how much so depending upon the status of the officer in the Klan hierarchy. The robe of a Grand Dragon, for example, was of orange satin trimmed with military braid and embroidered in silk. Together with an orange satin peaked hood, it cost $40. . . .

Klan Beliefs

Naturally, it was expected of every individual who took the sacred oath of allegiance to the Invisible Empire, Knights of the Ku Klux Klan to know and fully accept the beliefs of the order. The main tenets in the creed of the secret fraternity were the following: (1) memorialization of the original Klan; (2) white supremacy; (3) anti-Semitism [hatred of Jews]; (4) anti-foreign-bornism; (5) anti-Catholicism; (6) "pure" Americanism; (7) Protestantism and strict morality. . . .

The twentieth century Klan copied a great deal from its precursor—the hierarchy of officers, subdivisional structure, regalia, silent parades, and mysterious language. There was only one thing, however, taken over from the original Klan by the twentieth century order which was ideological in nature rather than ritualistic or ornamental—and that was the belief in white supremacy.

A quick and highly satisfactory method by which to approach the Klan's thinking on the Negro (as well as on such topics as the Jew, foreign-born, Catholic, or Americanism) is to dip into a few of the writings of, addresses by, and interviews with [Hiram Wesley] Evans, for as Imperial Wizard he spoke officially for every man in the order. In an article for *The North American Review,* Evans declared:

"The world has been so made that each race must fight for its life, must conquer, accept slavery or die. The Klansman believes that the whites will not become slaves, and he does not intend to die before his time.

". . . the future of progress and civilization depends on the continual supremacy of the white race. The forward movement of the world for centuries has come entirely from it. Other races each had its chance and either failed or stuck fast, while white civilization shows no sign of having reached its limit. Until the whites falter, or some colored civilization has a miracle of awakening, there is not a single colored stock that can claim even equality with the white; much less supremacy.". . .

The very heart of the Klan's thinking on the foreign-born in America can be found in a single passage from one of Evans' articles for *The Forum:*

"We believe that the pioneers who built America bequeathed to their own children a priority right to it, the control of it and of its future, and that no one on earth can claim any part of this inheritance except through our generosity. We believe, too, that the mission of America under Almighty God is to perpetuate and develop just the kind of nation and just the kind of civilization which our forefathers created. . . . Also, we believe . . . that the American stock, which was bred under highly selective surroundings, has proved its value and should not be [through intermarriage with the foreign-born] mongrelized. . . . Finally, we believe that all foreigners were admitted with the idea, and on the basis of at least an implied understanding, that they would . . . adopt our ideas and ideals, and help in fulfilling our destiny along those lines, but never that they should be permitted to force us to change into anything else.". . .

The Klan believed that only through a public educational

system which stressed the "value and beauty of true citizenship" could a mighty and vibrant America be created. Therefore, the order swore to fight for the extension of the public school system all over the nation, in spite of the continuous refusal of certain bodies, such as the Catholic Church, to give up their own private educational programs.

The Klan's interest in education, however, went deeper than a concern for the protection of the public elementary and secondary school system. As a matter of fact, the order felt so strongly about education for the preservation of Americanism that it made two separate attempts to set up a Klan college, the first during [William J.] Simmons' Imperial Wizardship and the second during Evans'. In August, 1921, the Klan acquired Lanier University in Atlanta, the Baptist institution where Simmons had once been an instructor in Southern history. Co-educational, and open to the children of native-born, white Protestants only, the new school dedicated itself to the teaching of "pure, 100 per cent Americanism." Failing to gain an adequate enrollment, the Klan gave up this academic enterprise, only to negotiate, two years later, for the taking over of Valparaiso University in Valparaiso, Indiana. In this instance, however, all attempts to acquire the institution met with failure.

The Klan cherished a belief in Protestant Christian doctrine. Although it did not require an applicant to hold church membership, it did insist upon his embracing the tenets of Protestantism. The Klan endorsed no one religious denomination. Many Knights, however, were adherents to "the old-time religion," with its faith in the Bible as the literal and unalterable word of God. So many Klansmen (especially those of the South) belonged to the evangelical sects that the public came to think that one of the articles of faith of the Klan was Fundamentalism [belief in the Bible as a factual historical record]. . . .

Methods to Promote the Klan

Of all the practices of Klansmen, the one most often and vehemently criticized was the taking of a meddling or terroristic course of action in an attempt to prescribe personal conduct. It appears that each local Klan decided its chief task was the regulation of the morals of the community in which it existed. A typical chapter operated something like this: every Knight considered himself a detective whose duty it was to go about the community spying on the morals of his fellow residents, the objects of the surveillance being entirely unaware of it, as only Klansmen knew who the members of the order were. When the chapter met, every Knight reported the information he had collected on his neighbors' morals. The assembled body then passed judgment on each case, after which it decided the course of action necessary and proper for the reforming of immorality.

The local Klan's course of action in the reforming of personal conduct usually resulted in the chapter's appointing a select committee which remonstrated with the delinquent on the evil of his ways. If this approach failed to bring about an improvement in conduct, the chapter then reported him and his sins to the police, offering to those officials its full moral support. Should the law authorities fail to act (in which case the local Klan attempted to retire them from office and fill their places with individuals deemed more worthy, preferably Klansmen), and should the wrongdoer still remain unregenerate, the chapter then turned to a more extreme measure—ostracism, perhaps.

The local Klan expected its program of ostracism to force the wrongdoer into self-imposed exile. An actual case of a chapter's use of ostracism is worth citing. In a town of an eastern state, a hardworking, rather reliable young man was engaging in an illicit sexual relationship with a notoriously wanton woman. Threatened by telephone that he would regret it if he did not leave his mistress within three days, he chose to remain with her. Four days later his employer fired him. The following day his landlord demanded an exorbitant raise in rent. The milkman no longer went to the door. The butcher failed to stop his wagon. Merchants treated him with rudeness in their shops, some telling him bluntly that his patronage was no longer desired. By the end of the week only one grocer (in defiance of a telephone warning) would sell the man food, and this storekeeper was shortly brought into line by the loss of nearly three-quarters of his trade. Within two weeks the local Klan's program of ostracism had fully proved itself. The newly-created pariah moved to a hovel outside of town, where a few friends gave him aid and comfort until he was able to find employment and settle down elsewhere.

Rarely did any local Klan resort to a physical disciplining of an individual who had offended against its moral ideas. When a chapter did so, the press naturally gave the incident a great deal of coverage. Following are some illustrations of the Klan's use of corporal punishment. In October, 1920, an attorney from Yonkers, New York, Peter McMahon, while in the South to assist a client in a dispute over an estate, was taken from a train at Trenton, South Carolina, and beaten by a gang of individuals dressed as Klansmen. On April 1, 1921, a Negro bellhop from a Dallas hotel was abducted by a group of hooded men who branded him with acid on the forehead with the letters "K.K.K." Two months later, in Tenaha, Texas, a woman believed to have been committing adultery was seized, stripped of her clothing, and tarred and feathered. Another resident of the state, a woman from Goose Creek, was kidnapped by hooded and robed men who cut off her hair and tacked the tresses to a post in the center of town. On July 16, 1921, a sixty-eight-year-old farmer was whipped in Warrensburg, Missouri. The following day, in Miami, Florida, an archdeacon of the Episcopal Church was whipped, tarred and feathered. A few days later a man and woman at Birmingham, Alabama, received a flogging at the hands of a mob. In August, 1921, in Mason City, Iowa, persons who "preferred to be known as the Ku Klux Klan" forced a Socialist, Mrs. Ida Couch Hazlett, from a speaker's platform into a car, drove her to the outskirts of the city, and threw her out with a threat of greater physical violence if she returned. That same month, in Tulsa, Oklahoma, a ne'er-do-well by the name of Nathan Hantaman was dragged by Klansmen from his residence to a waiting car which deposited him just outside the city, where he was whipped until his back was a swollen mass of ugly welts. On August 24, 1922, near Mer Rouge, Louisiana, while returning from a picnic, two arch-critics of the local Klan of that town, Filmore Watt Daniels and Thomas F. Richards, were seized by hooded men. Two months later the badly decomposed corpses of Daniels and Richards were found floating on nearby Lake La Fourche.

Segregation in Housing: A Case Study

John F. Wukovits

Strides have been made to guarantee equal opportunity to all people, but in the 1920s African Americans daily felt the sting of bigotry. Though an array of laws kept blacks in an inferior position in the South, prejudice ran rampant in northern states as well. In Michigan, a man named Ossian Sweet learned that he had to fight for the basic right to own a home, then wage a second battle to stay out of jail. The nation's foremost defense attorney, Clarence Darrow, argued his case in front of a Detroit jury.

Historian and biographer John F. Wukovits recounts the events leading to Darrow's defense of Ossian Sweet in an article for a prominent national publication.

Ossian Sweet wasn't looking for trouble when he went shopping in Detroit for a house for his young family in the spring of 1925. "He just wanted to bring up his girl in good surroundings," his brother Otis later recalled. Sweet found what he wanted in a two-story bungalow at 2905 Garland Avenue, in a lower middle-class neighborhood of small businessmen and factory workers. But when Sweet, a black doctor with a thriving practice in the city, tried to move into his new home, his efforts triggered violent protests from white neighbors and led to two remarkable trials.

Excerpted from "A Case Close to My Heart," by John F. Wukovits, *American History*, December 1998. Reprinted with permission from the author.

Racial tension was high in Detroit that year. Henry Ford's introduction of the five-dollar-a-day wage in 1914 had spurred an exodus of poor, black Southerners to Detroit to build automobiles. When Ford raised his rate by a dollar in 1919 the migration increased; by the mid-1920s Detroit was home to the nation's fastest-growing black community. Whites reacted with increasing alarm. The city police department was responsible for the deaths of roughly 50 blacks between 1923 and 1925. Meanwhile, the Ku Klux Klan, buttressed by a similar movement north of poor southern whites, became involved in city politics and fielded a candidate in the 1925 mayoral race.

Racial Tensions

It was in this setting that Ossian Sweet started a family and career. The grandson of an Alabama slave, Sweet worked his way through Howard University Medical School in Washington, D.C., before opening a practice in Detroit in 1921. After marrying Gladys Mitchell the following year, Sweet treated his wife to a lengthy European honeymoon and studied in Vienna and in Paris under the renowned Madame Curie. Following the birth of a daughter, the Sweets returned to Detroit in 1924 and moved temporarily into the home of Mrs. Sweet's mother.

Sweet could afford a decent home for his family, away from the cramped, unhealthy conditions of Detroit's "Paradise Valley," where two-thirds of the city's black population resided. Although he had witnessed race-related violence in his Florida hometown and in Washington, Sweet did not initially anticipate trouble. His mother-in-law had lived peacefully in a partially integrated area for many years, and the owners of the house on Garland Avenue—the Smiths—were a white woman and a black man. Mr. Smith, however, was apparently so light-skinned that his neighbors never realized he was black.

Sweet soon saw signs of trouble. First the Smiths received warnings not to sell their house to a black family. In July, a local group called the Waterworks Improvement Association was formed to "render constructive social and civic service" to the neighborhood. The innocent-sounding name hid the group's real purpose, which was to keep the area free of blacks.

Other incidents that summer illustrated the increase in racial tension in the city. Another black physician named A.L. Turner was greeted by loud demonstrations when he moved into an all-white neighborhood. The police responded by directing that area's "improvement association" to deliver Turner's furniture back to his old house. Meanwhile, a crowd of angry whites pelted the home of a black waiter named John Fletcher with lumps of coal. Gunfire erupted from within the house, wounding a white teenager. Fletcher was arrested, but the charges were later dropped.

Resolving to "die a man or live a coward," Sweet informed the Detroit police department that he would move into his new home on September 8. He was not reassured by the department's reluctant promise to protect his rights and asked his brothers, Henry and Otis, and several of their friends to stay with him for a few days. He left his young daughter in the care of Gladys' mother for the time being. Among the items Sweet brought with him for the move were nine guns and a stockpile of ammunition.

Sweet Moves to Garland Avenue

Four policemen looked on as the Sweets carried furniture into their house on September 8. That night the Sweets and their friends waited anxiously by the windows, armed and ready to defend the house, but the gathering mass of people across the street was content to shout threats and taunts. The next morning, however, Ossian received word that the crowd had decided that "they are going to get you out of here tonight." Sweet asked three more friends to spend the night, and by evening the mood of the crowd had turned markedly sour. The small police contingent had doubled in size but did nothing when stones were hurled at the house.

Heavy traffic clogged the street outside Sweet's house as the men inside watched the growing crowd. Around 8:15

P.M., a taxi carrying Otis Sweet and a friend nudged through the gathering, and when the passengers stepped out they had to rush to the house amidst a torrent of rocks and cries of "Get them! Get them!" The raucous mob closed in on the house. Suddenly, gunfire erupted from inside. Across the street, two men fell with bullet wounds, one of whom—Leon Breiner—later died.

Inspector Norton N. Schuknecht rushed into the house and demanded, "What in hell are you fellows shooting about?" Sweet countered that he was just protecting his home and that there would be no more shooting. Schuknecht departed, not realizing that two white men had been shot. Shortly afterward, however, he returned with several other officers and arrested Sweet and his 10 companions, including his wife, on charges of first-degree murder.

For two days the police kept defense lawyers from conferring with their clients, and the confused defendants told contradictory stories about what had happened. Meanwhile, the police officers claimed that there had been no crowd or violence sufficient to justify the shooting. In light of the inflammatory state of racial feelings in the city, the assistant prosecutor argued against bail for any of the defendants, and all were sent to the Wayne County jail.

Darrow to the Defense

The National Association for the Advancement of Colored People (NAACP) quickly rallied to Sweet's defense. Convinced that only a prominent white lawyer could elicit sympathy from white citizens, the group sought the aid of renowned defense attorney Clarence Darrow.

Darrow had long been a champion of unpopular causes. He had represented radical union leaders, saved a pair of teenage killers from the death penalty, and had recently defended Tennessee school teacher John Scopes, on trial for teaching evolution. Long a protector of individual rights, Darrow came from a family known for its sympathy for blacks. His ancestors had supported the Underground Railroad, and Darrow often spoke in black churches, contending that "When it comes to human beings, I am color blind; to me people are not simply white or black; they are all freckled."

At the age of 68, however, Darrow was exhausted. The laborious Scopes "Monkey" Trial [concerning the teaching of evolution in public schools], in which he had battled head to head with the formidable William Jennings Bryan, had weakened the aging warrior. Bryan, in fact, had died within days of the trial's end. Darrow was tired of taking on cases "that required hard work and brought me into conflict with the crowd." He was ready to retire.

Darrow knew from the start, however, that his sympathy for the Sweets' plight would force him to accept the case. After NAACP Assistant Secretary Walter White explained its basic details, Darrow asked if the defendants had actually fired into the crowd. White hesitated, afraid the answer would cause Darrow to decline the case, but finally said yes. Darrow instantly accepted, adding that "If they had not had the courage to shoot back in defense of their own lives, I wouldn't think they were worth defending."

On October 12, Darrow arrived in Detroit with his associate, Arthur Garfield Hays. His first task was to convince the defendants that their state of mind during the shooting was crucial to their defense. Hays later stated that, because they were heroes to other blacks, "Not all of them cared to admit they had been scared."

The Trial Opens

Court convened on October 30, and spectators packed the courtroom to watch America's foremost defense attorney spar with District Attorney Robert M. Toms and his aggressive assistant, Lester S. Moll. Darrow's assistants argued that Sweet could not receive a fair trial in Detroit and urged a change of venue, but Darrow rejected their advice. He had been impressed by the impartiality of the presiding judge, Frank Murphy. Darrow believed a good lawyer "should be able to tell something about a man by looking at his face," and he liked what he saw in Murphy.

Darrow's judgment proved sound. Murphy, who later became governor of Michigan and an associate justice of the U.S. Supreme Court, consciously strove to ensure that any person who appeared before him—rich or poor, black or white—enjoyed the same rights. Darrow wrote after the trial that Murphy "proved to be the kindliest and most understanding man I have ever happened to meet on the bench. . . ."

Selecting an impartial jury proved difficult. Darrow questioned 150 potential jurors, attempting in the process to educate them in black history. He thought that if he could enlighten the 12 men chosen, his clients stood a chance. It took five weeks to choose the jury. "The case is won or lost now," Darrow remarked to his associates. "The rest is window dressing."

The state called 71 witnesses to support its assertion that the Sweets had "feloniously, willfully and of their malice aforethought" armed themselves with the intent to kill anyone threatening the house. Prosecuting attorneys said the shootings were unprovoked, that prejudice played no part in the drama, and that no unruly mob had assembled that night. Inspector Schuknecht testified that the neighborhood had been quiet and that he had told his men he would use "every man in the police station" to guard the Sweets' right to live in his new home.

Darrow worked on crossword puzzles at the defense table while the prosecution laid out its case, but he was paying close attention to the proceedings. Noticing that whites dominated the courtroom crowds, he told Judge Murphy that a larger percentage of blacks should be witnesses to a trial that meant so much to the black population. Murphy agreed. As the trial progressed, more and more blacks filled the courtroom.

During cross-examination, Darrow managed to pry a few crucial statements from the prosecution's witnesses. Police admitted that traffic outside Sweet's home was so congested that two men had been assigned to direct it. Each time a witness described the crowd as being no more than

25 or 30 people, Darrow pointedly asked why he had been in the neighborhood. After hearing the same response from almost every witness—that they were "curious"—Darrow sarcastically mused how odd it was that so many whites had been curious at the same time about a black family.

In a significant breakthrough for the defense, two teenage boys indicated that the crowd had indeed posed a threat to the Sweets. Urlic Arthur testified that he had watched four or five youths hurl rocks at the Sweet house. When Darrow quizzed a local boy named Dwight Hubbard about the crowd's size, Hubbard answered, "There was a great crowd—no, I won't say a great crowd, a large crowd—well, there were a few people there and the officers were keeping them moving." Darrow jumped on this confusion and asked if Hubbard had talked to anyone about the case. The boy admitted that he had forgotten to characterize the crowd as "a few people," as he had been coached to do.

There had been few emotional outbursts to that point in the trial. Prosecutor Toms made a point to be pleasant to Darrow, trying to prevent his opponent from erupting in one of his famed courtroom speeches. Hoping for the battle to heat up, though, a frustrated Darrow complained, "God damn it, Toms, I can't get going. I am supposed to be mad at you and I can't even pretend that I am."

The prosecution rested its case on November 14. Hays opened for the defense by citing PEOPLE v. AUGUSTUS POND, a landmark Michigan case from 1860. It had ruled that a man could employ any necessary method to defend his home, including homicide.

The Defense Argues Its Case

Darrow then went to work. He hammered home the point that his clients acted in self-defense and that "one is justified in defending himself when he apprehends that his life is in danger and when that apprehension is based upon reason." Explaining that Michigan law defined a mob as 12 or more armed or 30 unarmed persons, Darrow contended that his clients had ample reason to fear the whites outside the Sweet home, especially in light of recent events.

Philip A. Adler, a white reporter for the *Detroit News,* led the parade of defense witnesses. Adler had been in the area on the night of the shooting and estimated the crowd to be 400 to 500 people. After parking his car, he recalled, he had elbowed his way through the boisterous throng. Threats against those inside the house echoed about the neighborhood, and one person told Adler that a "Negro family has moved in here and we're going to get them out."

Three black witnesses who had driven together through the area then compared the crowd, that had pelted their car with rocks, to "a mob of howling Indians." Darrow's star witness, however, was Ossian Sweet. Darrow intended to quietly ask his client a few simple questions, then allow him to occupy center stage.

According to Sweet, he and his friends were playing cards at about 8:00 P.M. when "something hit the roof of the house." One of the men peered outside and saw people scurrying around the property, so Sweet dashed into the kitchen to check on his wife. While there he heard someone outside yell, "Go and raise hell in front; I am going back." Rocks peppered the house and Sweet grabbed a gun and ran upstairs. "Pandemonium—I guess that's the best way to describe it—broke loose," he explained calmly. "Everyone was running from room to room. There was a general uproar." Sweet added that the crowd moved forward "like a human sea. Stones kept coming faster. . . . Another window was smashed. Then one shot, then eight or ten from upstairs, then it was all over."

Darrow asked Sweet to describe his state of mind during the incident. Prosecutor Toms immediately jumped to his feet and objected that such material was irrelevant. Courtroom observers leaned forward in their seats, sensing that a crucial moment had arrived. Judge Murphy broke the tension by permitting the evidence on the grounds that such knowledge did have a bearing as to the defendants' motives.

As blacks in the courtroom listened "with strained and

anxious faces," Sweet spoke of growing up outside Orlando, Florida, where black-owned homes were burned and black men were killed. He referred to four brothers in Arkansas who had been yanked from a train and murdered, and to a Texas man who surrendered to police to escape a threatening mob of whites but was then turned over to that same mob and burned at the stake.

When he opened the door to let in his brother "and saw that mob," said the soft-spoken physician, "I realized in a way that I was facing that same mob that had hounded my people through its entire history. I realized my back was against the wall and I was filled with a peculiar type of fear—the fear of one who knows the history of my race."

In his closing argument on November 24, Moll labeled the shooting "a cowardly act" and declared that each defendant "took a hand in the killing of Breiner in cold blood." Darrow then stepped forward. His voice "tense with emotion," he argued that his clients were on trial for only one reason—the color of their skin. "If it had been a white man defending his home from a member of a Negro mob," he declared, "no one would have been arrested nor put on trial." He discounted the testimony of prosecution witnesses—"there is not an honest person in the whole bunch," he said—and he castigated the police department for its ineffective control of what the prosecution refused to call a mob. "Gentlemen, the State has put on enough witnesses who said they were there, to make a mob."

Darrow asked the jurors to try to put themselves in the defendants' position before they passed judgment on them. "The Sweets spent their first night in their new home afraid to go to bed," he said. "The next night they spent in jail. Now the state wants them to spend the rest of their lives in the penitentiary."

Finally, with many in the audience moved to tears, Darrow ended his powerful plea. "I speak to you not only in behalf of them, but in behalf of the millions of black faces who look to these 12 white faces for confidence and trust and hope in the institutions of our land. . . . I ask you in the name of the future to do justice in this case." Judge Murphy could barely contain his emotions as Darrow returned to his chair. One lawyer later said he had heard "about lawyers making a judge cry but Darrow is the first man I actually saw do it."

Though Toms was in the unenviable position of following Darrow, he delivered a strong closing statement. The jury's responsibility, he noted, was not to solve the race issue but to determine who had killed Breiner, whose right to live was more important than Sweet's "right to live where you please, in a certain house on a certain street." Toms directed his final remarks to his opponents. "Back of all your sophistry and transparent political philosophy, gentlemen of the defense, back of all your prating of civil rights, back of your psychology and theory of race hatred, lies the stark body of Leon Breiner with a bullet hole in his back."

Murphy instructed the jury to consider the defendants' race and color, and the fact that a man's home is his castle "whether he is white or black." They should also ask themselves, he added, if they had reasonable cause to sense danger. If such a belief existed, he said, "the shooting would be justifiable and the defendants would be not guilty."

Darrow believed these instructions had "scarcely left a chance for them to do anything but acquit," but the jury thought otherwise. Deliberations lasted 46 hours and were punctuated by loud arguments. People outside the jury room sometimes heard angry voices shouting phrases such as, "What's the use of arguing with these fellows?", "Two of you had these fellows convicted before you came in here," and "I'll stay here 20 years, if necessary, and I am younger than any of you." In the end, they could not agree on a verdict, and Murphy was forced to discharge them.

A New Trial

Toms immediately stated his intention to re-try the defendants. For the second trial Darrow switched tactics. Instead of defending all 11 at the same time, he would represent each one separately. The State chose first to prosecute Henry

Sweet, who was the only one to admit firing his gun. Darrow was confident that if he could gain an acquittal for Henry, the other cases would crumble.

The second trial opened in April 1926. Testimony generally followed the same lines as the first trial, although Darrow learned from one state witness that at a meeting of the Waterworks Association, a representative from a similar neighborhood group had promoted violence to drive out the Sweets. Violence, the man told the group, worked when they wanted to keep their street white.

Few people in any courtroom ever experienced anything similar to Darrow's closing. Although exhausted by the two trials, Darrow delivered an epic eight-hour speech that captivated his audience. "One could have heard a pin drop in the crowded courtroom," marveled one observer. "Sometimes his resonant, melodious voice sank to a whisper. Sometimes it rose in a roar of indignation."

Darrow pulled few punches in characterizing Breiner as "a conspirator in as foul a conspiracy as was ever hatched in a community; in a conspiracy to drive from their homes a little family of black people." He compared Breiner to ancient Romans who eagerly rushed to the Coliseum to watch lions mangle Christians. "He was there waiting to see these black men driven from their homes, and you know it; peacefully smoking his pipe, and as innocent a man as ever scuttled a ship."

But the central issue was prejudice, which Darrow had fought all his life. Disagreeing with the prosecution's contention that this was a murder case, not a question of race, Darrow countered, "I insist that there is nothing but prejudice in this case; that if it was reversed and eleven white men had shot and killed a black while protecting their home and their lives against a mob of blacks, nobody would have dreamed of having them indicted. . . . Now, that is the case, gentlemen, and that is all there is to this case. Take the hatred away, and you have nothing left."

Finally, the emotionally drained Darrow tied up his summation. "I ask you, on behalf of this defendant, on behalf of these helpless ones who turn to you. . . . I ask you, in the name of progress and of the human race, to return a verdict of not guilty in this case!" Darrow apologized for the length of his remarks and admitted "this case is close to my heart."

Reaction in the courtroom almost equaled the speech in passion. Fighting tears, Judge Murphy grasped a friend's hand after the summation and claimed, "This is the greatest experience of my life. That was Clarence Darrow at his best. I will never hear anything like it again. He is the most Christ-like man I have ever known." The NAACP so esteemed the summation that it reprinted the entire text for distribution. Even Darrow, who had delivered some of the finest court-room speeches ever heard, called this "one of the strongest and most satisfactory arguments that I ever delivered."

As the jury left the room to begin its deliberations, Dar-row studied one juror who had shown little emotion one way or the other. "That is the most stubborn man I have ever run up against," he said, "I didn't make any impres-sion on him. His mind is made up, and I don't think any-thing could have changed him. I wonder if he is for or against us."

The Jury Frees Sweet

He quickly found out. Less than four hours later the jury re-turned with its verdict. Darrow tilted forward in his chair and stared at the floor while waiting for the decision. When he heard "Not Guilty," he slumped so low that Toms feared he had fainted. Darrow quietly told his opponent, "Oh, I'm all right. I've heard that verdict before." Darrow learned later that the juror who worried him had walked into the jury room, lit a cigar, opened a book, and told the others not to bother him until they were ready to acquit Henry Sweet.

Tears streamed down the faces of Darrow and Henry Sweet. Toms appeared surprised with the verdict, while Mrs. Breiner angrily responded, "My husband was mur-dered and the murderers go free." The NAACP hailed this decision as "one of the most important steps ever taken in the struggle for justice to the Negro in the United States."

Judge Murphy ended the trial by telling Henry Sweet, "I believe it is a just and reasonable verdict, and may God bless you."

In July 1927, Murphy dismissed all charges against the other defendants. Though justice had triumphed in this case, tragedy haunted Ossian Sweet throughout his remaining days. For several years he lived in the home for which he had fought, but it harbored only misery. His daughter and wife died of tuberculosis within two years of the second trial, and his brother Henry succumbed to the same disease in 1940. Ossian remarried twice and ran several times for public office, without success. On March 19, 1960, broken in health and spirit, Ossian Sweet took his own life.

A Jailed Teacher: John Scopes and the Antievolution Law

Don Nardo

Clarence Darrow fashioned a career out of defending unpopular causes. He especially battled in behalf of a person's right to think or hold beliefs with which others might not agree. When a Tennessee teacher, John Scopes, was imprisoned in 1925 for teaching the theory of evolution to his high school classes, Darrow rushed to his defense.

In this article, writer Don Nardo relates the events of the Scopes trial and concludes with an analysis of the trial's impact today.

B eads of perspiration formed on the bald pate of the portly man in the witness chair. Sixty-five-year-old William Jennings Bryan, golden-throated orator, former U.S. secretary of state, and three-time national presidential candidate, was known as the Great Commoner because he had long championed the interests of everyday American workers against big business. Often, he toured the country, speaking to legions of adoring fans at political rallies and religious revival or "tent" meetings. Now, on this July day in 1925, he sat, sweating profusely in nearly one-hundred-degree heat, on the front lawn of the courthouse in the tiny rural town of Dayton, Tennessee.

Bryan had volunteered to lead local prosecutors in try-

---

ing a Dayton high school teacher, John T. Scopes, who stood accused of breaking a new state law. This law forbade the teaching of Charles Darwin's theory of evolution, which holds that all living things, including humans, descended from lower life-forms. Like many other Americans, Bryan was disturbed that such a "godless" idea was commonly taught in most American biology classes. He saw evolution, which he called the "brute theory," as dangerous because it might make children "lose the consciousness of God's presence in our daily life." In his view, the events described in Genesis, the first book of the Bible, constituted the one true version of creation and this was what schools should be teaching. "You may trace your ancestry back to the monkey if you find pleasure or pride in doing so," he had declared on more than one occasion, "but you shall not connect me with your family tree without more evidence than has yet been produced." It was this firm antievolution stance that had made Bryan the logical choice to come to Dayton and set an example for other "modernists" and "atheists" who might try to subvert and degrade wholesome American values and traditions.

All present at the Dayton courthouse that day were surprised to see Bryan testifying because it was, and still is, unusual for the head prosecutor in a trial to be called as a witness. This legal ploy, which would soon prove to be a brilliant and devastating maneuver, was the work of Scopes's chief defense counsel, sixty-eight-year-old Clarence Darrow, at the time the most famous trial lawyer in the United States. Darrow had come to Dayton with the same zeal and sense of purpose that had animated Bryan. "For the first, the last, the only time in my life," Darrow would later recall,

> I volunteered my services in a case . . . because I really wanted to take part in it. . . . An organization calling themselves "fundamentalists" had been very actively seeking to control the schools and universities of America. The members of this body claimed to believe that the . . . Bible . . .

was virtually written by the Almighty and is in every part literally true. . . . [Legislative] bills were prepared to forbid the teaching of evolution, or any doctrine in conflict with the Genesis story, in any school wholly or in part supported by public funds. . . . I was in New York not long after the arrest of Mr. Scopes, and saw that Mr. Bryan had volunteered to go to Dayton to assist in the prosecution. At once I wanted to go. My object, and my only object, was to focus the attention of the country on the program of Mr. Bryan and the other fundamentalists in America. I knew that education was in danger from the source that has always hampered it—religious fanaticism.

Selecting John Scopes

The American Civil Liberties Union, an organization dedicated to protecting the rights of citizens, believed that Tennessee's antievolution law was illegal. All the organization needed was a teacher willing to test the law. They found one in John Scopes.

On May 7 John Scopes was arrested. Three days later he had a preliminary hearing before three squires. It was charged that on April 24 he had taught the theory of evolution to his class. It was shown that Hunter's *Civic Biology* contained such sentences as: "We have now learned that animal forms may be arranged so as to begin with the simple one-celled forms and culminate with a group which contains man himself." The justices decided there was ample evidence, and Scopes was bound over to the grand jury that would meet the first Monday in August. Bond was fixed at $1,000.

Roger Baldwin announced in New York for the American Civil Liberties Union: "We shall take the Scopes case to the United States supreme court if necessary to establish that a teacher may tell the truth without being thrown in jail."

Ray Ginger, *Six Days or Forever?*: Tennessee v. John Thomas Scopes. Chicago: Quadrangle Books, 1958.

Indeed, exposing the fundamentalists' leading spokesman as a fanatic who refused even to consider the worth of non-biblical explanations of creation had been Darrow's strategy in putting Bryan on the stand. "Do you claim that everything in the Bible should be literally interpreted?" Darrow asked, leaning toward his opponent in the witness box.

"I believe that everything in the Bible should be accepted as it is given there," Bryan declared proudly.

"When you read that the whale swallowed Jonah, how do you literally interpret that?"

"When I read that a big fish swallowed Jonah, I believe it, and I believe in a god who can make a whale and can make a man and make them both do what he pleases." The Commoner fanned himself, grinned, and forcefully added, "One miracle is just as easy to believe as another."

Bryan maintained this confident air for a while; but relentless grilling under the merciless midday sun began to have its effect. Barraged by question after pointed question about why so many biblical claims seemed to go against scientific evidence and just plain common sense, Bryan seemed increasingly confused and unsure.

The Length of a Biblical Day

After more than an hour on the stand, Bryan showed not only that he was ignorant of history, but that he knew practically nothing of the established and universally accepted facts of archaeology, geology, astronomy, and other scholarly disciplines. The man who had so vigorously advocated limiting the teaching of science in the schools had just demonstrated that he had not the foggiest notion of what science was all about. The reactions from the crowd were mixed. Those few who had long maintained that Bryan was shallow and ignorant felt vindicated. Among his far more numerous supporters, some looked befuddled and many others seemed to feel sorry for him; but most were at least thankful for his continued unflagging defense of God and a literal interpretation of the Bible.

But then Bryan said something that even many of his

staunchest advocates saw as a betrayal of the fundamentalist cause. Seeing that his opponent was now clearly tired, listless, nervous, and confused, Darrow returned to the subject of the Bible. "Do you think the earth was made in six days?" he asked.

"Not six days of twenty-four hours," Bryan answered. At the sound of these six fateful words, shocked gasps came from various sections of the crowd. "What does he want to say that for?" someone in the rear of the throng demanded. At the heart of the fundamentalist doctrine lies the belief that every word in the Bible was a truth to be accepted exactly as stated, so that when the Book of Genesis said that God had shaped the earth in six days, it meant six ordinary days, *days of twenty-four hours*. Yet the great champion of biblical literalists everywhere had just denied this "holy truth."

Darrow immediately realized the import of his opponent's unfortunate remark and pounced on the opportunity. Sounding astonished, the chief defense attorney asked, "Doesn't the Bible say so?"

"No sir," Bryan repeated, eliciting more gasps from the audience.

Prosecutor Stewart realized that his colleague was in serious trouble and attempted to rescue him. "What is the purpose of this examination?" Stewart demanded, leaping to his feet.

But before either Darrow or the judge could answer, Bryan answered for them. "The purpose is to cast ridicule on everybody who believes in the Bible!" the witness said in a loud and angry voice.

Darrow answered this charge with equal gruffness. "We have the purpose of preventing bigots and ignoramuses from controlling the education of the United States and you know it—and that is all!"

Evening and Morning Without Sun?

At this point a lengthy argument erupted among the prosecutors, defense lawyers, and the judge. Dudley Malone charged that Bryan was trying to get biblical "evidence" into the court record to distort or disprove the scientists' statements that Hays had earlier read aloud. After Bryan angrily denied this, Stewart again tried to convince Judge Raulston to terminate the interrogation of Bryan. Raulston agreed with Stewart that the questions Darrow had been asking were not proper testimony for a jury but said that he would permit them for the record. This greatly pleased the defense because any and all statements in the record could be used later, if Scopes were found guilty, to open up and conduct an appeal to a higher court. Upset and indignant, Bryan wanted to make it clear to all present that he had not taken the stand to aid some future defense appeal. "I want the Christian world to know," he bellowed, "that any atheist, agnostic, unbeliever, can question me any time as to my belief in God, and I will answer him!"

And so, Darrow's questioning of Bryan continued. Darrow shrewdly continued to emphasize the witness's uncertainty and flexibility about the length of a biblical day. The defender read aloud that passage from Genesis that states, "The morning and the evening were the first day." Then he turned to Bryan and asked, "Do you think the sun was made on the fourth day?"

"Yes."

"And they had evening and morning without the sun?"

"I am simply saying it is a period," corrected Bryan. He seemed to be digging himself in ever deeper and Darrow took advantage of it by asking if by a "period" he meant that the creation might have lasted a long time, perhaps longer than six ordinary days? The creation "might have continued for millions of years," Bryan admitted. Still more gasps came from the audience. Many of the onlookers were just plain mad at Bryan for his apparent heresy against fundamentalist doctrine; but at least a few people began to realize that if a biblical day was actually millions of years long, then the earth might be as old as the evolutionists and geologists claimed. God might have created the world and then given plants and animals plenty of time to change and develop, in which case religion and evolution might be reconciled after all; and if so, what was all the fuss about?

Darrow continued the grilling until the exhausted and flustered Bryan, on hearing another derisive laugh from the crowd, lost whatever composure he had left. In an emotional outburst, the Great Commoner told the judge, "Your honor, I think I can shorten this testimony. The only purpose Mr. Darrow has is to slur at the Bible, but I will answer his questions, I shall answer them at once. I want the world to know that this man, who does not believe in a God, is trying to use a court in Tennessee—"

"I object to your statement," Darrow interrupted loudly. "I am examining you on your fool ideas that no intelligent Christian on earth believes!"

Triumph and Tragedy

And then it was suddenly over. Distressed that the questioning had degenerated into little more than a shouting match, Judge Raulston ended the interrogation, excused Bryan, and adjourned court for the day. For the two giants who had just clashed, it was a moment of triumph for one and tragedy for the other. Hundreds of people pressed in to congratulate Darrow, most of them passing by and ignoring the crestfallen Bryan. Darrow later recalled:

> Much to my surprise, the great gathering began to surge toward me. They seemed to have changed sides in a single afternoon. A friendly crowd followed me toward my home. Mr. Bryan left the grounds practically alone. The people seemed to feel that he had failed and deserted his cause and his followers when he admitted that the first six days might have been periods of millions of ages long. Mr. Bryan had made himself ridiculous and had contradicted his own faith. I was truly sorry for Mr. Bryan. But I consoled myself by thinking of the years through which he had busied himself tormenting intelligent professors with impudent questions about their faith, and seeking to arouse the ignoramuses and bigots to drive them out of their [teaching] positions.

To many it seemed as if Darrow had won a conclusive victory that day. But the reality was that the Scopes trial was not yet over, and neither was the controversy that had inspired it.

In the evening of July 20, 1925, only hours after the devastating confrontation between Darrow and Bryan in Dayton, late newspaper editions across the country carried stories and editorials about the showdown. The vast majority were very critical of Bryan and his support for efforts to change and censor school curricula. Typical were the comments made by the great American humorist Will Rogers in his popular syndicated newspaper column:

> Now personally, I like Bill [Bryan], but when he says that he will make this his life's issue and take it up through all the various courts and finally get it into the Constitution of the United States . . . he is wrong. More wrong than he has ever been before. These other things he was wrong on [in his testimony] didn't do much harm, but now he is going to try to drag . . . the Bible into a political campaign. He can't ever do that. He might make Tennessee the side show of America, but he can't make a street carnival of the whole United States.

But though Bryan had taken a beating at the hands of Darrow and the press that day, the next day it was the turn of Darrow and Scopes's other attorneys to suffer a setback. When court reconvened on the morning of Tuesday, July 21, Judge Raulston ruled that Bryan could not go back on the stand. What is more, all Bryan's testimony from the preceding session had to be stricken from the court record. This was a definite blow to the defense because it had no further means of presenting its position on the issue of evolution versus the Bible. The Scopes trial was over and nothing remained but for the jury to render its verdict.

The Verdict and Closing Statements

After the judge summoned the jury that morning, Darrow asked that he might address the panel. Darrow was worried that the jurors might find Scopes not guilty, in which case the defense would lose its right to appeal the case to a higher court and the Butler Act would remain on the books. The efforts of Darrow, the ACLU, and the others to stop the campaign against the teaching of evolution in American schools would come to nothing. For this reason, Darrow emphasized to the jury that Scopes had broken the law and that they had no other choice but to find him guilty; and Judge Raulston also gave the jurors instructions to the same effect.

The jury then promptly did its duty and delivered a guilty verdict. Since the Butler Act provided for a minimum penalty of $100, the judge sentenced John Scopes to pay a fine in that amount. A few seconds later, all eyes in the courtroom focused on the former teacher, who, wearing a white shirt and a bow tie, stood before the judge's bench to make the closing statement the law allowed him. "Your honor," he began,

> I feel that I have been convicted of violating an unjust statute. I will continue in the future as I have in the past, to oppose this law in any way I can. Any other action would be in violation of my ideal of academic freedom—that is, to teach the truth as guaranteed in our constitution, of personal and religious freedom. I think the fine is unjust.

Next, Arthur Hays made the official request that the court permit the defense to appeal the case and the judge granted it without discussion. After several of the attorneys, including Darrow and Bryan, made short closing statements, Judge Raulston made his own, the fair and noble tone of which impressed Darrow greatly. The judge did not name Scopes specifically, but there could be little doubt that the speech was aimed at the man who had just been found guilty. "It sometimes takes courage," Raulston declared,

> to search diligently for a truth that may destroy our preconceived notions and ideas. It sometimes takes courage to declare a truth or stand for an act that is in contravention to [goes against] the public sentiment. A man who is big

enough to search for the truth and find it and declare it in the face of all opposition is a big man.

With these words, what nearly everyone in the world at that time perceived as the "trial of the century" officially ended.

The Trial's Immediate Aftermath

Over too was the Dayton carnival. The Bible sellers and hot dog vendors packed up and left, and the tents and banners of the revivalists came down, so that within a few days the town's main squares gave little or no hint that they had so recently harbored a world-class event. After the transformation, a Knoxville journalist reported: "A lonesome quietness seemed to hover over the little Tennessee village. The only visitors to the courthouse were now and then some who had attended the trial and left some of their belongings in the courtroom."

One important visitor stayed on in Dayton, however. William Jennings Bryan, his once gleaming reputation now tarnished, remained in hopes of delivering a long oration he had not been allowed to present on the last morning of the trial. Five days after the judge's gavel had closed the proceeding, Bryan, following his personal habit, ate a huge afternoon meal and then lay down to take a nap. This time he never woke up. On hearing the news of his passing, some of his remaining supporters proposed that after his terrible humiliation on the witness stand he had "died of a broken heart," while Darrow was quoted as saying, "Broken heart nothing; he died of a busted belly." The actual medical diagnosis was stroke, probably related to Bryan's diabetes.

Thus, Bryan did not live to see the results of the appeal, which Darrow and the other defense attorneys brought to the Tennessee Supreme Court almost a year later. Of the four justices who heard the case, two ended up declaring the Butler Act constitutional; one ruled that the law was constitutional but that Scopes had not actually violated it; and the remaining justice decided that the statute was unconstitutional. With a three-to-one vote upholding its legality, the Butler Act remained on Tennessee's books. There was an ironic footnote, however. On a technicality, the justices overruled Judge Raulston's sentence and revoked Scopes's $100 fine.

Scopes himself, who had never felt comfortable in the public limelight, then returned to an obscure private life, although he never again taught high school; after attending the University of Chicago, he thereafter made his living as a geologist. As for Clarence Darrow, he moved on to more controversial cases, including one involving the revenge murder of an accused rapist. He published a widely read autobiography in 1932 and died in Chicago in 1938 at the age of eighty. After that, he and his chief opponent in the Scopes trial, William Jennings Bryan, developed images even more legendary than they had enjoyed in life. Now a part of American folklore, their characters still argue about the length of a biblical day in countless stage productions, as well as the film version, of *Inherit the Wind*, the drama based on the infamous eight-day Dayton Monkey Trial.

Darwin Under the Desk

The legacy of the Scopes trial itself, in the sense of who ultimately won and lost, has been mixed. On the one hand, Darrow's side—the cause of science and academic freedom—benefited greatly over time, even though the Tennessee high court upheld the validity of the Butler Act. A similar law passed in Mississippi in 1926; however, that same year the Kentucky and Louisiana legislatures rejected antievolution bills. The press, as well as scientists and academic spokespersons across the nation, continued to depict those who advocated such laws as backward and ignorant. In the wake of what seemed to be a moral victory for Scopes and his defenders and supporters, the fundamentalist drive to censor science in the schools steadily lost steam. By the 1940s, the conflict between evolution and the Bible had become a largely forgotten issue. And in the 1960s, the U.S. Supreme Court finally overturned the Butler Act (and the few remaining antievolution laws in other states) by ruling that the teaching of evolution is constitutional.

On the other hand, the fundamentalists won what might be termed a silent victory. Even though the campaign to ban the work of Darwin from the public schools had been more or less discredited, many southern teachers, school administrators, and textbook publishers remained anxious and fearful about teaching evolution. For almost thirty-five years after the Scopes trial, only a handful of high school biology texts in the country retained sections on Darwin and evolution; and most high school biology teachers either mentioned the topic only briefly or skipped it altogether.

A few enterprising teachers did manage to slip Darwin into the curriculum "through the back door." In some Tennessee towns, for example, instructors mentioned Darwin and his famous book in literature classes, since by discussing its literary merits they were technically not "teaching the theory that man has descended from a lower order of animals," as forbidden in the Butler Act. Yet in the same towns, librarians usually kept their copies of the *Origin of Species* under the front desk and loaned them out by special request only. Not

ON

THE ORIGIN OF SPECIES

BY MEANS OF NATURAL SELECTION,

OR THE

PRESERVATION OF FAVOURED RACES IN THE STRUGGLE FOR LIFE.

BY CHARLES DARWIN, M.A.,
FELLOW OF THE ROYAL, GEOLOGICAL, LINNÆAN, ETC., SOCIETIES;
AUTHOR OF ' JOURNAL OF RESEARCHES DURING H. M. S. BEAGLE'S VOYAGE ROUND THE WORLD.'

LONDON:
JOHN MURRAY, ALBEMARLE STREET.
1859.

The right of Translation is reserved.

The title page of Charles Darwin's controversial book

until the Soviet launch of the satellite *Sputnik I* in 1957 had jolted the United States into a feverish campaign to promote science education did most school textbooks and biology classes once more routinely devote time to evolution, as they had before the mid-1920s.

The Rise of Creationism

But with Darwin's return to the classroom came a new surge of fundamentalist concern about children being exposed to a doctrine that seemed to contradict the biblical story of creation. By the late 1960s, the number of fundamentalists in the United States had grown to an estimated fifty million. Many, like their predecessors in Dayton, Tennessee, wanted to see evolution excluded from classrooms; but with laws like the Butler Act now ruled unconstitutional, that was no longer possible. There was also no way to teach the Bible in public schools because that violated the First Amendment's intent with respect to separation of church and state. To get around these obstacles, as scholar Michael Ruse explains, some hard-core fundamentalists changed their approach and in the process redefined themselves:

> They would like to exclude evolution, but they cannot. They would like to include Genesis, but they cannot. As a compromise, therefore, they try to slide Genesis into classrooms, sideways. They argue that . . . all of the claims of Genesis can be supported by the best principles and premises of empirical science. In other words, *as scientists*, people can argue for instant creation of the universe, separate ancestry for man and apes, short time span for the earth (between approximately 6,000 and 20,000 years), and a universal flood over everything, at some later date. Hence, we have the growth of "Scientific Creationism" or "Creation Science."

All through the 1970s, the creationists lobbied for "equal time" and "balanced treatment" in classrooms, arguing that evolution was only "one of the theories" for human origins. The biblical creation was another and equally worthy theory, they insisted, and should therefore be taught right alongside evolution in biology classes. These efforts were unsuccessful until 1981 when a bill, titled Act 590, came before the Arkansas legislature. Act 590 provided that, if human origins were discussed in a public classroom, the teacher must cover "Creation-science" along with "Evolution-science." On March 19 of that same year Governor Frank J. White signed the bill into law.

Immediately, many groups and individuals came out against the new law. Among them were several southern clergymen, who felt that religion was the province of churches, not schools, and also many local business organizations, which feared that a blow to science education might discourage lucrative high-tech companies from migrating to Arkansas. With the aid of the ACLU, which had been instrumental in the Scopes case, they challenged Act 590 on the grounds that it violated the doctrine of separation of church and state, that it infringed on teachers' "academic freedom," and that the law was vague from a legal standpoint.

These arguments against Act 590 eventually won out. On January 5, 1982, the judge hearing the case ruled that "Creation-science" was religion, not science, and could not be taught in public classrooms. The state of Arkansas did not appeal the decision. Later, in 1987, the U.S. Supreme Court made an almost identical ruling that struck down a pro-creationist act that had recently passed in Louisiana.

A Grand View of Life

But despite these setbacks, advocates of creationism remained active. In the 1990s, as they continued their efforts to gain equal time with evolutionists, some conservative politicians aided them with supportive public statements. Early in 1996, Republican presidential hopeful Pat Buchanan told an ABC reporter, "I believe you're a creature of God. I think [parents] have a right to insist that Godless evolution not be taught to their children or their children not be indoctrinated in it." Encouraged by such support, politically active creationists worked to chip away at what they saw as an unfair evolutionist stranglehold on education. In March 1996, the Tennessee legislature considered a bill that would require school boards to dismiss teachers who present evolution as scientific fact. And in Alabama, creationists successfully pushed to get biology textbooks to include a disclaimer saying that evolution is a "controversial theory" that only "some scientists" accept. (Opponents say this statement is ludicrous, pointing out that virtually all reputable scientists accept evolution.)

Thus, the controversy that Charles Darwin ignited in 1859, which flared up again in the 1925 Scopes trial, continues to smolder. Darwin himself would, no doubt, be perplexed at the longevity of these arguments, for he easily reconciled the concept of God with that of evolution. "To my mind," he wrote in the moving finale of the *Origin of Species*, "it accords better with what we know of the laws impressed on matter by the Creator, that the production and extinction of the past and present inhabitants of the world should have been due to secondary causes." Because modern animals and people could trace their lineage back for hundreds of millions of years, he said, it was obvious that no catastrophe had ever managed to destroy the thread of life; and this showed that God's design of natural selection assured that life would survive far into the future. Finally, Darwin suggested that God's conception of a process as fantastically complex, productive, and durable as evolution was far more awesome than that of a sudden and simple miraculous creation. "There is grandeur in this view of life," he stated, describing evolution,

> having been originally breathed by the Creator into a few forms or into one; and that, whilst this planet has gone cycling on according to the fixed law of gravity, from so simple a beginning endless forms most beautiful and most wonderful have been, and are being evolved.

Sacco Guilty, Vanzetti Innocent?

Francis Russell

The 1920s featured a string of high-profile criminal trials, among them the Leopold-Loeb murder case, the Scopes trial, and the Ossian Sweet murder trial. Another courtroom drama that grabbed headlines, both during the trial and for years afterward, involved Nicola Sacco and Bartolomeo Vanzetti, Italian immigrants who were accused of murdering two men in a robbery attempt. Both were eventually found guilty and put to death for the crimes, even though a large segment of American society believed in their innocence.

Author Francis Russell spent much of his career examining the case. In 1962 he arrived at a surprising conclusion.

The murders for which Nicola Sacco and Bartolomeo Vanzetti were convicted and finally executed were quick, simple, and brutal. On the afternoon of April 15, 1920, in the small shoe manufacturing town of South Braintree, Massachusetts, a paymaster, Frederick Parmenter, and his guard, Alessandro Berardelli, were shot and robbed as they walked down Pearl Street with the Slater & Morrill Shoe Company payroll—some fifteen thousand dollars in two metal boxes.

The paymaster and the guard, each carrying a box, had crossed the railroad tracks near the front of the Rice & Hutchins factory when two strangers who had been lean-

---

Excerpted from "Sacco Guilty, Vanzetti Innocent?" by Francis Russell, *American Heritage,* vol. 13, no. 4, June 1962.

ing against the fence there suddenly stepped toward them. The strangers were short, dark men. One wore a felt hat and the other, a cap. In a flash the first man whipped a pistol from his pocket and fired several shots into Berardelli. The guard dropped to the ground. Parmenter, a step in advance, turned and when he saw what was happening, started to run across the street. Before he reached the other side he was shot twice. He dropped his box and collapsed in the gutter. Witnesses—of which there were a number in the factory windows and along Pearl Street—were afterward uncertain whether one man or two had done the shooting, but most thought there had been two.

With Parmenter and Berardelli lying in the gravel, one of their assailants fired a signal shot, and a Buick touring car that had been parked near the Slater & Morrill factory now started jerkily up the rise. As it slowed down, the two bandits picked up the money boxes and climbed into the back seat. Berardelli had managed to get to his hands and knees. Seeing him wavering, a third man sprang from the car and fired another shot into him. It was a death wound.

The Buick continued along Pearl Street with five men in it, a gunman in the front seal firing at random at the crowd drawn by the sound of the shots. No one was hit, although one bystander had his coat lapel singed. The car gathered speed, swung left at the top of Pearl Street, and one of the men in the rear seat threw out handfuls of tacks to hinder any pursuit. The speeding car was noticed at intervals along a ten-mile stretch of road; then it vanished. Two days later it was found abandoned in the woods near Brockton, a dozen miles away.

Berardelli died within a few minutes, the final bullet having severed the great artery issuing from his heart. Parmenter too had received a fatal wound, a bullet cutting his inferior vena cava, the body's largest vein. He died early the following morning. At the autopsy two bullets were found in Parmenter and four in Berardelli. The county medical examiner, Dr. George Burgess Magrath, removed the bullets from Berardelli's body, scratching the base of each with a Roman numeral. The bullet that had cut the artery and that, from the angle of its path, he determined must have been fired while Berardelli was down, he marked III. It had struck the hipbone obliquely and was slightly bent from this glancing contact.

Of the six bullets, five had been fired from a .32 caliber pistol or pistols with a right-hand twist to the rifling. These bullets were of varied manufacture—three Peters and two Remingtons. The remaining bullet, the one Dr. Magrath marked III, was a Winchester of an obsolete type having a cannelure, or milling around the edge. It had been fired from a .32 caliber pistol with a left-hand twist. Only a Colt, among American pistols, had such a reverse twist. Four spent cartridges of the same caliber as the bullets were picked up in the gravel near Berardelli's body. Two of these were Peters, one a Remington, and one a Winchester later known as Shell W.

No weapons were found on the bodies, although Berardelli customarily carried a revolver with him. On March 19, 1920, he had taken his gun to the Iver Johnson Company in Boston to have it repaired. According to his wife, it needed a new spring. Lincoln Wadsworth, in charge of the repair department, recorded that on that day he had received a .38 caliber Harrington & Richardson revolver from Alex Berardelli and had sent the gun upstairs to the workshop. There the foreman, George Fitzemeyer, for some reason marked it as a .32 caliber Harrington & Richardson requiring a new hammer and ticketed it with a repair number.

No one at Iver Johnson's recorded the revolver's serial number. The store manager testified a year later at the trial that the company did not keep a record of deliveries of repaired guns, but he was certain this particular revolver had been delivered. All weapons in the repair department not called for by the year's end were sold and a record made of each sale. Since Berardelli's revolver was no longer in the store, and there was no record of its being sold, the manager insisted it must have been called for.

Several witnesses of the shooting said at the inquest that they saw one of the bandits stoop over Berardelli. Peter McCullum, peering out of the first floor cutting room of Rice & Hutchins after he heard the shots, saw a man putting a money box into the Buick while holding a "white" revolver in his other hand. A Harrington & Richardson revolver was nickel-plated and might well have seemed white in the sunlight. This may have been Berardelli's. It seems unlikely that the guard would have accompanied the paymaster without being armed. And if he had a revolver, it is possible that one of the men who shot him may have reached down and taken it.

Sacco and Vanzetti were arrested almost by chance on the night of May 5, 1920. They had met earlier in the evening at Sacco's bungalow in Stoughton—a half-dozen miles from South Braintree—with two anarchist comrades, Mike Boda and Ricardo Orciani, to arrange about gathering up incriminating literature from other comrades for fear of government "Red" raids. Until a few months before this, Boda had been living in West Bridgewater ten miles away with another anarchist, Ferruccio Coacci, who had been taken away for deportation on April 17. Not until Coacci was at sea did the police come to suspect that he and Boda might have been concerned in the South Braintree holdup. Boda had left an old Overland touring car in a West Bridgewater garage to be repaired, and the four men were planning to pick it up that evening. Orciani and Boda left Stoughton on Orciani's motorcycle. Sacco and Vanzetti went by streetcar. Once they had arrived, Boda was unable to get the car from the forewarned proprietor. As the men argued, the proprietor's wife telephoned the police.

Sacco and Vanzetti were arrested in Brockton while rifling back to Stoughton on the streetcar. The police found a .32 caliber Colt automatic tucked in Sacco's waistband. In the gun's clip were eight cartridges, with another in the chamber. Sacco had twenty-three more loose cartridges in his pocket. These, though all .32 caliber, were of assorted makes—sixteen Peters, seven U.S., six Winchesters of the obsolete type, and three Remingtons. Vanzetti was found to be carrying a Harrington & Richardson .38 caliber revolver, its five chambers loaded with two Remington and three U.S. bullets.

The day following their arrest the two men were questioned at some length by the district attorney, Frederick Katzmann. Sacco told Katzmann he had bought his automatic two years before on Hanover Street in Boston under an assumed name. He had paid sixteen or seventeen dollars for it, and at the same time he had bought an unopened box of cartridges.

Vanzetti said he had bought his revolver four or five years before, also under an assumed name, at some shop on Hanover Street and had paid eighteen dollars for it. He had also bought an unopened box of cartridges, all but six of which he had fired off on the beach at Plymouth.

At their trial fourteen months later the two men told very different stories. They both admitted they had lied when they were first questioned, but explained that they then thought they were being held because they were anarchists. They had lied, they said, partly because they were afraid and partly to protect their comrades. Indeed they had good reason to feel apprehensive about their anarchism, for there were rumors of new government Red raids, and only a few days before their arrest their comrade Salsedo had died mysteriously in New York while being held by federal agents.

Sacco's revised trial story was that he had bought the pistol in 1917 or 1918 in the small town where he was working. He had bought a box of cartridges on Hanover Street shortly afterward. The man who sold him the box filled it with various makes because of the wartime scarcity of cartridges.

Vanzetti now said that he had bought his revolver a few months before his arrest. Often he carried a hundred dollars or more with him from his fish business, and he felt he needed a gun to protect himself because of the many recent holdups. He had bought the revolver from a friend, Luigi

Falzini. It was loaded when he bought it, and he had never fired it.

Falzini appeared in court, identified the revolver by certain rust spots and scratches as having belonged to him, and said he had bought it from Orciani. Another witness, Rexford Slater, testified that the revolver had originally belonged to him and that he had sold it to Orciani in the autumn of 1919.

Orciani had been arrested the day following the arrests of Sacco and Vanzetti. However, as he was able to provide a timecard alibi for his whereabouts on April 15, he was released. During the early part of the trial he acted as chauffeur for one of the defense attorneys, but although he was in the courthouse almost daily, he did not take the stand. Yet he was, as the district attorney pointed out in his summing up, the missing link in the revolver's chain of ownership.

At the trial the prosecution contended that the automatic found on Sacco was the one that had fired Bullet III and that Vanzetti's revolver had been taken from the dying Berardelli. Several days before the ballistics testimony, two experts for the prosecution, Captain William Proctor of the Massachusetts State Police—then no more than a detective bureau—and Captain Charles Van Amburgh from the Remington Arms Company in Connecticut, fired a number of test shots from Sacco's automatic into oiled sawdust. Proctor and Van Amburgh were joined in these experiments by a defense expert, James Burns. After the test bullets were recovered they were then compared with Bullet III.

The trial testimony of the firearms experts on both sides was involved and confusing, "a wilderness of lands and grooves" as one reporter noted. In the opinion of the Gunther brothers, whose book on firearms identification has become a legal classic, all the ballistics evidence offered was so primitive as to be worthless.

Each tooled gun barrel, with its hundreds of minute striations, is unique. The one certain method of determining whether two separate bullets have been fired through any particular barrel is the use of a comparison microscope.

Through this instrument the ends of the two bullets are brought together in one fused image. If the striations match, then it is practically certain that both bullets were fired from the same weapon.

Today the comparison microscope is the standard method of bullet identification. In 1920 it was just beginning to come into use, but it was not used in the Sacco-Vanzetti trial. There the experts attempted to measure the bullets with calipers and compare them with measurements made of a cast of the barrel of Sacco's pistol. It was a useless, haggling proceeding. . . .

In the six years that had elapsed between the conviction of Sacco and Vanzetti and the passing of the death sentence on them in 1927, the case had expanded from its obscure beginnings to become an international issue of increasing turbulence. Finally in June, 1927, the governor of Massachusetts appointed a three-man committee headed by President A. Lawrence Lowell of Harvard to review the case.

The ballistics issue had remained dormant since Judge Thayer's rejection of the Proctor-Hamilton motion. Just before the Lowell Committee hearings, still another expert, Major Calvin Goddard, arrived in Boston with a comparison microscope, with which he offered to make without charge what he maintained would be conclusive tests on the Sacco-Vanzetti shells and bullets. The prosecution had no objections. William Thompson, the conservative Boston lawyer who had taken charge of the defense, would not approve of the tests but agreed not to try to prevent them.

Goddard made his tests June 3 before Professor Gill, a junior defense lawyer, an assistant district attorney, and several newsmen. His findings were:

1. That Shell W was fired in the Sacco pistol and could have been fired in no other.

2. That the so-called "mortal" bullet, Bullet III, was fired through the Sacco pistol and could have been fired through no other.

Professor Gill, after spending some time looking through the comparison microscope, became convinced of the parallel patterns of Bullet III and a test bullet, but felt that these would have shown more clearly if Bullet III could have been cleaned of its encrusted grime. Thompson, for the defense, refused to give permission to have this done. Shortly afterward Gill wrote to Thompson that he now doubted his testimony at the Hamilton-Proctor motion and wished to sever all connection with the case. His disavowal was followed by another from the trial defense expert James Burns.

Goddard's findings, though unofficial, undoubtedly had much influence on the Lowell Committee. When Thompson later appeared before the committee, he made the novel accusation that the prosecution had juggled the evidence by substituting a test bullet and cartridge fired in Sacco's pistol for the original Shell W found in the gravel and Bullet III taken from Berardelli's body. As an indication of this he pointed out that the identifying scratches on Bullet III differed from those on the other bullets, being wider apart and uneven—as if made with a different instrument. . . .

In July, 1927, the Sacco-Vanzetti guns and bullets were brought to Boston from the Dedham Courthouse, where they had been in the custody of the clerk of court since the trial, to be examined by the Lowell Committee. Then they disappeared. When in 1959 I tried to see them, they were nowhere to be found. The Dedham clerk of court had a record of their having been sent to Boston but no record of their return. The Massachusetts attorney general's office had no idea where they were, nor did the Commissioner of Public Safety at state police headquarters.

It took me six months of poking about before I finally managed to discover where they had gone. Apparently, after they had been examined by the Lowell Committee, they were sent to the ballistics laboratory of the state police and placed in the custody of Captain Van Amburgh. He put all the exhibits, each triple-sealed in its official court envelope, in a cardboard box and locked them away. The box remained there almost twenty years. Then when Van Amburgh retired he took several ballistics souvenirs with him, among them the box of Sacco-Vanzetti exhibits.

Van Amburgh—who died in 1949—was succeeded in the laboratory by his son. The son in turn retired in 1951 to Kingston, a small town near Plymouth, about forty miles from Boston. When I telephoned him to ask about the Sacco-Vanzetti exhibits, he refused at first to say whether he had them or not. But after I had persuaded the Boston *Globe* to run a feature article on the missing exhibits, he admitted to reporters that he did have them but regarded himself merely as their "custodian." The *Globe* story was a Sunday sensation. Among the paper's early readers was the Commissioner of Public Safety, J. Henry Goguen. The Commissioner at once sent two state troopers to Kingston to demand the surrender of the exhibits. The next day the guns and bullets, still in their box, were back in the state police laboratory.

When I at last saw the exhibits at the laboratory they were relatively free from corrosion, although the clips that fastened them in their triple envelopes had rusted into the paper. Apparently they had not been disturbed since 1927. What I first planned to do was to have comparison tests made of Bullet III and a bullet fired from Sacco's pistol, and similar comparisons made with Shell W. Then I hoped to determine whether or not the other bullets and shells had been fired from a single gun. . . .

I thought there would be no difficulty in arranging these tests, but when I discussed the matter with Commissioner Goguen I found out otherwise. Even in 1959, it seemed, the Sacco-Vanzetti case was still an explosive political issue—as the spring legislative hearings requesting a posthumous pardon for the two men had demonstrated—and the Commissioner wanted to stay out of it. Each time I asked for permission to have properly qualified experts conduct ballistics tests, he postponed any definite answer, telling me to come back in a month or two. At last, after a year, he announced flatly that he would allow no tests.

Not until Goguen's term of office expired and his successor, Frank Giles, took over was I able to arrange for the tests. Finally on October 4, 1961, Professor William Boyd of the Boston University Medical School examined the six bullets for blood. Unfortunately, because of slight oxidization of the bullets, he was unable to determine whether any blood traces remained. However, after Bullet III had been washed I was able to examine the base under the microscope. Previously the bullet had been covered with some foreign substance that obscured the markings on the base. With this removed I could see the three scratched lines clearly. Although they were farther apart than the lines on the other bullets, this could have been because Bullet III had a concave base whereas the bases of the remaining bullets were flat. In any case as I looked through the microscope successively at Bullets I, II, III, and IIII, I could see no notable difference between the scratches on Bullet III and those on the rest.

A week after Professor Boyd had made his blood tests, two firearms consultants came to Boston to make the ballistics comparisons: Jac Weller, the honorary curator of the West Point Museum, and Lieutenant Colonel Frank Jury, formerly in charge of the Firearms Laboratory of the New Jersey State Police. On October 11, 1961, Weller and Jury conducted their tests in the laboratory of the Massachusetts State Police.

Sacco's pistol, they found, was still in condition to be used. After firing two shots to clear the rust from the barrel, Colonel Jury fired two more shots which he then used to match against Bullet III in the comparison microscope. Making independent examinations, Jury and Weller both concluded that "the bullet marked 'III' was fired in Sacco's pistol and in no other." They also agreed, after comparing the breech-block markings of Shell W and a test shell that Shell W must have been fired in Sacco's pistol. The other five bullets, they concluded, were fired from a single unknown gun, probably a semiautomatic pistol. It is to be presumed that the three shells, also from a single gun, came from the same weapon as did the five bullets—although this, as Jury and Weller pointed out, cannot be demonstrated. . . .

In the light of the most recent ballistics evidence and after reviewing the inquest and autopsy reports, as well as the trial testimony, I felt I could come to no other conclusion than that the Colt automatic found on Sacco when he was picked up by the police was the one used to murder Berardelli three weeks earlier. About the gun found on Vanzetti there is too much uncertainty to come to any conclusion. Being of .38 caliber, it was obviously not used at South Braintree, where all the bullets fired were .32's. There is at least the possibility that it may have been taken from the dying Berardelli, but there is an equally strong if not stronger possibility that this is not so. A Harrington & Richardson was a cheap, common revolver, and there were several hundred thousand of them being carried at the time Vanzetti was arrested. No one today can be certain whether Berardelli's Harrington & Richardson was of .32 or .38 caliber, whether it had a broken spring or a broken hammer, whether it was ever called for at Iver Johnson's, whether in fact Berardelli had a gun with him the day he was murdered. Jury and Weller found it impossible to determine if the hammer of Vanzetti's revolver had been replaced.

Whether Sacco himself pulled the trigger of his automatic that day in South Braintree, whether he was even present, cannot be established definitely. But if he did not fire it, and if in fact he was not there, then one of his close associates must have been the murderer. The ballistics evidence leaves no alternative.

When a few years ago I wrote an article, "Tragedy in Dedham" (*American Heritage*, October, 1958), I was convinced that the two men were innocent, victims if not of a judicial frame-up at least of an ironic fate. But after the ballistics tests of 1961 I felt that, at least in the case of Sacco, I could no longer hold to my opinion. It has been pointed out that Vanzetti, just before he died, solemnly proclaimed his innocence. Sacco, however, when he took his place in the electric chair, gave the traditional anarchist cry—"Long live anarchy!"

Whatever my altered views about Sacco, I still continue

to feel that Vanzetti was innocent. Besides various subjective reasons, and convincing talks with Vanzetti's old friends, I found what seemed to me the clinching evidence in the statement of the New York anarchist leader, Carlo Tresca. Tresca, a luminous and vivid personality, became the most noted anarchist in the United States after the deportation of Luigi Galleani in 1919. He was the admired and trusted leader to whom the anarchists confidently turned when they were in trouble. It was he who had selected the original trial lawyer for Sacco and Vanzetti. His influence remained vast over the years, not only among the dwindling anarchists but throughout the whole New York Italian colony.

During World War II the anti-Soviet Tresca was so successful in keeping the Communists out of the government's overseas Italian broadcasts that a G.P.U. [Italian pro-Communist organization] killer known as Enea Sormenti was imported to eliminate him. Tresca was shot down on a New York street in 1943. Several weeks before he died he happened to be talking with his long-time friend Max Eastman, who had earlier written a "Profile" of him for the *New Yorker*. The subject of Sacco and Vanzetti came up, and Eastman asked Tresca if he would feel free to tell him the truth about them.

Without hesitation Tresca replied: "Sacco was guilty, but Vanzetti was not." At that moment some people came into the room, interrupting the conversation, and Eastman never saw Tresca again. Yet the reasons for Tresca's answer must have been profound. He could easily have avoided the question or even denied his comrade's guilt. And if any man should have known the truth of the case, Tresca was the man.

To my mind the most that can be said against Vanzetti is that he must have known who did commit the Braintree crime. Sacco, if he was guilty, was so out of no personal motive. But anarchist deeds of robbery and violence for the sake of the cause were not unknown. If he actually participated in the South Braintree holdup, it was to get money to aid his imprisoned fellow anarchists, and he must then have seen himself not as a robber but as a soldier of the revolution. But if someone else of his group was guilty, someone from whom he had received the murder pistol, he would have preferred death to betraying a comrade.

As far as the guns and bullets in the Sacco-Vanzetti case are concerned, the evidence is in, no longer to be disputed. The human problem remains.

CHAPTER 3

Prohibition

AMERICA'S DECADES

Prohibition Dries Up a Thirsty Nation

Page Smith

After years of heated debate, Prohibition went into effect in 1920. The proponents hoped that many of society's ills would disappear once alcohol was outlawed, while its detractors countered that Prohibition would only bring worse evils. Sentiment swayed back and forth until the advocates of Prohibition finally garnered sufficient support to pass the law.

Page Smith, who wrote a popular series of books covering American history, explains the background to Prohibition in this excerpt from one of his volumes.

Two of the most significant events of the postwar period were the Eighteenth and Nineteenth Amendments to the Constitution, the first forbidding the manufacture and sale of intoxicating liquors and the second giving the vote to women.

From the early days of the Republic the control or prohibition of liquor had been high on the agenda of reform. Most abolitionists, notably William Lloyd Garrison himself, had been teetotalers. At the height of the pre–Civil War movement for reform a number of states had passed prohibitory laws. There had been a strong temperance element in the Republican Party from its inception (Lincoln, the reader may recall, had been a temperance lecturer), and when it proved indifferent to the cause in the years following the war, the Prohibition Party had reasserted itself with marked effect on a number of Midwestern elections. Most Populists were prohibitionists or, at the least, temperance men and women; William Jennings Bryan was a prohibitionist and a teetotal abstinence man. Temperance and/or some form of prohibition had been a central issue in the women's rights movement from the first. Susan B. Anthony had started her public career as a temperance lecturer. Frances Willard had made prohibition the dominant issue for millions of reform-minded women. Most Spiritualists and all Methodists were advocates of some program or another to do away with alcohol. So it is not surprising that the Midwestern variety of Insurgency or Progressivism contained a strong element of prohibitionism. In a considerable degree it was an East-West issue.

Prohibition Gains Support

A revival campaign for a national Prohibition law was clearly a by-product of the era of reform. To the persistent Protestant evangel against the demon alcohol as an offense to God, as a social evil and a major impediment to the realization of a redeemed Christian republic, was added the new concern for the human body as "the Temple of God," to use the title of Victoria Woodhull's essay. The same refrain was carried by reformers of all orders and denominations, from Unitarians and Baptists to Presbyterians and Methodists, from Spiritualists to Christian Scientists and Christian Socialists (although the Socialist Party steered clear of the issue because of its desire to cater to the radical elements among the German and Irish workers). To drink, even in moderation, was to poison the body and compromise the fight for social justice. "Research" and "science" were recruited to strengthen the case for prohibition. Studies showed that insanity, criminal behavior, a variety of diseases, and early death awaited not only the alcoholic but anyone who indulged. Colleges began to insist that their athletes not drink.

A drive was also instituted in professional baseball to squelch drinking (an uphill battle), and Connie Mack, the famous manager of the Philadelphia Athletics, announced, "Alcohol slows a man down. I don't bother with youngsters that drink." Henry Ford and other industrialists instituted in their plants programs directed at informing their workers of the dangers of strong drink (the most serious danger for Ford workers was that they would be fired if they were even suspected of drinking to excess).

The Woman's Christian Temperance Union, the leader in so many social reforms, prevailed on (or bullied) publishers to include lurid accounts of the dangers of intemperance in school textbooks. The ancient link among alcohol, prostitution, and venereal disease was given fresh potency by "studies" that offered alarming statistics. A physician declared that 70 percent of venereal infections in men under the age of twenty-five were contracted while the men were inebriated. A group of prisoners in the Western Penitentiary at Philadelphia exhorted the state legislature to pass a prohibition law, declaring that 70 percent of the crime in the state was the consequence of drinking hard liquor. Of all divorces, 20 percent were attributed to alcoholism, and 45 percent of children in orphanages and children's homes were said to be the offspring of alcoholics. In addition, uncounted thousands of children were beaten and abused by drunken parents. The Committee of Fifty, composed of doctors and scientists devoted to the study of the effects of intemperance, reported that it was the sole cause of crime in 16 percent of all arrests, the primary cause in 31 percent, and a contributory cause in almost 50 percent.

Sociologists and psychologists, who were placing increasing emphasis on the environment as a determining factor in human behavior, argued that poverty was less the result of bad genes than of bad surroundings; saloons and drunken parents produced delinquent children. Virtually all the reform journals from *McClure's* (a leader in the fight for prohibitory laws) to *Harper's Weekly,* the *Atlantic Monthly,* the *Survey,* and *Collier's* carried frequent articles on the disastrous consequences of excessive, or even moderate, imbibing. Dr. Henry Smith Williams, an authority on the effects of alcohol, declared it the "most subtle, the most far-reaching, and judged by its ultimate effects, incomparably the most virulent of all poisons." If you were a drinker, you were "tangibly threatening the physical structure of your stomach, your heart, your blood-vessels, your nerves, your brain; . . . you are unequivocally decreasing your capacity for work in any field, be it physical, intellectual, or artistic; . . . you are, in some measure, lowering the grade of your mind, dulling your higher aesthetic sense, taking the finer edge off your morals . . . and . . . you may be entailing upon your descendants yet unborn a bond of uncalculable misery. . . . As a mere business proposition: Is your glass of beer, your bottle of wine, your high-ball, or your cock-tail worth such a price?"

The editor of the journal in which Williams's article appeared added that scientific investigation had shown that "every function of the normal human body is injured by the use of alcohol—even the moderate use, and that the injury is both serious and permanent."

In the face of such evidence it was a bold spirit who dared say a good word for "spirits." The consensus among the informed and the reform-minded on alcohol was virtually unanimous; the real question was what to do about it. Most socialists of various denominations took the line that alcoholism, like poverty, was a side effect of an exploitative capitalism that produced the conditions that drove workingmen to drink as the only escape from their misery (and others to drink because of the grindingly competitive character of American life) and that robbing the workingman of the consolation of his glass of beer was hardly the way to remedy the situation. In 1912 at the Socialist Convention the delegates adopted a resolution which read in part: "Poverty, overwork and overworry necessarily result in intemperance. . . . To abolish the wage system with all its evils is the surest way to eliminate the evils of alcoholism. . . ." Taking a contrary tack were such prominent Socialists as

John Spargo, who pointed out that European Socialists had taken a position in favor of Prohibition. Strong drink, according to Spargo, was one of the means by which capitalism diminished revolutionary ardor and kept the masses in a passive state.

Laws Implement Prohibition

Between 1900 and 1906 many states and counties passed antisaloon or prohibitory laws until, by some estimates, approximately 40 percent of the country's population was living in dry [supporting Prohibition; opponents were called "wets"—ed.] territory. In New Hampshire 183 out of 224 towns were dry and in Vermont, 221 out of 246. In Ohio 1,150 towns were dry; there were 708 dry towns in Wisconsin, and 26 counties in Illinois. The South followed suit; by 1907 two-thirds of the Southern counties were dry. Often conflicts developed where the rural populations of counties forced cities within their boundaries to go dry. Most of the Rocky Mountain states went dry in the years

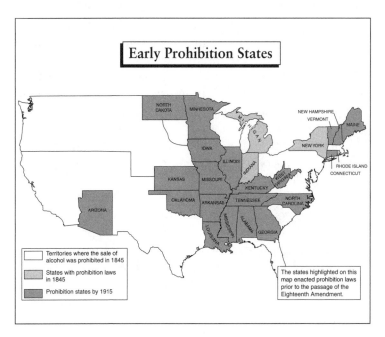

following, and the Prohibition movement seemed to have acquired an irresistible momentum. But soon there were defections. As had happened many times in the past, towns, counties, cities, even wards, backslid. Just when it appeared the tide had turned strongly against it, the cause of Prohibition was saved by the outbreak of the European War. Even before the entry of the United States into the conflict, the forces urging preparedness had called for "an entire or partial ban upon the liquor traffic," in the words of the *Bankers Magazine*. The argument for moral austerity was reinforced by the argument that the grain used to make alcohol was needed to feed the starving Belgians or the hungry British or French. The preparedness prohibitionists did all they could to identify opposition to Prohibition with the German-American population and thus, somehow, with Germany and, by extension, with treason. Undoubtedly the growing suspicion of and hostility toward those immigrants who had come from the nations that constituted the Central Powers gave added impetus to the Prohibition movement. It was almost like a rebuke by the old-time American-born reformers to the dangerous class of hyphenated Americans, many of whom strongly opposed the entry of the United States into the war.

With Prohibition increasingly identified with "loyalty" as well as austerity and morality, its opponents found themselves outmaneuvered. On December 18, 1917, Congress adopted and submitted to the states the Eighteenth Amendment, prohibiting the manufacture, transportation, or sale of liquors with an alcohol content of more than one-half of 1 percent.

Almost two years later, with the amendment ratified by a two-thirds vote of the states, Congress, in October, 1919, passed, over Wilson's veto, the Volstead Act, providing the enforcement apparatus. It was a strange moment in the history of the Republic. Vineyards and breweries and distilleries closed down all over the country. Tens of thousands of workers found themselves without jobs, and millions of Americans without the consolation of a sip or a nip.

The triumph of Prohibition in the United States was, in the mind of dedicated prohibitionists, simply the first step in the redemption of the world from alcohol. The Reverend A.C. Bane declared at a convention of the World League Against Alcoholism in 1917, "America will 'go over the top' in humanity's greatest battle, and plant the victorious white standard of Prohibition upon the nation's loftiest eminence. Then . . . we will go forth with the spirit of the missionary and the crusader to help drive the demon of drink from all civilization. With America leading the way, with faith in Omnipotent God . . . we will soon . . . bestow upon mankind the priceless gift of World Prohibition."

The redemptive zeal could not be suppressed. It manifested itself in Prohibition as surely as in the somewhat more sophisticated notion of the redemption of the world by the League of Nations. For better or worse, the relationship of Americans to strong drink is one of the most persistent and perplexing issues in our history. Outside of the issue of slavery and, subsequently, of the status of black Americans, no issue has more persistently troubled the mind and the consciousness of Americans than that of temperance, of the drinking or nondrinking of alcoholic beverages. As we have noted time and again, the forces of temperance endured from generation to generation, preserving in families unbroken lines of teetotalers from father to son to grandson. Few families failed to number among their members chronic alcoholics carried to early graves. The problem of alcoholism was not a figment of the imaginations of repressive-minded Puritans; it was one of the most enduring symptoms of the psychic cost of being an American. Decade after decade it seemed to give the lie to the proposition that Americans were a "happy" people.

An Amazing Pair of Prohibition Agents

Herbert Asbury

Once Prohibition became law, the government faced the monumental responsibility of enforcing it. At most times the task appeared insurmountable, and harried agents raided one illegal speakeasy only to learn that five more opened elsewhere. Individuals who would normally never consider violating a law freely purchased the illegal product. Consequently, overwhelmed enforcement officers wondered whether their actions made any difference.

An expert on Prohibition and the 1920s, Herbert Asbury, explains the incredible efforts of two agents, Isadore Einstein and Moe Smith, who carried out their duties in astounding, and sometimes hilarious, ways.

In a $14-a-month flat on Ridge Street, in New York's lower East Side, lived a bulbous little man named Isadore Einstein, whom everyone called Izzy. He had been a salesman, both inside and on the road, but was now a minor clerk at Station K of the New York Post Office. It required very shrewd management to feed, house, and clothe his family—his wife and four children and his father—on the meager salary of a postal employee. He was looking for something better, and decided that he had found it when he read in his newspaper about the government's plans to pay

Excerpted from "The Noble Experiment of Izzy and Moe," by Herbert Asbury (originally published as "When Prohibition Was in Flower") in *The Aspirin Age: 1919–1941*, edited by Isabel Leighton. Copyright ©1946 by the American Mercury Inc., ©1949 by Simon & Schuster, Inc. Reprinted with permission from Edith Asbury.

enforcement agents up to $2,500 a year.

But James Shevlin, Chief Enforcement Agent for the Southern District of New York, was not enthusiastic about Izzy. "I must say, Mr. Einstein," he said, "you don't look much like a detective." And that was the truth. Probably no one ever looked less like a detective than Izzy Einstein. He was forty years old, almost bald, five feet and five inches tall, and weighed 225 pounds. Most of this poundage was around his middle, so that when he walked his noble paunch, gently wobbling, moved majestically ahead like the breast of an overfed pouter pigeon.

But Izzy was accomplished. Besides English and Yiddish, he spoke German, Polish, and Hungarian fluently, and could make headway, though haltingly, in French, Italian, and Russian. He had even picked up a few words and phrases of Chinese. Moreover, Izzy had a knack of getting along with people and inspiring confidence. No one, looking at his round, jolly face and twinkling black eyes, could believe that he was a government snooper. Down on the lower East Side in New York he was the neighborhood cutup; whenever he dropped into the corner cigar stores and the coffeehouses his witticisms and high spirits never failed to draw an appreciative crowd.

"I guess Mr. Shevlin never saw a type like me," Izzy said afterward. "Maybe I fascinated him or something. Anyhow, I sold him on the idea that this prohibition business needed a new type of people that couldn't be spotted so easy."

Whatever the reason, Izzy got the job.

"But I must warn you," said Shevlin, "that hunting down liquor sellers isn't exactly a safe line of work. Some law violator might get mad and try to crack a bottle over your head."

"Bottles," said Izzy, "I can dodge."

Izzy's First Assignments

Izzy's first assignment was to clean up a place in Brooklyn which the enforcement authorities shrewdly suspected housed a speakeasy, since drunken men had been seen staggering from the building, and the air for half a block around was redolent with the fumes of beer and whiskey. Several agents had snooped and slunk around the house; one had watched all one afternoon from a roof across the street, and another had hidden for hours in an adjoining doorway, obtaining an accurate count of the number of men who entered and left. But none had been able to get inside. Izzy knew nothing of sleuthing procedures; he simply walked up to the joint and knocked on the door. A peephole was opened, and a hoarse voice demanded to know who was there.

"Izzy Einstein," said Izzy. "I want a drink."

"Oh, yeah? Who sent you here, bud? What's your business?"

"My boss sent me," Izzy explained. "I'm a prohibition agent. I just got appointed."

The door swung open and the doorman slapped Izzy jovially on the back.

"Ho! ho!" he cried. "Come right in, bud. That's the best gag I've heard yet."

Izzy stepped into a room where half a dozen men were drinking at a small, makeshift bar.

"Hey, boss!" the doorman yelled. "Here's a prohibition agent wants a drink! You got a badge, too, bud?"

"Sure I have," said Izzy, and produced it.

"Well, I'll be damned," said the man behind the bar. "Looks just like the real thing."

He poured a slug of whiskey, and Izzy downed it. That was a mistake, for when the time came to make the pinch Izzy had no evidence. He tried to grab the bottle but the bartender ran out the back door with it.

"I learned right there," said Izzy, "that a slug of hooch in an agent's belly might feel good, but it ain't evidence."

So when he went home that night he rigged up an evidence-collector. He put a small funnel in the upper left-hand pocket of his vest, and connected it, by means of a rubber tube, with a flat bottle concealed in the lining of the garment. Thereafter, when a drink was served to him, Izzy took a small sip, then poured the remainder into the funnel while the bartender was making change. The bottle wouldn't hold much, but there was always enough for analysis and to offer in evidence. "I'd have died if it hadn't been for that little funnel and the bottle," said Izzy. "And most of the stuff I got in those places was terrible."

Izzy used his original device of giving his real name, with some variation, more than twenty times during the next five years. It was successful even after he became so well known, and so greatly feared, that his picture hung behind the bar in many speakeasies, that all might see and be warned. Occasionally Izzy would prance into a gin-mill with his badge pinned to his lapel, in plain sight, and shout jovially, "How about a drink for a hard-working prohibition agent?" Seeing the round little man trying so hard to be funny, everyone in the place would rush forward to hand him something alcoholic, and Izzy would arrest them and close the joint. . . .

Moe Joins Izzy

After Izzy had been an enforcement agent for a few weeks, he began to miss his old friend Moe Smith, with whom he had spent many pleasant evenings in the East Side coffee-houses. Like Izzy, Moe was a natural comedian, and, also like Izzy, he was corpulent. He tipped the scales at about 235 pounds, but he was a couple of inches taller than Izzy and didn't look quite so roly-poly. Moe had been a cigar salesman, and manager of a small fight club at Orchard and Grand Streets, New York City, and had invested his savings in a little cigar store, where he was doing well. Izzy persuaded him to put a relative in charge of the store, and to apply for a job as enforcement agent.

Moe could probably have got on the enforcement staff by his own efforts, for his background and experience were at least as good as those of nine-tenths of the agents who were hired, but he obtained the post a little quicker through Izzy's recommendation. As soon as he was sworn in as an agent, he and Izzy teamed up together, and most of the time thereafter worked as a pair. Their first assignment took them to Rockaway Beach, near New York, where they confiscated a still and arrested the operator. This man apparently took a great liking to Izzy, for after he got out of jail he made several trips to New York especially to urge Izzy to go on a fishing trip with him.

"I'll take you three miles out to sea," he said. "You'll have quite a time."

But Izzy firmly declined the invitation. "Sure he'll take me out to sea," he said, "but will he bring me back? He could leave me with the fishes."

In those early days of the noble experiment everything that happened in connection with prohibition was news, and some of New York's best reporters covered enforcement headquarters. Casting about for a way to enliven their stories and provide exercise for their imaginations, they seized upon the exploits of Izzy and Moe. The two fat and indefatigable agents supplied human-interest material by the yard; moreover, they were extraordinarily cooperative. They frequently scheduled their raids to suit the convenience of the reporters and the newspaper photographers, and soon learned that there was more room in the papers on Monday morning than on any other day of the week.

One Sunday, accompanied by a swarm of eager reporters, they established a record by making seventy-one raids in a little more than twelve hours. On another they staged a spectacular raid for the benefit of Dr. John Roach Straton, a famous hell-buster of the period, and the congregation of the Calvary Baptist Church in West Fifty-seventh Street, of which Dr. Straton was pastor. Izzy and Moe timed their raid, on a small café near the church, to coincide with the dismissal of Dr. Straton's flock after morning services, and the members of the congregation reached the street in time to see the agents rolling barrels of whiskey out of the café and smashing them with hatchets. This raid made everybody happy, except, of course, the man who owned the whiskey. . . .

An Amazing Duo

What the newspapers enjoyed most about Izzy and Moe was their ingenuity. Once they went after a speakeasy where half a dozen dry agents had tried without success to buy a drink. The bartender positively wouldn't sell to anyone he didn't know. So on a cold winter night Izzy stood in front of the gin-mill, in his shirt sleeves, until he was red and shivering and his teeth were chattering. Then Moe half-carried him into the speakeasy, shouting excitedly:

"Give this man a drink! He's just been bitten by a frost!"

The kindhearted bartender, startled by Moe's excitement and upset by Izzy's miserable appearance, rushed forward with a bottle of whiskey. Moe promptly snatched the bottle and put him under arrest.

One of Izzy's most brilliant ideas was always to carry something on his raids, the nature of the burden depending upon the character of the neighborhood and of a particular speakeasy's clientele. When he wanted to get into a place frequented by musicians, for example, he carried a violin or a trombone, and if, as sometimes happened, he was asked to play the instrument, he could do it. He usually played "How Dry I Am." On the East Side and in the poorer sections of the Bronx, if the weather permitted, Izzy went around in his shirt sleeves carrying a pitcher of milk, the very pattern of an honest man on his way home from the grocery. Once in Brooklyn he was admitted to half a dozen gin-mills because he was lugging a big pail of dill pickles. "A fat man with pickles!" said Izzy. "Who'd ever think a fat man with pickles was an agent?"

When Izzy operated on the beaches around New York he always carried a fishing rod or a bathing suit; he had great success one day at Sheepshead Bay with a string of fish slung over his shoulder. The doorman of the Assembly, a café in Brooklyn which catered to judges and lawyers, let him in without question because he wore a frock coat and carried a huge tome bound in sheepskin. Once inside, Izzy opened his book and adjusted a pair of horn-rimmed spectacles and, with lips moving and brow furrowed, marched with stately tread across the room and barged into the bar. Without lifting his eyes from the book, he called sonorously for "a beverage, please," and the fascinated bartender poured a slug of whiskey before he realized what he was doing. When Izzy and Moe visited Reisenweber's, a famous and expensive resort on Broadway, they carried two lovely blondes and wore "full-dress tuxedos," with rings on their fingers, sweet-smelling pomade on their hair, and huge imitation-pearl studs in their shirt fronts. The headwaiter asked them for references when they ordered liquor, and Izzy searched his pockets and pulled out the first card he found. It happened to be the card of a rabbi, with which Izzy planned to ensnare a sacramental-wine store. But the headwaiter, a man of scant perception, bowed deferentially and sold them a bottle of whiskey. "He deserved to be arrested," said Izzy, indignantly. "Imagine! A rabbi with a blonde and no beard!"

Up in Van Cortlandt Park, in New York City, near the public playing fields, was a soft-drink establishment which was suspected of being one of the retail outlets of a big rum ring. Many complaints were made to enforcement headquarters that customers had become tipsy after a few shots of the soda water sold in the place; one woman wrote that by mistake her milk shake had been filled with gin. Bad gin, too, she added. The job of getting the evidence was given to Izzy. It proved a difficult task, for the owner of the joint would sell liquor to no one he didn't know personally. So on a Saturday afternoon in November Izzy assembled a group of half a dozen dry agents, clad them in football uniforms, and smeared their arms and faces with fresh dirt. Then Izzy tucked a football under his arm, hung a helmet over his ears, and led them whooping and rah-rahing into the suspected speakeasy, where they shouted that they had just won the last game of the season and wanted to break training in a big way. The speakeasy owner, pleased at such a rush of business, sold each agent a pint of whiskey. "Have fun, boys," he said. "The same to you," said Izzy, handing him a summons.

Flushed with this striking success, which showed that at

heart he was a college boy, Izzy went to Ithaca, N.Y., to investigate a complaint by officials of Cornell University that some soda fountains near the campus were not confining their sales to pop. Izzy disguised himself as an undergraduate by putting on a little cap and a pair of white linen knickers, not so little, and for several days strolled about the campus. He hummed snatches of Cornell songs which he had learned, and played safe by addressing everyone with a mustache as "Professor," and everyone with a beard as "Dean." Having located the soda fountains which sold liquor, he dashed into them one by one, establishing himself as a student by shouting, "Sizzle Boom! Sizzle Boom! Rah! Rah! Rah!" The speakeasy boys thought he was a comedian, which indeed he was, and they gladly sold him all the booze he wanted, after which he went from place to place distributing "diplomas," or summonses.

From Cornell, and without the blessing of the student body, Izzy rushed into Harlem to investigate a complaint about a grocery store. "The man charged me two dollars for a can of tomatoes," a woman wrote to enforcement headquarters, "and when I got it home I found there was nothing in it but a lot of nasty-smelling water. My husband he grabbed it and ran out of the house and I ain't seen him since. I want you to arrest that man." Izzy disguised himself as a Negro, with his face blackened by burnt cork and a rich Southern accent rolling off his tongue. He visited the store and awaited his turn in a long line of impatient customers. He found that to buy a half-pint of whiskey (four dollars) a customer asked for a can of beans. If he wanted gin (two dollars) he asked for tomatoes. Izzy bought both beans and tomatoes and came back next day with a warrant and a truck. Besides the groceryman, he hauled away four hundred bottles of gin, some empty cans, a canning machine, three barrels of whiskey, and a barrel of pickles which contained one hundred small bottles of gin. "Pickles was a kind of hobby of mine," he said, "and I could always tell if anything was wrong with a barrel."

The trail of illegal liquor led Izzy and Moe into some

mighty queer places, but they followed wherever it led, and were always ready with the appropriate disguise. Dressed as a longshoreman, Izzy captured an Italian who used his cash register as a cellarette; its drawers were filled with little bottles of booze. In the guise of a mendicant, Izzy pawned an old pair of pants for two dollars in Brooklyn, and snooping about the pawnshops a bit found ten thousand dollars' worth of good liquor wrapped in clothing that had been left as pledges. He got into the Half Past Nine Club, on Eighth Avenue, as a prosperous poultry salesman, playing tipsy and carrying a sample, and found a large stock of liquor in a stuffed grizzly bear. . . .

One of Izzy's largest and most important hauls came as the result of a visit to a graveyard on the outskirts of New York. He had gone to the cemetery to attend the burial services of a friend, and, as usual, kept his eyes open. Just as the car in which he was riding turned into the cemetery gates, he saw two men come out of the back door of a house across the street, look furtively about, and then carry a large galvanized can across the yard into a shed. This looked suspicious, so when the services were over, instead of returning to New York, Izzy hid in some shrubbery. At sundown, when the cemetery gates had been closed, he moved to a tombstone directly across from the house, and crouched behind it. For three hours he watched and listened. Several times he thought he caught a whiff of mash, but nothing happened.

Izzy returned to New York about midnight, but without evidence to justify making a raid or asking for a warrant. So he evolved a scheme, for he was convinced that dirty business was afoot in the house. Next day he and Moe appeared at the cemetery office, two very seedy-looking characters, clad in rags and obviously down on their luck. They asked for work as gravediggers. The superintendent said there were no jobs open but changed his mind when they offered to dig graves for half price. They worked in an obscure corner of the cemetery until the time came to close the gates, then they told the superintendent that they needed money badly and would like to work overtime. He agreed, and left them there with their picks and shovels. After he had gone they moved to an unused area near the fence, across from the house, and began to dig. About an hour later a man came out of the house, stood on the porch watching them for a few minutes, then crossed the road and leaned idly against the fence.

"Hard work, ain't it, boys?" he asked.

"Yeah," said Moe. "Thirsty work, too. I'd give ten dollars for a pint right now."

"Five, anyway," said Izzy.

The man said nothing, and after a few minutes went back into the house. Then Izzy had another idea. He and Moe quickly dug three or four shallow holes, and were working on a fifth when the man returned. When he got within hearing distance Moe called to Izzy:

"How many more we got to dig tonight?"

"Ten," said Izzy.

"My God!" exclaimed the man. "What happened? Somebody blow up a hotel?"

"Well, that's the way it goes," said Izzy. "Sometimes nobody dies for a long time, then all of a sudden a lot of people make up their minds at the same time."

"It wouldn't be so bad," said Moe, "if we could get a drink."

"You boys come over to the house after a while," the man said. "Maybe I can fix you up."

Half an hour later Izzy and Moe put away their tools, climbed the fence, and strolled across the road. The man greeted them cordially, and introduced them to two others as hard-working gravediggers. The party adjourned to the kitchen, where Izzy bought a pint of whiskey for six dollars, having beat the price down from ten. Then while Moe covered the three prisoners with his gun, Izzy kicked in the door of an adjoining room, from which came the heavy odor of fermenting mash. There he found three big stills running full blast, fifty-one barrels containing alcohol, and a dozen bottles of essences and chemical coloring, used to give the new hooch the appearance, and something of the flavor, of the real stuff. In another room Izzy discovered a large quantity of counterfeit labels and government revenue stamps. The hosts had the job of carrying all this stuff out and loading it on a truck.

A Fabulous Career Ends

For more than five years the whole country laughed at the antics of Izzy and Moe, with the exception of the ardent drys, who thought the boys were wonderful, and the bootleggers and speakeasy proprietors, who thought they were crazy and feared them mightily. And their fear was justified, for in their comparatively brief career Izzy and Moe confiscated 5,000,000 bottles of booze, worth $15,000,000, besides thousands of gallons in kegs and barrels and hundreds of stills and breweries. They smashed an enormous quantity of saloon fixtures and equipment, and made 4,392 arrests, of which more than 95 per cent resulted in convictions. No other two agents even approached this record.

Nearly all of their victims were small-fry bootleggers and speakeasy operators, although they raided and confiscated a considerable number of large stills and breweries. Their largest single haul was 2,000 cases of bottled whiskey and 365 barrels of whiskey and brandy, which they found in a Bronx garage. And they made one terrifying swoop up and down Broadway which put the finishing touches to such celebrated night-life resorts as Jack's, the Ted Lewis Club, Shanley's, the Beaux Arts, and Reisenweber's. . . .

Izzy didn't approve of guns, and never carried one. Moe lugged a revolver around occasionally, but in five years fired it only twice. Once he shot out a lock that had resisted his efforts, and another time he shot a hole in a keg of whiskey. Izzy said later that guns were pulled on him only twice. The first time was on Dock Street, in Yonkers, N.Y., where he had spent a pleasant and profitable evening with raids on five speakeasies. To make it an even half dozen, he stepped into a sixth place that looked suspicious, bought a slug of whiskey for sixty cents, and poured it into the funnel in his vest pocket. While he was arresting the bartender, the owner of the joint came into the bar from another part of the house.

"He pulled an automatic from behind the bar," wrote Izzy. "She clicked but the trigger jammed. It was aimed right at my heart. I didn't like that. I grabbed his arm and he and I had a fierce fight all over the bar, till finally I got the pistol. I don't mind telling you I was afraid, particularly when I found the gun was loaded."

On another occasion an angry bartender shoved a revolver against Izzy's stomach. But Izzy didn't bat an eye; he calmly shoved the gun aside.

"Put that up, son," he said, soothingly. "Murdering me won't help your family."

Fortunately, the bartender had a family, and Izzy's warning brought to his mind a vision of his fatherless children weeping at the knee of their widowed mother, who was also weeping. He stopped to think. While he was thinking, Moe knocked him cold. . . .

During the summer of 1925 the almost continual stories about Izzy and Moe in the newspapers got on the nerves of high prohibition enforcement officials in Washington, few of whom ever got mentioned in the papers at all. National headquarters announced that any agent whose name appeared in print in connection with his work would be suspended, and perhaps otherwise punished, on the ground that publicity brought discredit to the service. At the same time a high official called Izzy to Washington and spoke to him rather severely. "You get your name in the newspaper all the time, and in the headlines, too," he complained, "whereas mine is hardly ever mentioned. I must ask you to remember that you are merely a subordinate, not the whole show." For a while Izzy really tried to keep away from the reporters and out of the papers, but both he and Moe had become public personages, and it was impossible to keep the newspapermen from writing about them. When they refused to tell what they had done, the reporters invented stories about them, so a stream of angry denials and protests continued to come from Washington.

Finally, on November 13, 1925, it was announced that Izzy and Moe had turned in their gold badges and were no longer prohibition agents. Izzy's story was that he had been told he was to be transferred to Chicago. He had lived in New York since he was fifteen years old, and had no intention of ever living anywhere else, so he refused to go, and "thereby fired myself." Government officials, however, said that Izzy and Moe had been dismissed "for the good of the service." Off the record they added, "The service must be dignified. Izzy and Moe belong on the vaudeville stage." Most of the newspapers took the position that the whole problem of enforcement belonged on the vaudeville stage. The New York *Herald Tribune* said, "They [Izzy and Moe] never made prohibition much more of a joke than it has been made by some of the serious-minded prohibition officers."

Both Izzy and Moe went into the insurance business, and did well. They dropped out of the public eye, and remained out except for an occasional Sunday feature story, and a brief flurry of publicity in 1928, when Izzy went to Europe and returned with some entertaining accounts of his adventures. Izzy died in New York on February 17, 1938, by which time his four sons had all become successful lawyers.

America Ignores the Law

Edward Behr

Even though Prohibition became the law of the land, many Americans refused to obey it. People intended to have their bottle of beer, shot of whiskey, or glass of wine no matter what the government declared. In this excerpt, however, Edward Behr describes the methods individuals and groups developed to ensure a steady flow of alcohol.

Prohibition turned Andrew J. Volstead, an otherwise obscure Republican congressman from Minnesota, into a household name. It was commonly assumed that because the Eighteenth Amendment to the Constitution introducing nationwide Prohibition bore his name it was largely his doing. In fact, Volstead was its facilitator rather than its architect. [Wayne] Wheeler himself, as he would later boast, conceived, drafted, and copiously rewrote it. Its many weaknesses, and omissions, are largely attributable to him.

Volstead, a dour Lutheran of Norwegian origin, with a huge bristling mustache, was not even part of the hard core of dry advocates in Congress and, in his long political career, had never used the Prohibition platform as part of his election campaign strategy. On two occasions, his unsuccessful challengers to his House of Representatives seat had even been Prohibition candidates. As county prosecutor in his earlier days, he had prosecuted many cases involving illicit liquor because Minnesota had been a dry state long before 1917, but he had done so routinely, with no dogmatic belief in Prohibition's inherent virtues. It was in this same spirit, as chairman of the Senate Judiciary Committee, that he oversaw its passage, after the Supreme Court had narrowly (by five votes to four) validated its constitutionality.

Prohibition Becomes Law

Introduced on May 27, 1919, the bill was passed (255 to 166) after a three-month debate. The Senate vote followed on September 5, and, as part of routine procedure, it then went back to the House, to be adopted on October 10 by 321 to 70 votes. An already desperately ill President Wilson, further weakened by his losing fight to keep America within the League of Nations, vetoed it, on both constitutional and ethical grounds. "In all matters having to do with personal habits and customs of large numbers of our people," he wrote, "we must be certain that the established processes of legal change are followed." But that same day, the veto was overridden in Congress, and the act became law. Henceforth, the act determined, "No person shall manufacture, sell, barter, transport, import, export, deliver, furnish or possess any intoxicating liquor except as authorized in this act." The act replaced all previous dry legislation measures in force in the various states.

On the face of it, the Volstead Act was both all-encompassing and foolproof, though it did contain specific exemptions—regarding industrial alcohol, sacramental wine, certain patent medicines, doctors' prescriptions (but no more than a pint at a time per patient within a ten-day period), toilet preparations, flavoring extracts, syrups, vinegar, and cider. Brewers could remain in business provided they confined themselves to making "near-beer," with a maximum 0.5 percent alcohol content. Penalties for improper use were to be fines and prison terms—$1,000 or 30 days for the first offense, rising to $10,000 and a year for further convictions.

The act also banned liquor advertising, and the use or sale of anything that might lead to its manufacture. "Any room, house, building, boat, vehicle, structure or place where intoxicating liquor is manufactured, sold, kept or bartered in violation of this title . . . is hereby declared a common nuisance," it said, outlining the scale of fines and jail sentences for transgressors. Liquor stored for sale or vehicles used for transport were to be seized and destroyed. But the act was mute concerning the actual consumption of liquor in private homes—the one concession to individual liberty. . . .

In retrospect, the Volstead Act was hopelessly inadequate, because it grossly underestimated the willingness of the lawbreakers to risk conviction, the degree of human ingenuity displayed to get around its provisions, and the ease with which the lawbreakers would be able to subvert all those whose job was to enforce it. Above all, its failure resulted from a naive American belief in the effectiveness of law: the drys, whether ASL [Anti-Saloon League] or church activists, politicians, law enforcers, or simply individuals of strong moral convictions, were convinced that Americans, as law-abiding citizens intensely respectful of established authority, would obey the provisions of the Volstead Act, even if, as drinkers and as advocates of personal, individual liberty, they deeply resented it. . . .

Widespread Violations Begin

Although Prohibition had been in the cards for several years, many Americans simply did not know what to expect. Whereas Colonel Daniel Porter, a New York supervising revenue agent, announced that he was confident "there will not be any violations to speak of," New Jersey Governor Edward I. Edwards said he hoped to keep New Jersey "as wet as the Atlantic ocean." In truth, the Volstead Act was flagrantly broken from the moment it became law, and continued to be flouted for the next thirteen years.

The nation's legislators and law enforcers professed to be completely taken aback, after 1920, by the extent of Prohibition-related lawbreaking—and the concomitant, almost immediate proliferation of speakeasies, bootleggers, rumrunners, moonshiners, and hijackers, all bringing violence in their wake. They need not have been so surprised.

Had they bothered to look at those towns and states where Prohibition had already become law *before* 1920, they would have realized what was in store. In 1916, for instance, Prohibition had finally become a reality in Wash-

A federal agent smashes a barrel of beer in 1924. The agents assigned to enforce Prohibition were unable to keep up with the tide of illegal activity that prevailed during the 1920s.

ington State, and immediately the new law there (very similar in content to the Volstead Act) had been totally ignored or subverted. A month after Spokane, then a town of 44,000 registered voters, became dry, 34,000 liquor permits had been issued, and soft-drink shops selling under-the-counter liquor were doing a roaring trade, with sixty-five brand-new drugstores—all selling liquor—competing for business. Moonshine liquor was freely available, there was a constant stream of smuggled liquor from across the nearby Canadian border, and a drugstore-owning couple whose establishment was, Carry Nation style, "hatchetized" by Prohibition vigilantes, promptly went into another line of business, running a company shipping rum from Cuba to Canada, but in fact smuggling it back into the twenty-eight dry states.

What had happened in Spokane four years before national Prohibition became law was to become the norm all over America. "A staggering increase in liquor prescribed as medicine occurred during the first five months throughout the country." In Chicago alone, as soon as the Volstead Act became law, over 15,000 doctors and 57,000 retail druggists applied for licenses to sell "medicinal" liquor, and in the next three years there would be 7,000 (mostly new) "soft-drinking" parlors, actually dispensing liquor. Scores of clandestine breweries also set up shop, and small fortunes were made by printers supplying fake whiskey labels, carpenters making fake wooden crates for brand-name whiskey, and pharmacists selling ingredients for homemade stills (yeast, juniper oil, fusel oil, iodine, and caramel). Americans bought huge quantities of malt syrup, essential for turning "near-beer" into the real thing, and the Prohibition Bureau estimated that several hundred million gallons of homemade 2.5-degree beer were consumed every year. There was a run on anything containing alcohol that could be used as a basis for homemade liquor—embalming fluid, antifreeze solution, solidified and rubbing alcohol, bay rum—often with horrendous consequences, for, inexplicably, old rules requiring denatured alcohol to bear the POISON warning were discontinued.

The ingenuity of clandestine liquor manufacturers was considerable. In the Midwest, the liquid residue of silos was collected and turned into liquor. New brands sprang up: Panther Whiskey, Red Eye, Cherry Dynamite, Old Stingo, Old Horsey, Scat Whiskey, Happy Sally, Jump Steady, Soda Pop Moon, Sugar Moon, and Jackass Brandy, supposedly made of peaches. In the South, a brand called Squirrel Whiskey got its name because it was so strong it was supposed to make consumers climb trees. In the ghettos, a popular drink was known simply as nigger gin. "Sweet whiskey" was made with nitrous ether—alcohol mixed with nitric and sulfuric acid. Yack-yack Bourbon, a popular Chicago drink, was made with iodine and burnt sugar. From Mexico came "American" whiskey, made from potatoes and cactus, and from Jamaica a 90-proof alcohol concoction known as Jamaica ginger, or Jake. *Colliers* reported that victims of Jake paralysis lost control of their extremities: ". . . the victim has no control over the muscles that normally point the toes upward."

Although some Californian vineyards were ruined by Prohibition, certain Napa Valley wine-making families became exceedingly wealthy. In fact, grape production, far from declining, increased tenfold between 1920 and 1933, the main reason being the manufacture of dried grape and "raisin cakes." These were allowed, under a provision of the Volstead Act, to prevent farmers from going under entirely. The aim was, officially, to allow householders to make "nonintoxicating cider and fruit juices for home consumption to the extent of 200 gallons annually."

The raisin cakes were easily turned into something else. Wholesalers used demonstrators (often attractive, well-spoken young women) in large stores to draw attention to the wine-making possibilities of their cakes (or "bricks") while ostensibly warning against fermentation—their straight-faced cautionary patter urging buyers "not to place the liquid in a jug and put it aside for twenty-one days because it would turn into wine . . . and not to stop the bottle with a cork because this is necessary only if fermentation occurs." The bricks were sold with a label that read "Caution: will ferment and turn into wine." The biggest beneficiary of all was Beringer Vineyards in Napa Valley, whose owners, Charles and Bertha Beringer, were the first to take advantage of the obscure Volstead Act loophole. Bertha Beringer, only 32 when Prohibition began, and recently wedded to Charles, was the real brains behind the scheme, saving the family business—and inspiring countless later competitors. . . .

New York Restaurants Evade the Law

In New York, whereas many great restaurants simply closed down (their owners reluctant to break the law and unwilling to provide meals without vintage wines), speakeasies proliferated on a truly startling scale. By 1922, there would be at least 5,000, and by 1927, over 30,000—twice as many as all legal bars, restaurants, and nightclubs *before* Prohibition. Some of them—such as the Twenty-One and the Stork Club—would survive repeated closures to become fashionable post-Prohibition restaurants, just as prominent bootlegging personalities such as William "Big Bill" Dwyer and "impresario" Larry Fay would eventually become respected, adulated "café society" figures.

The career of Sherman Billingsley, the owner-founder of the Stork Club—in its day the most famous speakeasy in America—revealed the extent of Prohibition's "window of opportunity"—and how pre-1920 dry legislation provided bold entrepreneurs with valuable experience in skirting the Volstead Act's laws. Oklahoma-born Billingsley began selling bootleg liquor in a drugstore when he was twelve. He was sixteen when he was first arrested, in Seattle, for contravening the local liquor laws. Soon afterward, he was running bootleg liquor from Canada and managing three speakeasies in Detroit; at nineteen, in New York, he was running a Bronx drugstore selling medicinal whiskey.

Billingsley opened the Stork Club, with money from Frank Costello, New York's leading gangster, in 1927, and the nightly presence there of Walter Winchell, America's most famous syndicated gossip columnist (his drinks, and meals, were on the house), made it *the* place to be seen. A raid in 1931 led to its temporary closure, but the "right people" soon flocked to the new address on Fifty-third Street, undeterred by sky-high prices (a $20 cover charge, $2 for a carafe of plain water).

There were hundreds of lesser-known private drinking clubs, where affluent members could store their own liquor. According to humorist Robert Benchley (himself a serious drinker), there were thirty-eight speakeasies on East Fifty-second Street alone, and potential buyers were so convinced that every house there was a speakeasy that one house-holder—rather in the manner of today's New York car owners, notifying potential burglars of "no radio"—put up a notice on her front door: "This is a private residence. Do not ring." McSorley's saloon in Greenwich Village never bothered to reduce its potent beer to "near-beer"—its popularity with the police and local politicians such that it was never raided once. A new type of nightclub became fashionable: the expensive, barely clandestine night spot run by socialites (Sherman Billingsley's Stork Club) and showbiz veterans (Belle Livingstone's Country Club on East Fifty-eighth Street and "Texas" Guinan's El Fay Club on West Forty-fifth Street). These typically included cabaret shows, dancing girls, and exotic acts. Prohibition encouraged the emergence of uniquely colorful women, whose wit and toughness attracted huge numbers of admiring customers. Belle Livingstone, a much-married ex-Broadway showgirl (her husbands included a paint salesman, an Italian count, a Cleveland millionaire, and an English engineer), charged a $5 entrance fee and $40 for a bottle of champagne. Mary Louise "Texas" Guinan was a former star of silent westerns, ex-circus rider, and vaudeville singer whose generous disposition was legendary. She even urged Walter Winchell, one of her devoted admirers, to promote, in his columns, speakeasies owned by less fortunate competitors.

The trashing of the Times Square area of New York, once the site of large numbers of respectable bars and restaurants, began with Prohibition, for not all speakeasies were furnished in the Louis XV style like the luxurious five-story Country Club. Most were dark, sordid clip joints haunted by bar girls pushing foul drinks in exchange for the promise of spurious sex to come. In Cincinnati, the attractive Across the Rhine beer gardens soon became a distant memory.

Some Prohibition advocates felt that "wide-open" towns such as New York and Chicago should be brought to heel, and called for more Prohibition agents and harsher laws (which were in fact introduced in 1925). Others became disenchanted for different reasons. Senator Thomas B. Watson (Democrat, Georgia), a lifelong dry, shocked the Senate by drawing attention to "murder and other outrages carried out by Prohibition agents" in his state.

There was an almost immediate, nationwide change in drinking habits. It became the thing to do, among students, flappers, and respectable middle-class Americans all over the country, to defy the law—as much a manifestation of personal liberty as a thirst for alcohol.

Other changes manifested themselves. The saloon had been an almost exclusively male preserve, but the new speakeasies welcomed women. The cocktail was largely born as a result of Prohibition, because this was the only way of disguising the often horrible taste of homemade gin or flavored wood alcohol. And tens of thousands of people would die before Prohibition was over, poisoned by wood alcohol and moonshine.

CHAPTER 4

Culture and
Entertainment

AMERICA'S DECADES

Women Enjoy a New Morality

Frederick Lewis Allen

One of the most powerful changes that emerged from the 1920s was the increased freedom enjoyed by females. Instead of being confined to the home, American women joined the labor force and experimented with ways of behavior that would have been unthinkable a few years before.

In this excerpt from his book, *Only Yesterday: An Informed History of the Nineteen-Twenties*, Frederick Lewis Allen describes the vast change in lifestyle for the nation's females.

A first-class revolt against the accepted American order was certainly taking place during those early years of the Post-war Decade, but it was one with which [Russian leader] Nikolai Lenin had nothing whatever to do. The shock troops of the rebellion were not alien agitators, but the sons and daughters of well-to-do American families, who knew little about Bolshevism and cared distinctly less, and their defiance was expressed not in obscure radical publications or in soap-box speeches, but right across the family breakfast table into the horrified ears of conservative fathers and mothers. Men and women were still shivering at the Red Menace when they awoke to the no less alarming Problem of the Younger Generation, and realized that if the Constitution were not in danger, the moral code of the country certainly was.

This code, as it currently concerned young people, might

have been roughly summarized as follows: Women were the guardians of morality; they were made of finer stuff than men and were expected to act accordingly. Young girls must look forward in innocence (tempered perhaps with a modicum of physiological instruction) to a romantic love match which would lead them to the altar and to living-happily-ever-after; and until the "right man" came along they must allow no male to kiss them. It was expected that some men would succumb to the temptations of sex, but only with a special class of outlawed women; girls of respectable families were supposed to have no such temptations. Boys and girls were permitted large freedom to work and play together, with decreasing and well-nigh nominal chaperonage, but only because the code worked so well on the whole that a sort of honor system was supplanting supervision by their elders; it was taken for granted that if they had been well brought up they would never take advantage of this freedom. And although the attitude toward smoking and drinking by girls differed widely in different strata of society and different parts of the country, majority opinion held that it was morally wrong for them to smoke and could hardly imagine them showing the effects of alcohol.

The war had not long been over when cries of alarm from parents, teachers, and moral preceptors began to rend the air. For the boys and girls just growing out of adolescence were making mincemeat of this code.

Females Shatter Previous Standards of Behavior

The dresses that the girls—and for that matter most of the older women—were wearing seemed alarming enough. In July, 1920, a fashion-writer reported in the *New York Times* that "the American woman . . . has lifted her skirts far beyond any modest limitation," which was another way of saying that the hem was now all of nine inches above the ground. It was freely predicted that skirts would come down again in the winter of 1920–21, but instead they climbed a few scandalous inches farther. The flappers wore thin dresses, short-sleeved and occasionally (in the evening) sleeveless; some of the wilder young things rolled their stockings below their knees, revealing to the shocked eyes of virtue a fleeting glance of shin-bones and knee-cap; and many of them were visibly using cosmetics. . . .

The current mode in dancing created still more consternation. Not the romantic violin but the barbaric saxophone now dominated the orchestra, and to its passionate crooning and wailing the fox-trotters moved in what the editor of the Hobart College *Herald* disgustedly called a "syncopated embrace." No longer did even an inch of space separate them; they danced as if glued together, body to body, cheek to cheek. Cried the *Catholic Telegraph* of Cincinnati in righteous indignation, "The music is sensuous, the embracing of partners—the female only half dressed—is absolutely indecent; and the motions—they are such as may not be described, with any respect for propriety, in a family newspaper. Suffice it to say that there are certain houses appropriate for such dances; but those houses have been closed by law."

Supposedly "nice" girls were smoking cigarettes—openly and defiantly, if often rather awkwardly and self-consciously. They were drinking—somewhat less openly but often all too efficaciously. There were stories of daughters of the most exemplary parents getting drunk—"blotto," as their companions cheerfully put it—on the contents of the hip-flasks of the new prohibition régime, and going out joyriding with men at four in the morning. And worst of all, even at well-regulated dances they were said to retire where the eye of the most sharp-sighted chaperon could not follow, and in darkened rooms or in parked cars to engage in the unspeakable practice of petting and necking.

It was not until F. Scott Fitzgerald, who had hardly graduated from Princeton and ought to know what his generation were doing brought out *This Side of Paradise* in April, 1920, that fathers and mothers realized fully what was afoot and how long it had been going on. Apparently the "petting party" had been current as early as 1916, and was now widely established as an indoor sport. "None of the Victorian mothers—and most of the mothers were Victorian—had any idea how casually their daughters were accustomed to be kissed," wrote Mr. Fitzgerald. ". . . Amory saw girls doing things that even in his memory would have been impossible: eating three-o'clock, after-dance suppers

Prohibition, coupled with the younger generation's more rebellious attitude, led to a new moral standard during the 1920s. Here, a flapper reveals her secret hiding place for illegal liquor—an ankle flask.

in impossible cafés, talking of every side of life with an air half of earnestness, half of mockery, yet with a furtive excitement that Amory considered stood for a real moral letdown. But he never realized how widespread it was until he saw the cities between New York and Chicago as one vast juvenile intrigue." The book caused a shudder to run down the national spine; did not Mr. Fitzgerald represent one of his well-nurtured heroines as brazenly confessing, "I've kissed dozens of men. I suppose I'll kiss dozens more"; and another heroine as saying to a young man (*to a young man!*), "Oh, just one person in fifty has any glimmer of what sex is. I'm hipped on Freud and all that, but it's rotten that every bit of real love in the world is ninety-nine per cent passion and one little *soupçon* of jealousy"?

It was incredible. It was abominable. What did it all mean? Was every decent standard being thrown over? Mothers read the scarlet words and wondered if they themselves "had any idea how often their daughters were accustomed to be kissed.". . .

The forces of morality rallied to the attack. Dr. Francis E. Clark, the founder and president of the Christian Endeavor Society, declared that the modern "indecent dance" was "an offense against womanly purity, the very fountainhead of our family and civil life." The new style of dancing was denounced in religious journals as "impure, polluting, corrupting, debasing, destroying spirituality, increasing carnality," and the mothers and sisters and church members of the land were called upon to admonish and instruct and raise the spiritual tone of these dreadful young people. President Murphy of the University of Florida cried out with true Southern warmth, "The low-cut gowns, the rolled hose and short skirts are born of the Devil and his angels, and are carrying the present and future generations to chaos and destruction.". . .

Not content with example and reproof, legislators in several states introduced bills to reform feminine dress once and for all. The *New York American* reported in 1921 that a bill was pending in Utah providing fine and imprisonment for those who wore on the streets "skirts higher than three inches above the ankle." A bill was laid before the Virginia legislature which would forbid any woman from wearing shirtwaists or evening gowns which displayed "more than three inches of her throat." In Ohio the proposed limit of decolletage was two inches; the bill introduced in the Ohio legislature aimed also to prevent the sale of any "garment which unduly displays or accentuates the lines of the female figure," and to prohibit any "female over fourteen years of age" from wearing "a skirt which does not reach to that part of the foot known as the instep."

Meanwhile innumerable families were torn with dissension over cigarettes and gin and all-night automobile rides. Fathers and mothers lay awake asking themselves whether their children were not utterly lost; sons and daughters evaded questions, lied miserably and unhappily, or flared up to reply rudely that at least they were not dirty-minded hypocrites, that they saw no harm in what they were doing and proposed to go right on doing it. From those liberal clergymen and teachers who prided themselves on keeping step with all that was new, came a chorus of reassurance: these young people were at least franker and more honest than their elders had been; having experimented for themselves, would they not soon find out which standards were outworn and which represented the accumulated moral wisdom of the race? Hearing such hopeful words, many good people took heart again. Perhaps this flare-up of youthful passion was a flash in the pan, after all. Perhaps in another year or two the boys and girls would come to their senses and everything would be all right again.

They were wrong, however. For the revolt of the younger generation was only the beginning of a revolution in manners and morals that was already beginning to affect men and women of every age in every part of the country.

War's Impact Reaches Society

A number of forces were working together and interacting upon one another to make this revolution inevitable.

First of all was the state of mind brought about by the war [World War I] and its conclusion. A whole generation had been infected by the eat-drink-and-be-merry-for-tomorrow-we-die spirit which accompanied the departure of the soldiers to the training camps and the fighting front. There had been an epidemic not only of abrupt war marriages, but of less conventional liaisons. In France, two million men had found themselves very close to filth and annihilation and very far from the American moral code and its defenders; prostitution had followed the flag and willing mademoiselles from Armentières had been plentiful; American girls sent over as nurses and war workers had come under the influence of continental manners and standards without being subject to the rigid protections thrown about their continental sisters of the respectable classes; and there had been a very widespread and very natural breakdown of traditional restraints and reticences and taboos. It was impossible for this generation to return unchanged when the ordeal was over. Some of them had acquired under the pressure of war-time conditions a new code which seemed to them quite defensible; millions of them had been provided with an emotional stimulant from which it was not easy to taper off. Their torn nerves craved the anodynes of speed, excitement, and passion. They found themselves expected to settle down into the humdrum routine of American life as if nothing had happened, to accept the moral dicta of elders who seemed to them still to be living in a Pollyanna land of rosy ideals which the war had killed for them. They couldn't do it, and they very disrespectfully said so.

"The older generation had certainly pretty well ruined this world before passing it on to us," wrote one of them (John F. Carter in the *Atlantic Monthly*, September, 1920), expressing accurately the sentiments of innumerable contemporaries. "They give us this thing, knocked to pieces, leaky, red-hot, threatening to blow up; and then they are surprised that we don't accept it with the same attitude of pretty, decorous enthusiasm with which they received it, way back in the 'eighties.". . .

Freedom from the Household

The revolution was accelerated also by the growing independence of the American woman. She won the suffrage [right to vote] in 1920. She seemed, it is true, to be very little interested in it once she had it; she voted, but mostly as the unregenerate men about her did, despite the efforts of women's clubs and the League of Women Voters to awaken her to womanhood's civic opportunity; feminine candidates for office were few, and some of them—such as Governor Ma Ferguson of Texas—scarcely seemed to represent the starry-eyed spiritual influence which, it had been promised, would presently ennoble public life. Few of the younger women could rouse themselves to even a passing interest in politics: to them it was a sordid and futile business, without flavor and without hope. Nevertheless, the winning of the suffrage had its effect. It consolidated woman's position as man's equal.

Even more marked was the effect of woman's growing independence of the drudgeries of housekeeping. Smaller houses were being built, and they were easier to look after. Families were moving into apartments, and these made even less claim upon the housekeeper's time and energy. Women were learning how to make lighter work of the preparation of meals. Sales of canned foods were growing, the number of delicatessen stores had increased three times as fast as the population during the decade 1910–20, the output of bakeries increased by 60 per cent during the decade 1914–24. Much of what had once been housework was now either moving out of the home entirely or being simplified by machinery. The use of commercial laundries, for instance, increased by 57 per cent between 1914 and 1924. . . .

Up to this time girls of the middle classes who had wanted to "do something" had been largely restricted to school-teaching, social-service work, nursing, stenography, and clerical work in business houses. But now they poured out of the schools and colleges into all manner of new occupations. They besieged the offices of publishers and advertisers; they went into tearoom management until there threatened to be more purveyors than consumers of chicken patties and cinnamon toast; they sold antiques, sold real estate, opened smart little shops, and finally invaded the department stores. . . .

With the feeling of economic independence came a slackening of husbandry and parental authority. Maiden aunts and unmarried daughters were leaving the shelter of the family roof to install themselves in kitchenette apartments of their own. For city-dwellers the home was steadily becoming less of a shrine, more of a dormitory—a place of casual shelter where one stopped overnight on the way from the restaurant and the movie theater to the office. . . .

The Sexual Revolution

Like all revolutions, this one was stimulated by foreign propaganda. It came, however, not from Moscow, but from Vienna. Sigmund Freud had published his first book on psychoanalysis at the end of the nineteenth century, and he and Jung had lectured to American psychologists as early as 1909, but it was not until after the war that the Freudian gospel began to circulate to a marked extent among the American lay public. The one great intellectual force which had not suffered disrepute as a result of the war was science; the more-or-less educated public was now absorbing a quantity of popularized information about biology and anthropology which gave a general impression that men and women were merely animals of a rather intricate variety, and that moral codes had no universal validity and were often based on curious superstitions. A fertile ground was ready for the seeds of Freudianism, and presently one began to hear even from the lips of flappers that "science taught" new and disturbing things about sex. Sex, it appeared, was the central and pervasive force which moved mankind. Almost every human motive was attributable to it: if you were patriotic or liked the violin, you were in the grip of sex—in a sublimated form. The first requirement of mental health was to have an uninhibited sex life. If you would be well and happy, you must obey your libido. Such was the Freudian gospel as it imbedded itself in the American mind after being filtered through the successive minds of interpreters and popularizers and guileless readers and people who had heard guileless readers talk about it. . . .

The principal remaining forces which accelerated the revolution in manners and morals were all 100 per cent American. They were prohibition, the automobile, the confession and sex magazines, and the movies.

When the Eighteenth Amendment was ratified, prohibition seemed, as we have already noted, to have an almost united country behind it. Evasion of the law began immediately, however, and strenuous and sincere opposition to it—especially in the large cities of the North and East—quickly gathered force. The results were the bootlegger, the speakeasy, and a spirit of deliberate revolt which in many communities made drinking "the thing to do." From these facts in turn flowed further results: the increased popularity of distilled as against fermented liquors, the use of the hip-flask, the cocktail party, and the general transformation of drinking from a masculine prerogative to one shared by both sexes together. The old-time saloon had been overwhelmingly masculine; the speakeasy usually catered to both men and women. As [reporter] Elmer Davis put it, "The old days when father spent his evenings at Cassidy's bar with the rest of the boys are gone, and probably gone forever; Cassidy may still be in business at the old stand and father may still go down there of evenings, but since prohibition mother goes down with him." Under the new régime not only the drinks were mixed, but the company as well.

Meanwhile a new sort of freedom was being made possible by the enormous increase in the use of the automobile, and particularly of the closed car. (In 1919 hardly more than 10 per cent of the cars produced in the United States were closed; by 1924 the percentage had jumped to 43, by 1927 it had reached 82.8.) The automobile offered an almost universally available means of escaping temporarily from the supervision of parents and chaperons, or from the influence of neighborhood opinion. Boys and girls now thought nothing, as the Lynds [prominent sociologists and authors] pointed out in *Middletown,* of jumping into a car and driving off at a moment's notice—without asking anybody's permission—to a dance in another town twenty miles away, where they were strangers and enjoyed a freedom impossible among their neighbors. The closed car, moreover, was in effect a room protected from the weather which could be occupied at any time of the day or night and could be moved at will into a darkened byway or a country lane. The Lynds quoted the judge of the juvenile court in "Middletown" as declaring that the automobile had become a "house of prostitution on wheels," and cited the fact that of thirty girls brought before his court in a year on charges of sex crimes, for whom the place where the offense had occurred was recorded, nineteen were listed as having committed it in an automobile.

Finally, as the revolution began, its influence fertilized a bumper crop of sex magazines, confession magazines, and lurid motion pictures, and these in turn had their effect on a class of readers and movie-goers who had never heard and never would hear of Freud and the libido. The publishers of the sex adventure magazines, offering stories with such titles as "What I Told My Daughter the Night Before Her Marriage," "Indolent Kisses," and "Watch Your Step-Ins," learned to a nicety the gentle art of arousing the reader without arousing the censor. The publishers of the confession magazines, while always instructing their authors to provide a moral ending and to utter pious sentiments, concentrated on the description of what they euphemistically called "missteps." Most of their fiction was faked to order by hack writers who could write one day "The Confessions of a Chorus Girl" and the next day recount, again in the first person, the temptations which made it easy for the taxi-driver to go wrong. Both classes of magazines became astonishingly numerous and successful. Bernarr McFadden's *True-Story,* launched as late as 1919, had over 300,000 readers by 1923; 848,000 by 1924; over a million and a half by 1925; and almost two million by 1926—a record of rapid growth probably un-paralleled in magazine publishing.

Crowding the news stands along with the sex and con-fession magazines were motion-picture magazines which depicted "seven movie kisses" with such captions as "Do you recognize your little friend, Mae Busch? She's had lots of kisses, but she never seems to grow *blasé*. At least you'll agree that she's giving a good imitation of a person enjoy-ing this one." The movies themselves, drawing millions to their doors every day and every night, played incessantly upon the same lucrative theme. The producers of one pic-ture advertised "brilliant men, beautiful jazz babies, cham-pagne baths, midnight revels, petting parties in the purple dawn, all ending in one terrific smashing climax that makes you gasp"; the venders of another promised "neckers, pet-ters, white kisses, red kisses, pleasure-mad daughters, sensation-craving mothers, . . . the truth—bold, naked, sen-sational." Seldom did the films offer as much as these ad-vertisements promised, but there was enough in some of them to cause a sixteen-year-old girl (quoted by Alice Miller Mitchell) to testify, "Those pictures with hot love-making in them, they make girls and boys sitting together want to get up and walk out, go off somewhere, you know. Once I walked out with a boy before the picture was even over. We took a ride. But my friend, she all the time had to get up and go out with her boy friend.". . .

Each of these diverse influences—the post-war disillu-sion, the new status of women, the Freudian gospel, the au-tomobile, prohibition, the sex and confession magazines, and the movies—had its part in bringing about the revolu-tion. Each of them, as an influence, was played upon by all the others; none of them could alone have changed to any great degree the folkways of America; together their force was irresistible.

The Growth of Black Pride

Geoffrey Perrett

Though African Americans constantly fought bigotry and prejudice throughout the decade, important advances occurred. Black artists and writers spurred a rebirth of culture in New York City, while thousands of other African Americans poured into northern states in search of better jobs. Geoffrey Perrett has written many respected histories in his career. In this excerpt, he describes African American achievements in the 1920s.

On the streets of a dozen American cities a nation in exile was being formed, flaunting its existence in a tangible, visible reality. It sported titles and decorations, and strutting at its head, beneath a hat with white plumes, wearing a uniform in the purple, black, and green colors of the new nation, was its provisional president, Marcus Garvey.

West Indian blacks, such as Garvey, were as a rule more self-reliant and better businessmen than American-born blacks, who scorned them as people lacking in soul. Garvey was typical: assertive, articulate, and ambitious. The West Indians had grown up oppressed by poverty and racism. Yet, discrimination in the West Indies was subtler than in Alabama or even in New York and opportunities correspondingly greater. Harlemites grudgingly accepted them as the "shock troops" in the struggle to open the job market wider for urban blacks.

They entered the United States through a side door: the unused quota places assigned to the colonial powers, to which they retained a remarkable loyalty. British West Indians flew the Union Jack in their windows, to the disgust of the entire tenement. French West Indians held Bastille Day dances. West Indians had the lowest naturalization rate of any immigrant group. Coming as they did from black societies that were rigorously patriarchal, they felt infinitely superior to the black matriarchy of Harlem.

Black Pride Asserts Itself

The cause that Garvey preached, however, was blackness itself. He "set in motion what was to become the most compelling force in Negro life—race and color consciousness . . . the banner to which Negroes rally; the chain that binds them together." He was not without competitors. On the one side were integrationists, such as the NAACP; on the other, revolutionaries such as the "Abyssinians," led by Grover Cleveland Redding. For a time Redding seemed likely to outshine Garvey.

Redding's Ethiopian Mission to Abyssinia began to attract large numbers of blacks whom Garvey was trying to recruit. Then, in the summer of 1920, Redding rode a white stallion through the South Side of Chicago. He was dressed in a toga of brilliant colors so that the horse did not capture all the attention. He ended his ride by setting fire to an American flag, and before it vanished completely in smoke, he emptied a pistol into it. Redding prepared to do the same with another flag, but this time a white sailor and a black policeman attempted to stop him. Redding instantly shot them down.

The Abyssinians raced down the streets to attack policemen, killing two of them, wounding half a dozen more, while terrified, law-abiding blacks hurried into their houses. Redding was seized, tried for murder, convicted, and hanged, his great dream of leading an "armed train" into the South unrealized.

Garvey's Universal Negro Improvement Association grew

apace. In each city where there were more than 10,000 members (New York, Chicago, Detroit, Philadelphia, Pittsburgh, Cleveland, and Cincinnati) the UNIA opened a Liberty Hall. There, weddings, funerals, cultural events and social gatherings were held almost every day. A Garveyite civil service handled such matters as UNIA passports. There were UNIA courts, dealing chiefly with domestic disputes. The Garveyites were trying to create a black nation by acting as though one already existed. The provisional president's fame was international, as the poet Langston Hughes discovered when he went to sea in 1923. "The name of Marcus Garvey," he found, "was known the length and breadth of the West coast of Africa."

Like most West Indians, Garvey was proud of his blackness. There was not a single white ancestor in his family, he claimed. He gloried in being entirely black, a descendant of the Maroons, those escaped slaves who had fled into the mountains of Jamaica and there fought three generations of British soldiers to a standstill. According to Garvey, it had been a black nation, the Cushites, who introduced civilization into Egypt, Phoenicia, and ancient Greece. If God was made in man's image, then God had to be black for any black man to worship him, Garvey decided. Christ was similarly black. The emphasis on blackness was unrelenting. Any Garveyite who married someone white was immediately expelled. He ridiculed anyone who believed that blacks and whites could live peacefully within the same society. Whites were too thoroughly racist ever to be amenable to reasoned pleas for justice.

Garvey's Collapse

Garvey's ardent separatism won the praise of some white racists and led him into an amazing blunder. In 1922 he traveled to Atlanta to meet in secret with Edward Young Clarke. UNIA organizers were being harassed in the South. By making clear that the movement wanted separation, not mixing, perhaps the Klan would leave his organizers alone? Or so he seems to have reasoned. He could not have been more mistaken. Klan floggers were not interested in the finer points of black liberation.

When the news leaked out that Garvey had supped with the devil, there was anguish among his million followers and supporters, joy among his many enemies. Garveyites and anti-Garveyites brawled on Harlem street corners. Several of Garvey's closest aides left him flat. Others remained within the UNIA to intrigue against him. Long-suppressed hostility between American blacks and West Indians broke into the open and nearly tore the UNIA apart.

Meanwhile, the UNIA's business ventures were about to collapse. In 1919 Garvey had launched a Negro Factories Corporation. It ran a chain of grocery stores, a publishing house, a restaurant, and various other businesses. He had proposed at the same time to create a black shipping line. The war had left the United States with thousands of ships for which there was no demand, and some were being sold for next to nothing. Garvey's proposed Black Star Line fired the imaginations of his followers as nothing else ever did. Before any attempt had been made to buy a ship, ticket requests, accompanied by money, poured into UNIA offices. Garvey had envisaged a line that would devote most of its efforts to carrying cargo between the United States and the West Indies, with passage to Africa for those who wanted to return to the ancestral land. The Back-to-Africa passion that surged through the movement was spontaneous.

The Black Star Line raised $750,000 through stock offerings, and only blacks were allowed to buy. This would have been enough to launch most types of business, but it was far from enough to create a shipping line. A succession of incompetent or crooked BSL officers succeeded in wasting most of the money anyway, or simply stole it. The BSL tried to operate its three ships with all-black crews. This proved impossible, so three white captains were hired. One of the ships sank, one was seized to satisfy a creditor, and the third was abandoned in Cuba after a fortune in repairs failed to make it seaworthy.

In 1923 Garvey and three other BSL officers were tried

for using the mails to defraud in their sale of BSL stock. The government produced only one witness, who claimed to have been sold a $5.00 share by mail. The evidence consisted of an empty envelope. There was no letter on BSL or UNIA stationery, no stock certificate, no proof of payment. Garvey was convicted, his three codefendants acquitted, on the same evidence, the same testimony.

The usual sentence for mail fraud was one year. Judge Julian Mack, a member of the NAACP, gave Garvey the maximum, five. His appeal was denied. In 1925 he entered Atlanta penitentiary to serve his sentence, utterly penniless. Although some of his aides in the UNIA had kept their fingers wedged firmly in the till, Garvey was an honest man.

The Growth of Harlem

Long after the war ended, the black migration northward continued at full spate. It involved more women than men. For their entire history, blacks had been an agricultural people: the land was what they had known in slavery, the land was what they had known before slavery. In one generation they were becoming urbanized. Something new came into existence—the black ghetto in the heart of the city. "Church, lodge, respect of friends, established customs, social and racial, exercise controls in the small Southern community," observed [political and social commentator] Charles S. Johnson. In the ghetto, these controls collapsed. The new freedom was both exciting and traumatic.

Supreme among all the new black communities stood Harlem. Until 1900 almost entirely white, it was by 1925 almost entirely black. A turn-of-the-century building boom had left the area with streets of empty apartments. Landlords began to take black tenants. After the war, as thousands of people migrated into New York from the South each week, there was a severe housing shortage. Real estate values rose sharply. Most of the buildings dated from a time when Harlem had been an upper-middle-class area, when large families lived in large rooms and were waited on by live-in servants. Few black families could live like that. Instead, they took in lodgers, partitioned the handsome, high-ceilinged rooms, and sang the words of a popular song, "What you gonna do when the rent comes 'round?" The lodgers were often the rootless and ruthless. In exchange for a little help with the rent, many a family got a lot of trouble.

Rapacious landlords, black and white, were making a killing out of what was turning into a slum boom. Working-class blacks earned less than working-class whites, yet were paying 50 percent more for housing. Street after street in Harlem was filling up with ignorant, poor farm families, accustomed to living amid clutter and filth, innocent of urban ways, their desire for self-improvement completely satisfied by their translation to the city.

Wartime emergency housing laws, designed to control rents, provided little relief. Landlords could always find ways to outflank them. Harlem's permanent rent crisis gave birth to the rent party. Throughout the Twenties there were notices like this in Harlem store windows or tacked to telephone poles:

If you're looking for a good time,
Don't look no more.
Just ring my bell
And I'll answer the door.

> Given by Charley Johnson and
> Joe Hotboy, and How Hot!

Tickets cost anything from a nickel to a quarter. The admission fee produced less money, however, than the sale, once the party got going, of illicit liquor and homemade soul food. Some parties were as exuberant and picaresque as whites fondly imagined. Others ended in stabbings and shootings.

Before the Twenties were out, New York had a black population of 300,000 or more. In the 1920 census there were not even 50,000. Roughly two-thirds of the city's black population was concentrated in Harlem. And as Harlem was transformed into a slum, it became at the same time the center of black cultural and intellectual life. It was the most diverse black community in the world, and in history; peopled with Africans, West Indians, blacks from the North, blacks from the South. It was probably the most race-conscious place on the planet.

White people also discovered Harlem, the new Harlem. They fled to it as a refuge from the dullness, the orderliness, the narrowness of middle-class life. And it was so convenient—only a taxi ride away for most New Yorkers. There, whatever was forbidden elsewhere was easy to find—marijuana, cocaine, sex. When the sun went down, Harlem was integrated.

By attracting nearly every black writer and intellectual, Harlem was graced with what was known as the "Black Renaissance." It was characteristic of the place, the time, and the magnetic attraction that one of the major works of this cultural outpouring was called *Home to Harlem,* yet was written by a Jamaican, Claude McKay. His fellow Jamaican's newspaper, Marcus Garvey's the *Negro World,* was important to the Harlem Renaissance. Garvey's paper circulated widely throughout the United States and the West Indies. It was mainly a propaganda organ for black nationalism. In the pages of the *Negro World* blacks for the first time were able to see Africa portrayed in a flattering light. The *Negro World* spurned the financial mainstay of the rest of the black press—advertisements for hair straighteners and skin lighteners. And it opened its pages to budding black writers, such as Claude McKay.

With the awakening of black pride went a new interest in black history and art. There were even black dolls for black children to play with. Ironically, however, there was only one important figure in the Harlem Renaissance who took an interest in jazz and that was Langston Hughes, Columbia dropout and onetime able-bodied seaman. For him this Renaissance had begun with the first all-black revue on Broadway, a show called *Shuffle Along,* which opened in 1921. "To see *Shuffle Along* was the main reason I wanted to go to Columbia," he confessed.

A far different figure was Alain Locke, Rhodes scholar, professor of philosophy at Howard, something of a dandy, but with a gentle, reflective manner. His editing of *The New Negro*, which made much of the nation's intelligentsia aware of the profound changes taking place among blacks, and his energetic cheerleading for black intellectuals and artists made him the pope of the Harlem Renaissance. To people such as Locke, high culture was the perfect bridge between the races, not a barricade behind which a few gifted blacks might carve out a comfortable niche for themselves.

The trouble was that like every renaissance it depended on patronage. In this case, white patronage. When the novelty wore off, the Harlem Renaissance was suddenly over. It had never been an easy way to make a living. The best novel to come out of it, Jean Toomer's *Cane*, now widely conceded to be one of the best books of the Twenties, sold fewer than 500 copies in its first year of publication. Toomer gave up writing.

Ray, the educated black man in *Home to Harlem*, typified the dilemmas faced by people such as McKay. Ray was crippled by education instead of being freed by it. High culture provided him with all the anxieties and doubts of the sensitive man, while denying him the emotional release of the ordinary black worker—cheap music, casual sex, rotgut liquor, gambling, dope. Educated to middle-class ideas of what he should do with his life, he was nevertheless forced to work as a waiter, a mess boy, a railroad cook. The more he learned, the less he loved life.

Blacks in the Labor Force

The northward migration spread near-panic in the South. During the war most states passed "work or fight" laws. Men of draft age who were not in uniform had to take jobs. Southern towns and counties passed similar laws affecting everyone, regardless of sex, regardless of age. This legislation was never enforced against whites, only against blacks. It assured a large work force of domestic servants and field hands. What it amounted to was peonage in the guise of patriotism.

To check the continuing outflow, labor agents were fined and imprisoned. Migrants who made their way to railroad stations were met by gangs of local thugs and terrified into turning back. "Many a colored farm tenant (had) to flee by night in order to come North." Yet flee they did, despite intimidation. Black tenant farmers were systematically bilked by the white landowners who lauded the moral superiority of white culture and deplored the moral degeneracy of blacks. Cotton and tobacco continued to be grown under virtually the same conditions as under slavery. These crops could be grown by the least skilled field hands; were cash crops; could not be eaten by man or beast; were easily stored and shipped; could be held against a poor market; were hand-cultivated and hand-harvested. They had wedded the South to slavery for more than 200 years; they kept it in a similar liaison into the Twenties.

But now southern blacks were beginning to inch their way up the economic ladder as education and ambition trickled down. Industry was beginning to appear in the South. And there were the alluring cities of the North which beckoned. As blacks began to move out and up, they became a challenge to the poor whites clinging to the rung just above that bottom rung that had been the black's appointed station in southern life for the past 300 years. Violent hatred of blacks was at its most intense and murderous as one descended the southern social scale.

Hatred, however, threats, intimidation, even murder, failed to check the stirrings of hope that moved through black communities. There were jobs in the North; not enough jobs, true; not well-paid jobs; but better than being a domestic servant or half-starved handyman. The immigration laws created silent rejoicing in black communities. American industry had for decades relied on cheap imported white labor. Almost overnight blacks became the reserve army of American industry, from which they had long been shut out, except during strikes. Blacks were also moving in large numbers into government jobs. Hoover, at a stroke, abolished segregation in the Commerce Department, putting pressure on other departments to do the same.

It was easier for black women to get jobs in the North than for men. Sixty percent of the women in Harlem went to work. Even children seemed to stand a better chance of getting work than grown black men. Child labor was far more common among black children than among white. But there can be no doubt that large numbers of blacks were entering industry at last. There was no mystery as to why the black population of Detroit doubled between 1920 and 1925 (from 41,000 to 82,000).

The unions, licking their wounds from 1919 and losing their self-confidence, snubbed this new source of members. Only the UMW [United Mine Workers] and the immigrant-dominated garment workers' unions welcomed black workers. By the late 1920s total black membership in AFL-affiliated unions came to little more than 40,000. Independent black unions boasted only 12,000 more.

The most notable among these black unions was A. Philip Randolph's Brotherhood of Railroad Car Porters. As an elevator operator in his teens, the young Philip Randolph had tried to organize black elevator operators. He was discovered and fired. Then as a hotel waiter he had organized the Headwaiters and Sidewaiters Society of Greater New York. But again he was fired. With the help of a $10,000 gift from the Socialist party in 1925, he was able to launch the BRCP after dozens of porters asked him to create a union.

Pullman porters worked a 400-hour month. They asked for a reduction to 250 hours. The Pullman Company created a company union to fight the Brotherhood and claimed that the average porter earned $200 a month. Which was strange, seeing that the other demand of the porters was an end to tipping and a flat wage of $150 a month. Despite a combination of pressure and inducements, more than 7,000 of the Pullman Company's 11,000 porters voted to join the BRCP. By the late Twenties, however, the company had virtually broken the union and rejected its demands. The BRCP's experience was not one to encourage separate, black unions.

The world for black workers was a little wider than before. But work was still divided into black men's jobs and white men's jobs. On the railroads, for example, being a porter or a waiter was a job for a black man; being an engineer or conductor was for whites only. The time was still a long way off when blacks would be allowed to compete with whites for the same occupations.

Film Comedy Comes of Age in the 1920s

Gerald Mast and Bruce F. Kawin

The movie industry captivated the nation from 1910 to 1920 and continued its phenomenal growth in the 1920s. While adventure films and romance movies enticed thousands to local theaters, comedies flooded the market to appease the postwar appetite for lighthearted fare. Consequently, an array of stars such as Charlie Chaplin and Buster Keaton enjoyed immense popularity.

Two of the foremost students of film, Professors Gerald Mast of the University of Chicago and Bruce F. Kawin of the University of Colorado, explain the emergence of comedy films in the decade.

One other group of 1920s films maintained an inventiveness and individuality that remain as fresh today as they were over half a century ago. The silent film, which had already proved itself the ideal medium for physical comedy, continued to nurture its most legitimate children. Several new comic imaginations joined the established Sennett [Mack Sennett, legendary producer of silent films], who still supervised films, and Chaplin [Charlie Chaplin, silent film star], who had begun to make features: most significantly, Harold Lloyd, Buster Keaton, Harry Langdon, and Laurel and Hardy. Laurel and Hardy perfected their material late in the silent period, then became the most popular comic team of the sound era. Laurel and Hardy had been put together by Hal Roach, Sennett's major rival as a producer of comedies, who reasoned that one of his fat players and one of his thin ones might go well together. The premise was entirely Sennett-like, and indeed Laurel and Hardy's method was a return to the completely comic, externalized, surface world of Sennett gags.

Comedians Rule the Silent Screen

But Laurel and Hardy films were far more controlled and far more tightly structured than the Sennett romps. Their films demonstrate the "snowball" principle that [Henri] Bergson had developed in *Le Rire*. Like the snowball rolling down the mountain, the Laurel and Hardy film gathers greater and greater momentum and bulk as it hurtles toward the valley. Their films demonstrate the classic structure of farce—from [Roman dramatist] Plautus to [French dramatist] Feydeau: to begin with a single problem and then multiply that problem to infinity. If an auto gets dented in a traffic jam at the start of the film, every car on the highway gets stripped by the end of it; if a Christmas tree branch gets caught in a door at the start of the film, the tree, the house, the salesmen's car must be totally annihilated by the end of it; if the two partners have trouble with a few nails and tacks when starting to build a house, the film must inevitably end with the house collapsing into a pile of rubble. There is an insane yet perfect logic about the whole process.

As does every great silent-film comedy, the Laurel and Hardy films depend on physical objects; the visual medium demands the use of concrete, visible things. But for Stan Laurel (the brains of the team and, like Chaplin, a Fred Karno alumnus) and Oliver Hardy, an object is something to throw, fall over, or destroy; most of their films are built around breaking things. The "adults" of this world are all overgrown, spiteful children squashing each other's mud pies. Stan is the weepy, puling, sneaky, why-blame-me, covertly nasty kid, while Ollie is the pompous, bullying, show-off, know-it-all, inherently incompetent kid. His dignity is as false and inevitable as Stan's tearfulness; they are both ploys to get away with something or get even. If the premise of the films is much thinner than Chaplin's, it is also true that the spiteful emotion they capture is a genuine one. They mirror our feelings when another car zips in to steal the parking place that we have been patiently waiting for. Their single-keyed emotion and their taut, unidirectional structure ensured their success in the short film. The best loved of their sound features are *Sons of the Desert* (1933), *Our Relations* (1936), and the great *Way Out West* (1937, in which Stan—exploiting the potential of the sound film to play with sound/picture relationships—sings a song in three voices, two of which are impossible but in perfect sync).

Harold Lloyd, another Hal Roach product, was almost a combination of Chaplin and Fairbanks. Like Charlie, he was a little guy, slightly inept, trying to succeed. Like Fairbanks, he was energetic, athletic, and engagingly charming, with a smile calculated to snare us as well as the girl. Like Charlie, he had trouble both with objects and with the world while trying to achieve his desires. But unlike Charlie—and like Doug—he invariably does achieve those desires, and they are the same material and romantic treasures that Doug always wins. Also like Doug—and unlike Charlie—Lloyd films never imply that the prize he has won was not worth the winning.

Rather than developing character or social commentary, Lloyd generates pure comedy from the situation, from topical satire, from his own limber body, and from the daring stunts he would dream up. In *High and Dizzy* (1920), the first of his high-rise comedies of thrills, he demonstrates the variety of his comedy. The film is constructed in three loosely related episodes. In the opening sequence, Lloyd plays a young doctor whose practice is so dismal that his phone is gathering cobwebs. He falls madly in love with a patient who, it turns out, walks in her sleep.

In the second sequence, he strolls down the hall and gets stinking drunk with another young doctor who has dis-

tilled some hooch in his medicinal laboratory. Lloyd's topical satire of doctors, admittedly rather gentle, is the same
kind that he would use to portray the twenties' college generation in *The Freshman* (1925). The comic premise of two
drunken doctors also allows Lloyd to demonstrate his ability and agility as pure physical comic, as the two friends,
one fat, one thin, dizzily weave down the street and into
their hotel, much like Charlie and Fatty in *The Rounders*.

Lloyd introduces his "comedy of thrills" in the film's
third section. It just happens that the sleepwalking patient
with whom he is in love lives in the same hotel. She starts
sleepwalking out on the hotel ledge, many frightening stories above the hard pavement below. Harold goes out on
the ledge to save her and, predictably, gets locked out there
when she decides to stroll inside. Lloyd tightropes, trips,
and stumbles on the ledge, playing on many emotions in us
at the same time. We feel suspense because he might fall;
yet we laugh because we know he won't. We wonder if he
was really on the ledge when he shot the sequence (the
camera angle and lack of editing trickiness make us suspect
he really performed the stunt). We laugh at the man's fright
and perplexity; we admire his underlying competence and
control. It was this same synthesis of cliff-hanging serial
and burlesque comedy that created the excitement and success of his feature *Safety Last* (1923).

Unlike the comedy of Chaplin and Keaton, Lloyd's remains content with emotional and psychological surfaces,
never cutting very deeply, never going beyond comic sensa-
tions to confront us with ironies and paradoxes. Lloyd's
films effectively distill the urges and values of American society as a whole in the 1920s—the success ethic of get up
and get. Further, the Lloyd comedies reveal an extremely
cunning and complex sense of comic construction, setting
up a comic problem, developing it clearly and cleverly, and
driving it to such dizzying heights (quite literally in the
high-rise films) that an audience becomes helplessly hyster-
ical in the presence of Lloyd's comic ingenuity (as opposed
to Chaplin's comic genius). . . .

The Imagination of Buster Keaton

Of the new comics, only Buster Keaton could rival Chaplin in his insight into human relationships, into the conflict between the individual man and the immense social machinery that surrounds him; only Keaton could rival Chaplin in making his insight both funny and serious at the same time. The character Keaton fashioned—with his deadpan, understated reactions to the chaos that blooms around him—lacks the compassionate yearnings and pitiable disappointments of Chaplin's tramp, but Keaton compensates for this apparent lack of passion with the terrific range of his resourcefulness and imagination. A vaudevillean from childhood, Keaton was far more a classic American type than the more European working-class tramp. Born in Kansas in 1895, Keaton's dour face and dry personality are reminiscent of Grant Wood's farmers in "American Gothic." Beneath this "Great Stone Face," Keaton's inventive brain conceived one outrageously imaginative gag after another, many of them based on bizarre machines and gadgets. The idol of Keaton's generation was Thomas Alva Edison, the supreme inventor as tinkerer, and Keaton loved to tinker with machines (especially trains) as much as anyone. One of those machines was the camera and, very unlike Chaplin, Keaton loved to find new ways to manipulate cinematic gadgetry. For his 1921 short *The Playhouse,* Keaton (together with his designer of special effects, Fred Gabourie) came up with a special matte box, capable of splitting the cinema frame into as many as nine fragments. The device allowed him to play every member of a minstrel line, every member of the orchestra, or an entire audience within the same shot. He was by far the most cinematically innovative comedian in film history, but he never saw himself as a genius; he just thought he was good at gags.

On the road to the success he achieves (like saving his train and sweetheart in *The General,* 1927, or growing up in *The Navigator,* 1924) or the goals he is forced to redefine (the house in *One Week,* 1920, will never be perfect and is wrecked by the end of the film, but the honeymooners are happy with each other), the environment throws staggeringly huge obstacles into Buster's path. While Chaplin typically plays with objects he can hold in his hand or sit on, Keaton plays against huge things: an ocean liner he must navigate by himself, a locomotive, a steamboat, a spinning house, a waterfall, a cyclone, a herd of cattle. When he runs into trouble with men, it is rarely with a single figure (an Eric Campbell); he runs into rivers of antagonists, into gangs of opponents: a whole tribe of jungle savages, the entire Union and Confederate armies. Like Charlie, Buster has his troubles with cops, but never with one or just a few cops; in *Cops* (1922), Buster runs into the entire police force. Given the size and complexity of his problems, Buster can take no reliable action, despite his most sensible, practical efforts. The perfect metaphor for the Keaton man is in the three-reel *Day Dreams* (1922) in which Buster, to avoid the police force, takes refuge in the paddle wheel of a ferryboat. The wheel begins turning; Buster begins walking. And walking. And walking. He behaves as sensibly as a man can on a treadmill that he cannot control, but how sensible can life on a treadmill ever be?

Keaton's most magnificent contrast between sensible human behavior and an absurd and uncooperative universe is *Sherlock Jr.* (1924), one of the greatest of comic movies about movies themselves. Buster plays a projectionist in a small town (similar to the town where Keaton was born) who falls asleep to dream himself into the movie he is projecting. The film-within-a-film that follows permits Buster to demonstrate spectacular physical skills; Keaton was one of the greatest performer-athletes in film history, and his chase sequences are among the greatest of cinema chases. As opposed to Sennett's miscellaneous chases of frantic mechanical puppets and Chaplin's chases as choreographed ballets, Keaton's chases (in *Sherlock Jr.,* in *Seven Chances,* 1925, and in *The General)* are breathtaking exercises by a single racing body—running faster, leaping higher, falling more gracefully than any human body ever seemingly could—or maneuvering a vehicle at top speed through an impossible situation.

In the most celebrated sequence of *Sherlock Jr.*, Keaton is not in motion but at rest. It is the world itself that moves, thanks to the cinema's ability to shift spaces instantaneously by means of editing. Buster, a mortal physical being, has been trapped in the universe of cinema, which

Sound Comes to the Movies

Americans loved film throughout the decade. They laughed at the antics of silent comedians like Charlie Chaplin, and swooned to the actions of Rudolph Valentino. However, in 1927 a new feature altered Hollywood forever.

The sound revolution was effecting a complete transition in the history of the movies. When sound films had become technically feasible, in the early 1920s, Hollywood had resisted the disruption and expense of changing its production and distribution methods. Then the Warner brothers, who were struggling to make their studio a major force on a shoestring budget, gambled on sound as a means of reproducing music without the expense of live performers. In 1926 they released *Don Juan* and several shorts with musical accompaniment on discs synchronized with each reel. Taking their cue, Fox introduced sound-on-film newsreels. But silent films were already accompanied by live music and sound effects. The missing link was dialogue, as shown by the growing popularity of radio. When Al Jolson [actor] improvised the line 'You ain't heard nothing yet' in *The Jazz Singer* (1927), the silent movie was destined for history as an art form.

The Jazz Singer was an enormous success, and Warner's daring gamble on the Vitaphone process paid off in a matter of months at the box office. By the summer of 1928, 300 theaters were wired to show the first 'talkies' and other studios rushed to secure equipment, build soundproof stages and force their silent stars to speak, with varying degrees of success. Some careers were ended, others took off like a comet. . . .

operates according to spatial and temporal laws unknown to physical reality. He simply stands, sits, or jumps, occupying the identical space within the frame, while the physical universe surrounding him switches from desert to ocean to mountain top to city street. It is perhaps the ultimate comic gag created by and commenting upon the cin-

---

Despite the fact that the clumsy new sound equipment had a disastrous effect upon the artistic quality of Hollywood films in the first few years, the image makers rushed to market with dialogue films and musicals. Broadway was raided for actors who could speak, and plays were transferred bodily to the cinema with little regard for their suitability to the medium. Many of the imported actors proved unsuited to the more intimate medium of film, although some enjoyed a success that led to a whole new generation of Hollywood stars, including Edward G Robinson, Fredric March, Paul Muni and James Cagney. Silent-film idols like Douglas Fairbanks Sr and Mary Pickford found their careers losing momentum, while other artists—Norma Shearer, Ronald Colman and Janet Gaynor, to name a few—were on the ascendant.

Some of the silent-screen giants proceeded cautiously into the new medium. Chaplin's *City Lights* (1931) and *Modern Times* (1936) were really silent films with some degree of synchronised musical and sound effects. Not until 1941 did Chaplin make a full-scale talking picture—*The Great Dictator*. Staple genres like slapstick comedy were on the wane, and new styles evolved. Laurel and Hardy made a successful transition to talking pictures, and the Marx Brothers invented a whole comic language. Beginning with *Broadway Melody* (1929), a new kind of film that owed its very existence to sound came into being, the Hollywood musical. And gangster films leaped into prominence with the addition of colorful speech idioms to the pictorial representation of the exciting Jazz Age underworld.

Robin Langley Sommer, *Hollywood: The Glamour Years, 1919–1940*. New York: Gallery Books, 1987.

ematic apparatus itself.

Chaplin and Keaton are the two poles of silent comics. Chaplin is sentimental; his gentle smiling women become idols to be revered. Keaton is not sentimental; he stuffs his females into bags and hauls them around like sacks of potatoes; he satirizes their finicky incompetence and even shakes the daylights out of the young lady in *The General* who feeds their racing locomotive only the unblemished pieces of wood—then he kisses her. It was especially appropriate and touching to see the two opposites, Chaplin and Keaton, united in *Limelight* (1952), both playing great clowns who were losing their audiences and feared they were losing their touch. It may be no accident that one of the most important theatre pieces of our era, *Waiting for Godot*, was produced in the same year as *Limelight* and used the same metaphor of two old tramps whose act (in *Godot* their act is their life) has become a bomb. If the Godot of Samuel Beckett's title suggests Charlot, it should also be remembered that Beckett wrote a film script especially for Buster Keaton, *Film* (1965, directed by Alan Schneider), and that in the 1930s Beckett studied the works of [Sergei M.] Eisenstein and [Vsevolod I.] Pudovkin.

The Comic Genius of Charlie Chaplin

No two films more clearly reveal the contrasting strengths and interests of the two clowns than *The Gold Rush* (1925) and *The General* (1927). Like Chaplin's short comedies, *The Gold Rush is* an episodic series of highly developed, individual situations. The mortar that keeps these bricks together is a mixture of the film's locale (the white, frozen wastes), the strivings and disappointments of Charlie, and the particular thematic view the film takes of those strivings (the quest for gold and for love, those two familiar goals, in an icy, cannibalistic jungle). *The Gold Rush* uses one of Chaplin's favorite figures, the circle, to structure the sequence of episodes: Prologue (the journey to Alaska), the Cabin, the Dance Hall, the Cabin, Epilogue (the journey home)—a perfect circle.

The movie industry witnessed phenomenal growth during the 1920s. Americans' demand for more comedies led to the popularity of comedic actors like Buster Keaton, Harold Lloyd, and Charlie Chaplin (pictured).

The individual sequences of *The Gold Rush* are rich both in Chaplin's comic ingenuity and in his ability to render pathos. Several of the comic sequences have become justifiably famous. In the first cabin scene, a hungry Charlie cooks his shoe, carves the sole like a prime rib of beef, salts it to taste, and then eats it like a gourmet, twirling the shoelaces around his fork like spaghetti, sucking the nails like chicken bones, offering his disgruntled partner (who has been chewing the upper half of the shoe as if it were just a shoe) a bent nail as a wishbone. This is the Chaplin who treats one object (a shoe) as if it were another kind of object (a feast), the same minute observation he used in dissecting the clock in *The Pawnshop;* it is also the definitive example of the tramp as a gentleman—that is, of comic contrast. And unlike the Sennett world where bullets can't kill, the funny business here has permanent consequences:

Characters really die in *The Gold Rush,* and once his boot has been boiled, Charlie spends the rest of the picture with his foot wrapped in rags.

But the comic business is matched by the pathos that Charlie can generate, often growing out of the comic business itself. Charlie's saddest moment is when Georgia (played by Georgia Hale), the woman he loves, whose picture and flower he preserves beneath his pillow, callously stands him up on New Year's Eve. When Charlie realizes that it is midnight and she is not coming, he opens his door and listens to the happy townspeople singing "Auld Lang Syne" (an excellent translation of sound—a song—into purely visual terms). The film cuts back and forth between Charlie, the outsider, standing silently and alone in a doorway, and the throng of revelers in the dance hall, clasping hands in a circle and singing exuberantly together. But this pathetic moment would have been impossible without the previous comic one in which Charlie falls asleep and dreams he is entertaining Georgia and her girlfriends with his "Oceana Roll." Charlie's joy, his naïve sincerity, his charm, his gentleness, all show on his face as he gracefully makes the two rolls kick, step, and twirl over the table on the ends of two forks. The happiness of the comic dream sequence sets up the pathos of the subsequently painful reality.

If the reality proves painful for Charlie, it is because the lust for gold makes it so. The film's theme is its consistent indictment of what the pursuit of the material does to the human animal; as in *Greed,* it makes them inhuman animals. Charlie has come to the most materialistic of places— a place where life is hard, dangerous, brutal, uncomfortable, and unkind. Unlike the life of Nanook, whose hardness becomes a virtue in itself, the men who have rushed for gold want to endure hardship only long enough to snatch up enough nuggets to go home and live easy. The quest for gold creates a Black Larsen who casually murders and purposely fails to help his starving fellows. It creates a Jack, Georgia's handsome boyfriend, who treats people like furniture. Just as Charlie's genuine compassion reveals the emptiness of

Jack's protestations of love, Chaplin's film technique makes an unsympathetic bully out of the conventional Hollywood leading man.

The rush toward gold perverts both love and friendship. Georgia herself, though Charlie perceives her inner beauty, has become hardened and callous from her strictly cash relationships with people in the isolated dance hall. And Charlie's partner, Big Jim McKay (Mack Swain), is one of those fair-weather friends whose feelings are the functions of expediency. When Big Jim gets hungry, he literally tries to eat Charlie; although Jim's seeing his buddy as a big chicken is comic, the implied cannibalism is not. Later, Big Jim needs Charlie to direct him to his claim; once again Charlie becomes a friend because he is needed. But when Jim and Charlie get stuck in the cabin that teeters on the edge of a cliff, the two men turn into dogs again, each trying to scramble out of the cabin by himself, stepping on the other to do so.

Keaton's Grand Movie

Whereas *The Gold Rush* combines a thematic unity with the episodic structure that exhausts individual situations, the thematic coherence of *The General* is itself the product of the film's tight narrative unity. *The General* is the first, probably the greatest comic epic in film form. Like every comic epic, *The General* is the story of a journey, of the road (albeit a railroad). As in every comic epic, (think of *The Odyssey* [Greek epic written by Homer]), the protagonist suffers a series of hardships and dangerous adventures before achieving the rewards and comforts of returning home. As in every comic epic (think of *Don Quixote* [famous novel of the Spanish author, Cervantes]), there is a comic insufficiency in the protagonist and a disparity between his powers and the task he sets out to accomplish—but Buster triumphs despite his insufficiencies. Everything in the Chaplin film, every gag, every piece of business, every thematic contrast, is subordinate to the delineation of the tramp's character and the qualities that make him both lonely and superior to the men who have betrayed their humanity to keep from being lonely. Everything in *The General*—every gag, every piece of business—is subordinate to the film's driving narrative, its story of Johnny Gray's race to save his three loves: his girl, his country, and, most important of all, his locomotive (whose name is "The General").

The great question posed by *The General* in the course of its narrative is how to perform heroic action in a crazy universe, where the easy and the impossible are reversed, as are the heroic and the mundane. Buster, with his typical deadpan expression, merely tries to go about his business while the world around him goes mad. A metaphor for the whole film is the shot in which Johnny/Buster is so busy chopping wood to feed his engine that he fails to notice that the train is racing past row after row of blue uniforms marching in the opposite direction; he has inadvertently crossed behind the enemy's lines. Johnny Gray simply wants to run his train; unfortunately, the Union Army has stolen the train and wants to use it to destroy his fellow Confederates. In the course of trying to save the train, Johnny rescues his lady love and accidentally wins a terrific victory for the South.

That heroism occurs as a series of frantic yet graceful accidents in *The General* is at the center of its moral thrust. It is an accident that the cannon, aimed squarely at Johnny, does not go off until the train rounds a curve, discharging its huge ball at the enemy instead of at the protagonist. It is an accident that Johnny's train comes to a rail switch just in time to detour the pursuing train. Just as wealth, material success, is accidental in *The Gold Rush* (and an accident not worth waiting for—whereas Georgia is), heroism and successful military strategy are accidental in *The General*. How less heroic, how less pretentious, less grand can a man be than the pragmatic and unassuming Buster?

The denigration, or redefinition, of the heroic is as constant an element in *The General* as the denigration of gold (the redefinition of wealth) is in *The Gold Rush*. The plot is triggered by Johnny Gray's rejection by the Confederate Army. He fears he has been found wanting, but the Confederacy vitally needs him at home, running his locomotive. Nevertheless, his girl and her family ostracize Johnny as an unheroic coward, a shirker, and the rest of the film demonstrates what heroism really is and what it is really worth. Johnny uses the most practical, least heroic of available tools to defeat the northern army: boxes of freight, pieces of wood, the locomotive's kerosene lantern. Hardheadedness and improvisation, not ego and gallantry, win the day.

Such antiheroism is common to all the Keaton comedies; he debunks chivalric mountain feuds in *Our Hospitality* (1923), pugilistic prowess in *Battling Butler* (1926), athletic prowess in *College* (1927), and riverboat romance in *Steamboat Bill, Jr.* (1928). What distinguishes *The General* is that the senseless object, the immense infernal machine of this film, is war. Men themselves have been transformed into a machine (an army), and the business of this machine is murder and destruction.

The film is as shrewd, as caustic, as hard-edged as Johnny Gray himself. His sweetheart (played by Marion Mack), a typical figure of sentiment and romance (her name is Annabelle Lee!), is degraded into an incompetent and feeble representative of romantic notions—until she learns the ropes. In the course of the film, pursuing "The General," Johnny becomes an actual general and Miss Lee grows up.

The ultimate proof of the power of *The Gold Rush* and *The General* is that they need not be referred to as great silent films; they are merely great films. For both of them, silence was not a limitation but a virtue. It is inconceivable that the two films could have been any better with talk; by removing our complete concentration on the visual they could only have been worse. With such control of physical business, thematic consistency, appropriate structure, placement of the camera, and functional editing, neither *The Gold Rush* nor *The General* requires speech to speak.

An Epic Feat: Gertrude Ederle Swims the Channel

Susan Ware

Sports heroes occupied newspaper headlines on a daily basis in the 1920s. Babe Ruth chased sixty home runs, Bill Tilden dominated tennis, Bobby Jones electrified the golf world. Possibly the most meaningful accomplishment, as far as its impact on society, was Gertrude Ederle's attempt to swim the English Channel.

Professor Susan Ware of Radcliffe College has written extensively about females in American history.

When Gertrude Ederle waded ashore near Dover on August 6, 1926, after swimming the English Channel in the record time of fourteen hours and thirty-one minutes, she went from being the unknown daughter of a German-American butcher to a worldwide celebrity overnight. Foreshadowing Charles Lindbergh's experience by more than a year, she had the right stuff for a sudden rise to fame in 1920s America, as the *New York Times* realized: Gertrude Ederle "has all the qualities that go to make up the kind of heroine whom America will ungrudgingly and freely worship and honor for her splendid achievement. The record of her 19 years shows her to be courageous, determined, modest, sportsmanlike, generous, unaffected and perfectly poised." Moreover, she was blessed with "beauty of face and figure" and "abounding health." After the largest and most enthusiastic ticker-tape parade ever given to an individual in New York City's history, Trudy, as she was called both out of affection and the need for punchy headlining, was showered by commercial offers approaching $1 million.

Ederle Shows Females Are the Equal of Males

It might seem strange that the mere fact of swimming the English Channel qualified this young woman, who never graduated from high school, for all this fame and fortune, but the 1920s was a sports-crazy era. Babe Ruth, Jack Dempsey, Bobby Jones, and Red Grange were household names. Sportswriter Paul Gallico noted that heroes' welcomes used to be reserved for admirals, generals, and visiting royalty, but the 1920s "produced a new royalty, the kings and queens of sport, as a vivid and thrilling demonstration of the workings of this unique democracy, where the poorest and the humblest could instantly become national heroes and heroines." Gertrude Ederle was the first swimmer, and one of the first women, to join this elite crowd.

Her channel swim had definite feminist implications. Not only was Ederle the first woman to complete the swim, she did it faster than any of the previous men. In other words, this young American girl had proved herself to be men's better in the water, thereby undermining, if not demolishing, rationales about women's being the weaker sex. Pity the London newspaper that by chance had chosen the very day of her channel swim to run an editorial that baldly stated, "Even the most uncompromising champion of the rights and capacities of women must admit that in a contest of physical skill, speed and endurance they must remain forever the weaker sex." That is, until Trudy proved them wrong. She saw her individual triumph as a victory for her sex, saying prophetically to a New York sports editor, "All the women of the world will celebrate, too." At a time when women were embracing dramatically expanded roles in public and private, Ederle's accomplishment became part of this larger story. As Will

Rogers [humorist and political commentator] quipped, "Yours for a revised edition of the dictionary explaining which is the weaker sex."

By the 1920s a certain degree of athleticism and competence at sports was considered desirable, even necessary, for young American women, in striking contrast to just several decades before, as suffrage leader Carrie Chapman Catt recalled: "It is a far cry from swimming the channel to the days to which my memory goes back, when it was thought that women could not throw a ball or even walk very far down the street without feeling faint." Catt was one of many to make the link "that women's freedom would go hand in hand with her bodily strength." Golfer Glenna Collett seconded this view: "The tomboy ideal is far more healthful than that of the poor little Goldilocks . . . who was forbidden vigorous activities lest she tear her clothes." And yet although sports and physical activity were encouraged for girls and young women, they rarely held the central role in girls' lives that sports did for the American male—except, of course, for Gertrude Ederle.

People wanted to swim the English Channel for the same reason they wanted to climb Everest or the Matterhorn [famous mountains]: it was there. The feat had first been accomplished by an Englishman, Captain Matthew Webb, in 1875; so amazing was his epic twenty-three-hour swim that it was not duplicated for another thirty-six years. After the second successful swim in 1911, there was another gap until 1923, when three men made it, lowering the time to around sixteen and a half hours. Ederle herself had tried and failed in 1925, done in not by physical exhaustion but by seasickness in the rough seas. And just the week before Ederle's second try, another American woman, Clarabelle Barrett of New Rochelle, New York, had come within several miles of succeeding, before being forced to turn back by the tides and poor weather. As Charles Lindbergh would find the next year when he made his solo transatlantic flight, luck and timing were often just as important as skill and preparation in becoming a hero.

Ederle's Emergence

Gertrude Ederle was born in 1906 in New York City to parents who had recently emigrated from Germany. Her father ran a small butcher shop and delicatessen on Amsterdam Avenue on Manhattan's West Side. The third of six children, she learned to swim at the age of nine on the New Jersey shore at Highlands, where her family vacationed. Her sister, Margaret, was also a competitive swimmer. Both girls received their swimming instruction at a remarkable institution called the Women's Swimming Association (WSA) of New York, which had been founded in 1917. In its tiny indoor pool on the Lower East Side, the WSA trained several generations of female swimmers who went on to national and Olympic success, including backstroker Eleanor Holm and future Hollywood star Esther Williams. At age thirteen, Trudy began serious training under WSA supervision. She benefited from a farsighted coach named L.B. de Handley, who revolutionized women's swimming by changing the leg action of the crawl stroke from a conservative four-beat flutter kick to a more powerful six- to eight-beat kick.

At this point swimming was just emerging as a serious competitive sport, and Ederle excelled. In 1924 she held eighteen world records for distances from fifty yards to a half-mile, and won three medals at the 1924 Paris Olympics: bronze medals in the 100- and 400-yard freestyle and a gold for the 4 × 100 relay. As early as 1922 she began to move into the endurance swimming that would be her claim to fame, beating the world's top female swimmers, American Helen Wainwright and Liverpool's Hilda James, in the prestigious three-and-a-half-mile Day Cup race in New York Bay as an unheralded fifteen-year-old. The next year she established a new record (seven hours, eleven minutes, thirty seconds) for the swim from the Battery to Sandy Hook, New Jersey.

Ederle's success in open water endurance swimming is an example of the advantage that women have in this athletic area. Because of women's lower center of gravity and higher percentage of body fat, they are anatomically better fitted for cold-water swimming over the long haul than men. Also critical to her success was the development, and popular acceptance, of one-piece bathing costumes for women that allowed them to swim, rather than just bob in the water weighted down by the pounds of waterlogged stockings, shoes, bloomers, and blouses demanded by Victorian modesty. This was part of a general revolution in women's clothing that freed female bodies from unnecessary con-

 The Immortal Babe

Of all the sports stars to fill the 1920s, none reached the height of success which Babe Ruth enjoyed in baseball. Millions followed the exploits of the man who restored dignity to a game that had been badly harmed by scandal.

This was the heroic era of American sports. Attendance at athletic events broke all records, and the champions of sport were known and loved throughout the land. "If St. Paul were living today," a prominent Methodist minister declared, "he would know Babe Ruth's batting average and what yardage Red Grange made."

And that applied to many others besides Ruth and Grange. Jack Dempsey, the grim Manassa Mauler, came out of the West to give boxing its first million-dollar gates. Bobby Jones and Bill Tilden took golf and tennis away from the country-club crowd and made them "important" sports. Swimmer Gertrude Ederle, Helen Wills, a tennis player, and golfer Glenna Collett showed that a woman's place was also in the sports pages.

One reason for the heightened interest in sport was the sudden emergence of the sports writer as a major figure on the literary scene—men such as Grantland Rice, Damon Runyon, Ring Lardner, Paul Gallico, John Kieran and Westbrook Pegler. These experts were occasionally assisted by outsiders like H.L. Mencken and even George Bernard Shaw (Shaw described the game of

straints. As Tom Robinson, a swimming instructor at Northwestern, noted of Ederle's triumph, "A woman could not possibly have accomplished this same feat thirty years ago, for corsets and other ridiculously unnecessary clothing hampered her physical condition and deprived her of the muscular effort so necessary in the development of a good swimmer."

Australian swimmer Annette Kellerman is credited with developing the first one-piece suit, which she proudly dis-

---

baseball as a combination of the "best features of that primitive form of cricket known as Tip and Run with those of lawn tennis, Puss-in-the-Corner, and Handel's *Messiah*.") The great writers recorded the deeds of the great athletes. One early beneficiary was that giant of giants, Babe Ruth. "After the Black Sox scandal," wrote W.O. McGeehan, "Babe Ruth with his bat pounded baseball back into popularity. He swings with the utmost sincerity. When he hits the ball it goes into wide-open spaces. When he misses, he misses with vehement sincerity."

By 1927, when he hit his high-water mark of 60 home runs, Babe Ruth was a better-known American to most foreigners than Calvin Coolidge, and he rivaled the dashing Prince of Wales as the most photographed man in the world. Kieran was moved to this bit of hero-worshipping doggerel, typical of the sports-page exaggeration of the era: "My voice may be loud above the crowd / And my words just a bit uncouth, / But I'll stand and shout till the last man's out: /'There never was a guy like Ruth!'"

The fact that the Babe was himself a bit uncouth—a wencher, imbiber, and notorious violator of training rules—bothered neither the writers nor the fans. He was simply the greatest ballplayer who ever lived, and he symbolized as no other man ever did the love affair that existed between the American public and the athletes of the 1920s.

Richard B. Stolley, *Our American Century: The Jazz Age, the 1920s*. Alexandria, VA: Time-Life Books, 1998.

played in swimming exhibitions throughout the United States in the 1910s and 1920s. Even her early bulky versions were liberating compared to the bathing costumes of old; by the 1920s, a trim one-piece suit was standard apparel for most young women. Paul Gallico's childhood memory of seeing Kellerman perform in a vaudeville routine well captures the intersection of swimming, sexuality, and women's bodies: "It made the question of how ladies were put together no longer a matter of vague speculation."

The National Media Discover Ederle

Newspapers and newsreels were finding out that swimming had sex appeal. Whereas editors would be barred from running photos of skimpily dressed showgirls in family magazines, they were free to run pictures of wholesome, fresh-faced American girls in their bathing costumes. Soon the bathing beauty would be as important as the girl athlete. It is no coincidence that the early 1920s saw both the launching of Ederle's competitive swimming career and the Miss America pageant.

Ederle did not present herself as glamorous, nor did the press feel the need to press her into that mold. Competitive swimming demanded hefty bodies, and Ederle carried close to 150 pounds on a frame of about five feet five inches. Because she did not have a heavily muscled body, however, and because slimness had not yet been established as an all-encompassing cultural norm, her appearance drew favorable comment from the press. Observed the *New York Times*, "In her street dress she looked like a healthy girl, a little on the bouncing order, but her dimensions were not very large." Paul Gallico noted that "her somewhat Teutonic chubbiness, round, dimpled face, and fair-brown bobbed hair, were offset by agreeable features and an extraordinarily sweet expression."

It was Ederle's wholesomeness that proved most appealing to the press. Even though she was once called a "bobhaired, nineteen-year-old daughter of the Jazz Age," she was no flapper. News coverage approvingly noted that she did not drink or smoke, and was not excessively interested in boys. In short, she was an excellent model for American girls. "American Girlhood Triumphs," headlined the *Syracuse Herald*. "The American girl is all right," said the *Washington Star*. It was President Calvin Coolidge himself who called her "America's best girl."

Although Ederle amassed an amazing amateur record, competitive swimming cost money, especially expensive undertakings like channel swims. The Women's Swimming Association had helped underwrite Ederle's unsuccessful 1925 attempt, but they could not finance a second try, so Ederle made the difficult decision to give up her amateur status and turn professional: she accepted commercial backing from the *Chicago Tribune* syndicate and the *New York Daily News*. In return for exclusive access to her story, she would receive a salary, her training and coaching expenses would be paid, and she would be eligible for a bonus if she succeeded. As with most exploits in fields like aviation and exploration, such commercial backing was absolutely necessary, but the public often conveniently overlooked those aspects and instead celebrated the accomplishment as that of a supreme individual, acting alone. That is certainly how the public reacted to Trudy's heroic battle against the elements on her record-breaking swim.

Ederle Makes Her Attempt

At 7:08 on the morning of August 6, 1926, Ederle, heavily greased against the chilly sixty-one-degree water, waded into the surf off Cape Gris Nez and began to swim at the steady rate of twenty-eight strokes to the minute. She wore a red bathing suit, cut deeply under the arms to free her powerful shoulders, goggles to protect her eyes from the sting of the saltwater, and a skull cap. She was accompanied by the tug *Alsace* containing her father (her mother was too nervous to make the trip), sister, trainer, and several fellow swimmers, who sometimes kept Ederle company in the water while she swam; a second boat filled with reporters and photographers followed closely. Both boats were equipped with wireless radio, so that reports of her progress could be relayed ashore, including back to a waiting America. Ederle took little sustenance during the swim, just some beef extract, chicken broth, chocolate, and sugar blocks, and luckily she escaped the seasickness that had plagued her earlier try. At times she sang "Let Me Call You Sweetheart" to keep up her rhythm; other times she was serenaded with songs from her supporters in the boat. If her spirits sagged, she could look up at the banner draped over the side of the tug, which said, "This Way, Ole Kid!" with an arrow pointing straight ahead.

The Ederle entourage had chosen the date of August 6 because of a favorable forecast, but the weather soon deteriorated into squall conditions and a heavy, rolling sea typical of the severe conditions that characterize that uncompromising body of water. After almost eleven hours in the water and with the weather still worsening, it was suggested that she give up and come out of the water. "What for?" she replied, to the cheers of the reporters in the press boat, who were understandably eager for a good story. Ederle kept swimming. In the end, her speed as well as her endurance won the day, because she caught the favorable tide that would take her into the English shore by only ten minutes.

When she waded ashore near the cliffs of Dover, she was greeted by bonfires and an enthusiastic crowd, plus an overzealous police officer who demanded to see her passport. After straightening out that bureaucratic snafu, she was free to relax in a hot bath, her first since her arrival in France in June to train. (She hadn't wanted to spoil herself for the chilly channel water.) She wasn't sore, she told reporters, adding that her only injury was a tender right wrist from shaking the hands of so many admirers.

Perhaps as the telegrams poured in, and the requests for interviews piled up, and the crowds thronged outside her hotel, she began to realize that she wasn't just little Trudy Ederle from Amsterdam Avenue anymore. She was on the front page of every newspaper in America, indeed throughout much of the world, an overnight sensation. The *New*

York Daily News, a tabloid paper heavily dependent on photos, organized the fastest and most expensive relay in the history of journalism to date to get photographs of her actual swim back to an eager American public. All the major news syndicates had placed sets of their developed photographs onboard express liners leaving Southampton for New York that day, but the *Daily News* trumped them by sending their pictures on a steamer bound for Montreal, which cut one day off the trip. From there, with a combination of sea and land planes, a racing car, a train, and even an ambulance for the last leg, the *News* got the packet showing Ederle emerging from the water near Dover into print twelve hours before its competitors. But their scoop was short-lived, since a rival paper simply photographed its front and back pages and reproduced the pictures in its next edition.

Two weeks later Ederle received a hero's welcome from her hometown of New York. Her ocean liner from Europe was met by Grover Whalen, the city's official greeter, who escorted her to the Battery in a city tug. From there she went by motorcade up Lower Broadway to City Hall, the streets lined with supporters and ticker tape showering out the windows of the skyscrapers. She was dressed in a lavender hat, a blue serge coat suit, a scarf from Paris, and gray silk stockings. A police officer noted the larger than usual number of women in the crowd, symptomatic of how Ederle's individual achievement meant something special to the nation's women. Ten thousand people and the mayor awaited her at City Hall. The only slightly sour note to the whole celebration was a dispute about how much prominence should be given to her German-American roots. At that point World War I was less than a decade old, and wounds were still fresh. The event was pointedly portrayed as an American, not a German-American, triumph. Ederle herself reinforced the patriotic theme by telling the crowd, "It was for my flag that I swam and to know that I could bring home the honors, and my mind was made up to do it."

Once the formal ceremony was over, Ederle was free to

go home to her own neighborhood at 106 Amsterdam Avenue (between Sixty-fourth and Sixty-fifth streets), where waiting for her outside her father's butcher shop was a bright red roadster, a gift from her backers. The newspapers quoted her agent, lawyer Dudley Field Malone, as saying that almost $1 million of potential endorsements and opportunities had been offered to Ederle, so she must have thought that the car was just the first of many riches that would flow her way. It did not turn out that way, and within that tale lies the downside to sudden celebrity: how hard it is to capitalize on sudden fame and how quickly the public forgets.

Ederle Fades into Retirement

In retrospect, it is clear that Ederle's finances were badly handled by Malone: instead of accepting offers while she was still hot property, he held out for more. But she was also hurt by a combination of factors that reinforce how ephemeral heroic status can be. Instead of hurrying home to America after her swim, she took time to visit her grandmother in Germany. In that period, an Englishwoman, and the mother of two children at that, swam the channel, although not as fast as Ederle. She was still the first woman, and the fastest human, but her salability was tarnished just a bit.

Most of Ederle's potential offers were in the area of entertainment. She traveled for a while with a vaudeville show, giving swimming exhibitions, and even auditioned for a part in Hollywood. (The studios quickly realized that her bulky frame, so necessary to long-distance swimming, was the antithesis of the streamlined, lithe look movie cameras wanted.) But Ederle found the strain of public performance unbearable, and there was talk that she might have had a nervous breakdown. Her lack of ease in public was exacerbated by the partial loss of hearing she had suffered as a result of the battering her body took during her swim. Very little of the money she made actually got to her, certainly not enough to make a difference for the rest of her life.

Since she had turned professional in order to make her

channel swim, Ederle could not return to amateur swimming, which precluded participating in the 1928 Olympics. She eventually took a job as a swimming instructor, and that was how she supported herself in the years to come. At one point she injured her back in an aquatic performance and spent many months in a cast. And her deafness grew worse. She did make a small appearance at Billy Rose's Aquacade at the 1939 New York World's Fair, but by then she had been long forgotten by the public.

Gertrude Ederle spent the rest of her life living in a small house in Flushing, Queens. She never married, and for many years shared her home with two other women. She never complained about her deafness or expressed bitterness about how she had lost out on the opportunities to cash in on her success. "Don't write any sob stories about me," she told a reporter in 1966. Although each August 6 there was usually some mention of her record-breaking channel swim, she made only infrequent public appearances. As a reporter put it in 1976, "In effect, Miss Ederle has gone from a legend in her own time to a relic in everyone else's, trotted out on anniversaries of her triumph to bask in the glow of an America that used to be."

In 1936 reporter Ishbel Ross captured the fleeting nature of Ederle's fame: "She flashed through the news columns, made the headlines, tasted the heady wine of extravagant publicity; then went out of sight with the speed of an expiring rocket." That is how the twentieth century has often treated its popular heroes, especially from the world of sports and entertainment. One day they are front-page news, the talk of the town. The next, they are practically forgotten, reduced to a single line in the record books and perhaps a few faint memories of a ticker-tape parade.

Gertrude Ederle didn't set out to be a hero; she just wanted to swim the English Channel. As she put it simply, "I knew I could do it. I knew I would, and I did."

CHAPTER 5

Science and Invention

AMERICA'S DECADES

A Musical Explosion

Page Smith

The 1920s saw the rapid growth of certain musical formats. Romantic ballads, jazz, and the blues added their own unique melodies and words to the national scene. Acclaimed historian Page Smith describes the musical outpouring in his account of the times.

Popular music was primarily the music of Tin Pan Alley [a section of New York City which housed many music publishers—ed.], songs of the type Americans had loved to sing since the era of "My Old Kentucky Home." The Gramophone (or Victrola) had given an enormous stimulus to the writing of such songs. Tin Pan Alley had been strongly influenced by Scott Joplin and ragtime. Will Marion Cook was a black songwriter whose popularity rivaled Scott Joplin's. Both his parents had gone to college (his mother was a graduate of Oberlin), and the musically precocious Cook grew up in Washington, D.C. At the age of eight his parents sent him to Berlin to study violin under the master Joseph Joachim. Back in the United States Cook discovered that the concert world of classical music was closed to blacks, and he began setting some of Paul Laurence Dunbar's poems to music. . . .

The first all-black revue that opened on Broadway was entitled *Shuffle Along* and featured songs by ex-Sergeant Noble Sissle, who had been the drum major of the black 369th Infantry, and Eubie Blake, who also played in the

---

Excerpted from *A People's History of the 1920s and the New Deal,* by Page Smith (New York: McGraw-Hill). Copyright ©1985 by Page Smith. Reprinted with permission from the Estate of Page Smith.

musical. Starring Florence Mills, *Shuffle Along* was a sensational success with white audiences. Sissle, Claude McKay wrote, "knows his range and canters over it with the ease and grace of an antelope. The Harmony Kings are in the direct line of the Jubilee Singers." The lovely Florence Mills was the "sparkling gold star of the show." James Reese Europe, another hero of the 369th, became one of the first of the big band kings, the rage of Harlem, of Broadway, and of France. In Claude McKay's words, "his heart was shot out during a performance in Boston by a savage buck of his own race."

Tin Pan Alley Entertains the Nation

Tin Pan Alley turned out a constant stream of popular songs, both sentimental and nonsensical. "Three little words / Eight little letters, just three little words, / That say 'I love you.'" "Yes, we have no bananas, / We have no bananas today." "Life is just a bowl of cherries, / Don't take it serious / It's too mysterious. / You work, you slave, you worry so, / But you can't take your dough / When you go, go, go. / So keep repeating it's the berries. . . ." Then there was Barney Google, "with his goo-goo-googly eyes."

A popular ditty was:

Just Molly and me
And baby makes three,
We're happy in my blue heaven.

There was also:

Tea for two and two for tea,
I'm for you and you're for me.

Other hits were "The Love Nest," "Hot Lips," "Burning Kisses," "Sweet Lips," "Kiss Before Dawn," "Baby Face," "I Need Lovin'." The years between 1920 and 1928 witnessed twenty-four Broadway musicals, among them *The Student Prince, No, No, Nanette, Show Boat,* and *Rio Rita,* all of which produced a spate of popular songs.

With the onset of the Depression popular songs often reflected the somber mood of the country. The classic song of the Depression era was "Brother, Can You Spare a Dime?"

> Once I built a railroad, made it run,
> Made it race against time,
> Once I built a railroad, now it's done.
> Brother, can you spare a dime?

Even musicals took on a social tone. The most successful was the garment workers' revue *Pins and Needles.* The opening number set the tone:

> Sing me a song of social significance,
> All other songs are taboo.

A former coed lamented:

> I used to be in a daisy-chain,
> But now I'm a chain-store daisy . . .
> I sell smart but thrifty corsets
> At three-fifty, better grade
> Four, sixty-nine.
> I sell bras and girdles
> To Maudes and Myrtles
> To hold in their plump
> Behind this counter.
> Once I wrote poems
> Put people in tears
> Now I write checks
> For Red Star brassieres
> I used to be in a daisy-chain
> But now I'm a chain-store daisy.

A showstopper was a black number in which parents and friends celebrate the birth of a son, singing that they intend to name him "Franklin D. Roosevelt Jones." "He will not be a dud / Or a stick in the mud / When he's Franklin D. Roosevelt Jones, / Yessiree, yessiree, yessireeeeeeee."

Jazz and Blues Make Their Marks

Then there was jazz, less to be sung than danced to. Americans had always loved to dance; foreign travelers almost invariably commented on the infatuation of Americans with dancing. Jazz captured America and then captured the world. There were also the blues and gospel and country music. Blues was a relatively recent secular offspring of spirituals. Gospel was black shoutin' music, music of praise to the Lord sung by black congregations, and it, like blues and jazz, was of relatively recent origin. Fortunately we do not have to decide whether jazz came up the Mississippi from New Orleans or down from St. Louis or east from Kansas City; it is enough that it became a permanent constituent of American music.

Country was white Southern music, vaguely derived from English ballads and folk songs preserved in the Southern mountains. It was the mournful music of love and betrayal and, not infrequently, murder. Although it spread into the "southern" Midwest, it remained stubbornly regional.

While black songwriters, as we have seen, wrote Tin Pan Alley songs, the alley was largely a white preserve; jazz was unmistakably black. Original New Orleans bands usually had piano, bass fiddle, banjo, and tuba or drums, with several wind instruments "out in front." Following the example of King Oliver and the early Louis Armstrong band, bands grew larger and larger—trombone, clarinet, drums, cornet, "vibes"—but the improvisational character of the early jazz bands was preserved. White bands learned from black bands, and jazz was one of the few areas of American life where blacks and whites mixed with some degree of freedom.

Robert Palmer, historian of the blues, ascribes their origin to the Mississippi delta near Clarksville, the Stovall plantation, and the Will Dockery plantation. . . . There Charley Patton began playing his own version of the blues. Robert Johnson, another delta bluesman, sang:

> You can call the blues, you can call the blues any old
>   thing you please,
> You can call the blues any old thing you please,
> But the blues ain't nothing but the doggone heart disease.

Muddy Waters, one of the fathers of the blues on the Stovall plantation in Mississippi, sang classic blues for Alan Lomax:

If I'm feelin' tomorrow
Like I feel today
I'm goin' to pack my suitcase
And make my getaway
I'm all worried in my mind
And I never been satisfied
And I just can't keep from cryin'.

While blues had an origin independent of jazz, it soon became a basic ingredient of jazz and the special province of black women vocalists. To Mezz Mezzrow, Bessie Smith was the mistress of blues singing—"Young Woman Blues," "Reckless Blues," "Empty Bed Blues." Mezzrow described her as "all woman, all the femaleness the world ever saw in one sweet package . . . tall and brown-skinned, with great dimples . . . dripping good looks . . . buxom and massive but stately too, shapely as an hour-glass. . . ." Bessie Smith died in 1937, when a white hospital in Mississippi refused to admit her after she had been badly injured in an auto-mobile accident. Other great blues singers were Billie Holiday, Ethel Waters, Mabs Moberly, and Pearl Bailey. Indeed, one of the most arresting facts about the jazz era was the number of black women involved, both as instrumentalists and vocalists. Linda Dahl's *Stormy Weather* is a history primarily of black jazzwomen. . . .

Jazz Goes Overseas

Like the movies, jazz was an American item of export. Josephine Baker was brought over to Paris by Caroline Dudley, a white woman, in *La Revue Nègre*. The musical created a sensation and made Baker the toast of Paris. In London and Berlin, in Moscow and Tokyo, jazz proved ir-resistible. Just as the twenties belonged to the silent films (or the silent films to the twenties), they belonged to the great black jazz bands. The thirties saw the birth of swing, a kind of formalized white derivative of jazz. White musicians took jazz, smoothed it out, and made big money. Harry James, the Dorsey brothers, Glenn Miller, Benny Goodman, Woody Herman all were excellent musicians, and they made good music, music for records and the radio. Underneath it black music continued. Some black bands (Jimmie Lunceford, Jimmy Rushing, Louis Armstrong, Duke Ellington) made it into the big band world and continued to do brilliant and innovative things, Ellington especially, but many of the great black jazzmen were reduced to working as day laborers or playing for tips in small jazz clubs. The end of Prohibition was a mayor blow to jazz. Speakeasies disappeared, and there were far fewer places to play.

Automobiles Fuel the Transportation Revolution

Fon W. Boardman Jr.

Transportation boomed during the 1920s. Railroads blanketed the country, ships steamed along both coasts, on rivers, and across the high seas, and aircraft made the skies accessible. The most dramatic impact upon society, though, came from the automobile, which provided Americans an increased freedom to leave the home and move about the country.

Historian Fon W. Boardman Jr., an expert in U.S. history in the 1900s, explains the transportation revolution that altered the face of American society.

The nation's railroads, whose thousands of miles of tracks had done so much to link the far-flung parts of the continent together, were the basic transportation system of the United States. This was clearly shown when the country entered World War I. Within months the many independent operating lines proved unable to provide the coordinated and unified transportation of goods and people necessary for the war effort to succeed. At the end of 1917 the Federal government took over the lines by Presidential proclamation and in March, 1918, Congress passed a law spelling out the terms of Federal operation.

Under William G. McAdoo as director general, govern-

Excerpted from *America and the Jazz Age: A History of the 1920s*, by Fon W. Boardman Jr. (New York: Random House, 1968). Copyright ©1968 by Fon W. Boardman Jr. Reprinted by permission of the author.

ment management was a great success, so that when the war ended there was some sentiment that the government should continue to operate the railroads and should take over ownership from the private companies. The railway labor unions favored this, but the owners wanted their property back, plus payment for wear and tear on equipment. The Transportation Act of 1920 abandoned the idea of government ownership but placed more power than previously in the hands of the Interstate Commerce Commission. Whereas in the past the general antitrust atmosphere had worked against the merging of railroads, the Commission was now instructed to help formulate consolidation plans that would bring about more efficient regional groupings of rail lines. In practice, though, nothing much came of this. The act also set up a Railroad Labor Board but since it had no power to enforce its decisions it was not effective. Another Railway Labor Act in 1926 did not prove any more practical.

The return of the railroads to their owners and the subsequent attempts to deal with their postwar problems came at a time when the railways were facing their first serious competition in almost a century. The automobile was beginning to cut heavily into rail passenger traffic, which declined by about a third by 1927. Transportation of freight by truck had been given a boost by the war, and the number and size of trucks continued to increase rapidly. At the same time pipe lines began to carry more and more liquid products. More and better highways were being built out of public funds while the railways had to use their own money for roadbeds and equipment. Even commercial aviation began to be a threat to the dominance of the railroads.

As in other areas, technological advances helped railways to compete. Automatic train controls were installed on a good deal of track mileage and centralized traffic control increased the capacity of the roads. Diesel locomotives appeared in the twenties in the form of small switching engines but it was the next decade before the large diesels came in.

A Shipbuilding Boom

The war, with its need for shipping millions of tons of goods across the oceans and its enormous loss of ships to German submarines, caused the government to enter the shipbuilding business. In the three years 1918–20 the United States launched about 8,500,000 tons of merchant shipping and by the end of the war had many more tons of shipping in relation to the British than in 1914. Nevertheless, when peace came and the demand for shipping space fell off, American merchantmen were once more unable to compete with British and other foreign operators whose costs were much lower.

There was considerable support for keeping up a substantial American merchant marine so that in case of another war the nation would not be dependent on other countries' ships. The controlling sentiment favored the government's getting out of the shipping business and turning it over to private interests. By mid-1920 the Shipping Board had about 1,500 ships which had been built at a cost of $3,000,000,000. The Merchant Marine Act of 1920 instructed the Board to sell its ships to American companies as soon as possible. Although sponsors of the legislation thought government ownership and operation was socialism, they did not mind subsidizing the private operators in various ways, such as exemption from certain taxes, generous payments for carrying the mail, and loans. In 1928 another law, the Jones-White Act, increased the mail subsidies and authorized another $250,000,000 of construction loans. Despite these efforts the American merchant fleet did not prosper.

In shipbuilding the main technological advance was the use of diesel engines in large vessels in place of steam power. In 1922 the United States Navy acquired its first aircraft carrier when it converted a collier into the U.S.S. *Langley.*

The Automobile Makes Its Mark

The significant transportation revolution of the decade took place on land where the automobile, its merits amply demonstrated by wartime use, rapidly changed from a rich man's toy to a necessity for millions. As recently as 1910 there had been only 458,000 cars in the entire United States. In ten years the number of passenger cars and trucks grew to nearly 9,250,000 and by the end of the 1920's the total had reached the astounding figure of just over 26,500,000. This meant that the whole population of the United States could go for an automobile ride at the same time.

Automobiles roll off the assembly line at the Ford factory in 1925. The automobile changed the way Americans traveled and spent their leisure time.

The automobile industry became a key factor in the economic life of the nation. By 1929 the value of its product was one-eighth of all manufactured goods. Without it such industries as steel, rubber, glass, and others could not prosper. About one million persons had jobs directly concerned with the motor vehicle industry while three times as many were indirectly dependent upon it. At the beginning of auto manufacturing in the early years of the century nearly two hundred persons or companies entered this very competitive field. By 1929, as a result of mergers and failures, only eleven survived. General Motors and Ford were already the two giants of the industry, with Chrysler third. There were still a few well-known smaller companies, such as Nash, Hudson, Packard, and Studebaker—the latter having ceased in 1920 to produce any more horse-drawn wagons, for which it had been well known for many years.

Ford was the best-known name and Henry Ford and his Model T auto became a part of American folklore. By the time he abandoned the Tin Lizzie [nickname for Model T] he had made fifteen million of them and in some single years his plants had turned out as many as two million. Ford consistently brought down the prices of his cars so that by the middle of the decade one could purchase a Model T for under $300. When he introduced an entirely new car in 1928—the Model A—it was somewhat more expensive, but it was the biggest news story of the year and more than half a million people signed up to buy one before they ever saw it. Ford was a lone wolf who would have nothing to do with Eastern bankers. Nor would he deal with labor unions, and he forced his retail dealers to try to sell more and more cars. But along with this he paid comparatively high wages and was one of the first leaders of industry to recognize that if mass production was to be successful there would have to be enough money paid out in wages and salaries so that there also could be mass consumption.

These vehicles that were transforming America were considerably different from their present-day descendants. At the start of the decade most passenger autos were open touring cars. Only about 10 per cent were closed. The proportion went up rapidly, partly because some highways were now kept open in winter so it was no longer necessary to lay up the family car for the season. One of the standard jokes about Henry Ford was that he said his customers could have his Model T in any color they wished so long as it was black. In 1925 other manufacturers began to offer a variety of colors, and so did Ford when he unveiled the Model A. Balloon tires came in about this time. Cars were getting more comfortable, but the average horsepower of passenger cars was only twenty.

Change Follows the Automobile

The automobile was changing American life in several ways. It became a status symbol as important as one's house or one's style of living. In fact some people preferred to have a modest house with a garage and a car than to have a more expensive dwelling. One sociological survey of a typical Middle Western city found that a number of families who did not have bathtubs owned autos, and one woman admitted she would go without meals before cutting down on buying gasoline to run the family car. The boy who could not borrow the family car to take his girl to a dance was soon dateless. In fact, in no area did the automobile bring about more change than in that of dating and courtship. Previously young couples had spent many hours in the home parlor; now the automobile became a parlor on wheels, taking them to more exciting places and away from parental supervision. Farmers were no longer isolated from the towns and cities. Entire families could take vacation trips to parts of the nation they might never otherwise see. This new and constant traveling in turn caused other changes. Service stations and roadside restaurants sprang up at every crossroad and before long the gas station and the garage for repairing autos were major businesses. Tourist cabins, the forerunners of today's plush motels, were built on what had been farm land.

The increasing number of owners and drivers of autos demanded more and better-paved highways—and the more roads that were built, the more incentive there was for still more people to buy and drive autos. Thus the coming of the motor vehicle also made the road construction industry and its suppliers, such as asphalt, cement, and machinery manufacturers, big business. During the 1920's the nation spent nearly $2,000,000,000 a year on its highways and streets. By 1927 there were fifty thousand miles of concrete roads, and by 1928 a man could drive from New York to

Kansas on paved highways. However, it was not advisable to try to go much farther west during the rainy season or in the winter.

The amazing increase in the number of cars also meant traffic problems in the cities, a need for new types of highways, and calls for more bridges and tunnels. The first traffic signals, manually operated, were used in New York City about 1920. Later, overhead red and green electrically operated signals, adapted from the railroad signal system, began to be used. The first parkway was the Bronx River Parkway in Westchester County, New York, which was opened in 1923. Parkways on Long Island and the Merritt Parkway in Connecticut also date from the twenties. Wacker Drive in Chicago, constructed between 1921 and 1925, made use of double-decking to carry traffic, while the first cloverleaf intersection was opened in New Jersey in 1928. The first long underwater tunnel designed specifically for motor vehicles was the Holland Tunnel under the Hudson River, which was built between 1920 and 1927. In Pittsburgh the Liberty tunnels for autos were cut through rock and opened in 1924. The George Washington Bridge over the Hudson River between New Jersey and New York City was started in 1927 and at the time was the longest suspension bridge in the world, with a span of 3,500 feet.

Aviation Joins the Fray

An even newer method of transportation than the auto was the airplane; and, as with the automobile, World War I provided a strong stimulus. The "aces," flying alone in their fragile fighter planes, were the romantic heroes of the war. More practical was the money and effort spent on making planes stronger and more powerful. Commercial airline companies began to try to turn aviation into a business, but progress was slow. As late as 1927 the airlines carried fewer than 10,000 passengers a year, but a new era was about to begin, for by the end of the 1920's the annual number of passengers had already risen to over 150,000.

A major source of encouragement to aviation was the

use of planes to carry the mail. At first the Post Office Department operated its own planes but the Air Commerce Act of 1926 gave power over commercial aviation to the Commerce Department, headed by Herbert Hoover. He began a campaign for better airports and better services, such as weather-forecasting. Gradually the airline companies took over the air mail and by 1929 Hoover could report regular flights of over 25,000,000 miles annually. At this time about 7,500 planes were being manufactured every year.

The 1920's were a great period for "firsts" in aviation and for competition that set new records in speed, endurance, and other categories. In 1923 two U.S. Army lieutenants made the first nonstop transcontinental flight in just under twenty-seven hours, flying from Long Island to San Diego, California. Commenting on the event, *Time* magazine (May 12) said: "Ultimately, no business will be able to afford any mail but air mail; no businessman any travel but air travel." The next year four Army planes took off on an around-the-world flight and five months and twenty-two days later two of them completed the journey. Actual flying time had been something over fifteen days. In 1926 a Navy officer, Richard E. Byrd, became the first man to pilot a plane over the North Pole. Two years later he added the South Pole to his accomplishments, and that same year Amelia Earhart became the first woman pilot to cross the Atlantic. In the last year of the decade five Army flyers—two of whom later became generals—set a world endurance record for sustained flight when they kept their three-motored plane in the air, with the aid of frequent refuelings, for 250 hours, 40 minutes, and 16 seconds. The first bad accident on an American commercial airline also occurred that year when a plane crashed in New Mexico, killing all five passengers and the crew of three. The flight of the decade that caused the greatest sensation was Charles A. Lindbergh's solo trip from New York to Paris in 1927.

During the 1920's the hydrogen- or helium-supported

dirigibles appeared ready to play an important part in air transportation. Many people believed they had more possibilities than heavier-than-air craft and the armed forces of several nations thought they might be the new dreadnought of the skies. The Germans pioneered with them during World War I and the British *R-34* made the first trans-Atlantic crossing in 1919. However, disaster seemed to follow the silvery, cigar-shaped craft. British, French, Italian, and American dirigibles all crashed or blew up during the 1920's. The U.S.S. *Shenandoah* broke apart over Ohio in September, 1925. The Germans were more successful with their commercial airships. The *Graf Zeppelin* made a round-trip flight between Germany and the United States in 1928 and the next year accomplished a flight around the world with twenty passengers.

Overall the 1920's was one of the most exciting decades in the history of transportation. Railroads and shipping showed no great technological advances and they had to face difficult economic problems. However, the motor vehicle powered by the internal combustion engine revolutionized land transportation, not only because of technological progress, but also because it made possible—in the United States at least—fast and nearly effortless personal transportation. In the same period air transportation not only improved mechanically but also became commercially feasible.

Charles Lindbergh Crosses an Ocean

Walter S. Ross

One of the most influential events of the century occurred in 1927, when a little-known pilot named Charles Lindbergh climbed in his aircraft, the *Spirit of St. Louis*, and flew nonstop from New York to Paris, France. By so doing, he became the first person to fly alone from North America to Europe.

In this excerpt taken from his biography of Lindbergh, magazine editor and author Walter S. Ross gives an account of Lindbergh's flight.

Usually, when Lindbergh put his head on the pillow, he went to sleep. But not this night. A poker game was going on among the correspondents at the hotel. Excitement mounted when the pot reached $400. Just at that point, Lindbergh came into the room and said, "Can't you let me get some sleep? I've got to get up early in the morning." Sam Schulman, a former International News Service cameraman recalls that this had little effect on the group.

Lindbergh went back to bed and twisted and turned, thinking of all the calculations he had made, all the decisions he had weighed. Had he done right to omit the radio? The parachute? To take on those extra pounds of gasoline? He had just begun to drift off when—slam!—his personal guard broke into the room with a completely irrelevant question. "Slim, what am I going to do when you're gone?" *That* murdered sleep.

He finally gave up and got up. He dressed and went downstairs into the hotel lobby and out on to the stone porch. It was about 2:45 A.M., The *New York Times* man covering the hotel, Johnny Frogge, saw him looking into the darkness at the dripping trees.

"Are you going this morning, Captain?" Frogge asked.

Lindbergh waited a minute. "I don't know," he said.

"When will you know?" Frogge asked, anxious to catch the last edition.

"I don't know," Lindbergh repeated.

He was, as Deac Lyman [New York newspaper reporter] said later, not being evasive, only honest. He really hadn't decided if he was taking off that day or not.

Lindbergh Heads to the Airfield

He drove out to Curtiss Field at three o'clock in the morning of May 20 without having slept. The weather was bad, but getting better. Nobody would take the plane from the hangar in the drizzle without Lindbergh's approval. He looked at the skies, smelled the wind, thought of what the weatherman had said about a high-pressure system moving in from the west, figured that if he started at dawn he could always turn back if he ran into too much bad weather. He ordered the plane hauled out of the hangar. Its tail was tied to a truck that would tow it the short distance to Roosevelt Field. It was not a happy occasion. The plane—shrouded against the weather, lurching tail first through the mud— seemed heavy and lifeless. Reporters, policemen, mechanics sloshed along on foot through the squelching ooze. To Lindbergh, it seemed more like a funeral procession than the beginning of a joyous adventure in the air.

A light east wind was blowing, so the *Spirit of St. Louis* was towed to the west end of the Roosevelt runway. At the other end of the runway was a steamroller that had been used to pack it down. Beyond that were telephone wires to clear, and beyond that Merrick Avenue.

Deac Lyman and C.B. Allen [New York newspaper reporter] walked down to the steamroller and crouched near it. "We knew the story would either be there or in Paris," Allen said recently, "and we wanted to be ready to help if necessary. The steamroller was plenty of protection for us.

The tanks were filled. Chief Abram Skidmore and Inspector Frank McCahill, of the Nassau County police, were worried about the danger. Everybody knew that the plane was loaded to the last ounce with gasoline. Harry Bruno agreed to follow the takeoff in his open car. Skidmore and McCahill were with him, holding fire extinguishers.

Lindbergh climbed into the cabin and closed the door. Ed Mulligan [mechanic] pulled the propeller, and Ken Boedecker [mechanic] held a booster coil to give the cold engine a hot spark. Once the engine started, he cut the wires to the coil, as Lindbergh would not need it again and did not want to carry the extra weight. The engine kicked over, and Lind-

Charles Lindbergh became the first person to fly nonstop across the Atlantic Ocean in 1927 when he flew from New York to Paris aboard his plane, the Spirit of St. Louis.

bergh kept opening and closing the throttle. It wasn't revving up as high as expected. "They never rev up on a day like this," Boedecker said, but his face looked worried. Lindbergh shut the engine off. Boedecker and Mulligan made a hasty check of fittings and connections. Everything was in order—the wires, the valve springs, the fuel lines.

Again Mulligan pulled the propeller, and once again Lindbergh tried to get the engine up to full power. It was still low. (Boedecker says it was fifty revolutions below optimum performance. But Lindbergh disputes this. He says it was thirty revolutions low. "If it was fifty low, I wouldn't have taken off," he told Boedecker many years later.) Adopting Lindbergh's figure, the Whirlwind was still about 1.5 per cent below full power. The plane was already overweight, its greased tires sinking into the rain-soaked clay of the runway.

Now, to complicate things further, the wind shifted from east to west, from head to tail. True, it was only the slightest breath of wind, barely enough to move the wind sock, but it was blowing the wrong way. It added another tiny element of danger to an already perilous situation. If Lindbergh decided to take off into the wind, the ship would have to be towed to the other side of the field. The engine was too light and would overheat if he taxied the heavy ship through the soft ground. Taking off westward also meant a hazardous course over hangars and houses, almost certain death if things went badly. And there would be the loss of vital time—just enough time, perhaps, to bring him to the Irish coast after dark instead of before sunset as he hoped.

Lindbergh Decides to Go

Everybody was watching him. The decision was his—his alone. Boedecker said that the engine was functioning as well as possible in that kind of weather. The test flights had shown that the plane had plenty of lift, but now he was asking it to lift a thousand pounds more than it ever had before—in mist, off a mud runway, with a tail wind. And with an engine at less than full power, and with moisture condensing on its lifting surfaces. Of course, Lindbergh could start his takeoff and then cut power at the halfway mark and hope not to crash by coasting to a stop. There were no brakes on the wheels, no reversible-pitch propeller such as today's aircraft have, to slow the plane on the ground.

Wind, weather, power, load—those were the thoughts churning in his mind. And then the churning stopped. "It's less a decision of logic than of feeling," he said later. "The kind of feeling that comes when you gauge the distance to be jumped between two stones across a brook." He knew that no one would blame him if he didn't take off; no one would doubt his courage. Still, "sitting in the cockpit . . . the conviction surges through me that the wheels *will* leave the ground, that the wings *will* rise above the wires, that it is time to start the flight."

He pulled down his goggles. Boedecker asked, "Do you want us to kick the blocks?" Lindbergh nodded. Boedecker and Mulligan knocked out the blocks. Lindbergh checked his instruments again and gave the engine full throttle. Eight or ten men pushed against the wing struts to help lift the plane loose from the gluey earth. *Spirit* began to move under its own power, at first agonizingly slow. It seemed that the overloaded plane could never rise above the ground; its wheels were cutting furrows in the clay instead of riding high and quick. At the halfway mark, the controls were mushy but tightening; he tried to lift the plane and the wheels did leave the ground for a split second. It was 7:52 A.M.

Bruno was following close behind in his roadster, with the policemen and the fire extinguishers.

Now Lindbergh was certain; he was committed. He continued to roar down the runway, picking up speed as he lurched along. He bounced into the air, still without enough flying speed. (A couple of "kangaroo leaps" was Bruno's description.) But at last the plane broke contact with the ground and Lindbergh nursed it slowly aloft. There was still a thousand feet to the telephone wires. He climbed very slowly, attaining speed as he went, and cleared the wires by twenty feet. Bruno and Skidmore turned toward each other in the front seat as the car skidded to a halt. "By God, he made it!" they shouted in unison.

Lindbergh flew along Long Island, and then, following the first leg of his great-circle course, he pointed across Long Island Sound toward Connecticut. He had never flown over so much water in his life, but he knew that between land and water there was always an area of turbulence. With his wings and fuselage overstrained, Lindbergh could not afford to add anything to the burden. He trembled with each shock of turbulence, watched his wing tips bend too much, waiting for the rending sound that would signal he had pushed things too far. Those were an uneasy few seconds, but a thousand feet out over the water the air became smooth as glass. The wings stopped vibrating. Now with each passing moment his ship became lighter as it consumed fuel, and a less likely prey to turbulence. He crossed the Sound and flew over Connecticut. At the end of his first hour he began to fill the hourly log that would tell him what he needed as he went along, particularly about fuel consumption. He recorded wind velocity (zero), true course, compass variation. His altitude was 600 feet, his air speed 102 m.p.h., the tachometer showed only 1,750 r.p.m., 50 below the normal cruising speed. He had plenty of reserve power as he cruised across Rhode Island and Massachusetts.

Between Massachusetts and Nova Scotia there were two hours of flight over open water. This would really test his navigating skill. If he could stay on course without familiar landmarks to guide him, he could be confident of doing the same thing over the North Atlantic. The drone of the engine seemed to emphasize the fact that he hadn't slept for more than twenty-four hours. Also, he had been flying for nearly four hours, a good day's flight. He began to get sleepy, very sleepy. And there were still thirty hours ahead of him, part of it at night and most of it over ocean. Overwater flight, he was learning, had a certain monotony that made sleep ever more desirable. His eyelids wanted to close. In fact, his eye did blink closed several times; perhaps he slept for a second or two without knowing it. During the third hour of flight, the cockpit was suddenly lit by warm sunlight. He looked out and saw a bit of mud on the wing, thrown up from Roosevelt Field by the wheels. It irritated him to think he had cut every unneeded ounce from his plane and was now forced to carry a tiny load of mud all the way to Paris.

Lindbergh Spots the Canadian Coast

Suddenly a green coast leaped at him, it was the shore of Nova Scotia. Checking his charts against the shape of the shore line, he found that he had made landfall at the mouth of St. Mary's Bay, only six miles off his course, only two degrees away from his calculated objective, well within the five-degree margin for error he had allowed himself. This was very good navigating indeed. A six-mile error here was the equivalent of a miss of about fifty miles at Ireland. And his plane had averaged a hundred and two miles an hour. Already it was about four hundred pounds lighter in fuel than when he started.

In his mind, Lindbergh had set three checkpoints which would determine his flight plan. The first one was halfway down the runway at Roosevelt. The second was this one, Nova Scotia. If he found it socked in by fog, or if he was totally lost—showing that flying by compass would not work—he planned to turn back to Long Island. His next and last would be halfway across the Atlantic, the point of no return. Before that, if he ran into trouble he could turn back; after that, he would have no choice but to press on.

Over Nova Scotia and Cape Breton Island he met heavy rain, fog, turbulent air. He began to worry about his wings again, and his lack of parachute. Why had he traded those twenty pounds of safety for extra gasoline? Why hadn't he put dump valves on his fuel tanks so he might lighten his load, if necessary, and save his plane? He knew the answers, but doubts began to gnaw at him. Had he made the right decisions? If he lived, he would know.

He flew for three hours over Nova Scotia, then headed out over another two hundred miles of open water toward Newfoundland. Once more, sleep began to overtake him; his eyes grew heavy, and he forgot to keep his plane on course. He began to dream of lying in a snowbank in Minnesota, that winter when he was seventeen and became snowbound with his pony. Those clouds looked so soft out there . . . just like the Minnesota snowbanks. But he wrenched himself awake to take an interest in the ice fields that appeared below. He began to make plans for a forced landing on ice. He adjusted his engine revolutions to allow for the lightened weight of fuel he was now carrying after nine hours of flight. At last the mountains of Newfoundland showed themselves, and Lindbergh had to make a decision. Should he fly off course a bit—only a few minutes off—to dip his wings to St. John's, the last settlement he would see before Ireland? Or should he stick to his rigid schedule?

No plane had ever flown from St. John's eastward without first landing there. It was there that Commander Read and his three flying boats refueled and took off for the Azores on the Navy flight eight years before, in 1919. It was from St. John's, too, that Alcock and Brown [aviators] had flown to Ireland the same year.

It would be fun to dive on St. John's and then continue across the Atlantic—another joke he could play. But this one had possibly serious consequences. After having cut everything to the bone to save fuel, he would be wasting a quarter of an hour's flight for a bit of fun. No, he couldn't do that. But then he continued to think—flying over the city would give the inhabitants one last fix on his plane and his course. They would know he had made it this far, which would reassure his partners, and they would know where he was heading and at approximately what speed. If he didn't get to Europe, they could figure he must be down somewhere along the route between St. John's and Ireland. This knowledge would narrow the search for him as he waited, floating on his rubber raft.

Lindbergh Tackles the Ocean

He altered course toward St. John's. It took only a moment to dive down over the edge of the city. Men looked up and saw him. Then he flew out to sea, nearly two thousand miles of it before him. As he broke his last tenuous connection with the land, he checked his fuel and his ignition. He was heading toward night.

"To the pilot of an airplane without flares or landing lights, night has a meaning that no earthbound mortal can fully understand," Lindbergh has written. "Once he has left the lighted airways there are no wayside shelters open to a flyer of the night. He can't park his plane on a cloud bank to weather out a storm, or heave over a sea anchor like the sailor and drag along slowly downwind. He's unable to control his speed like the driver of a motorcar in fog. He has to keep his craft hurtling through air no matter how black the sky or blinding the storm. To land without sight is to crash."

Now he was committed to the night and to the sea. After an hour he had to climb to get above fog. Then a storm began developing and he had to climb higher to get over it. He was at 10,500 feet. Suddenly he noticed how cold it was inside the plane, and this warned him through the haze of sleep that there was danger outside. Ice—ice that could deform the airy shape of a wing, that could overload the plane and force it into the sea—ice was forming. He could see some of it by the light of his flashlight. He was inside an ice cloud, one of those terrible, soft things that would not cause a plane to crash immediately but were an all-embracing threat. "They enmesh intruders," he wrote. "They're barbaric in their methods. They toss you in their inner turbulence, lash you with their hailstones, poison you with freezing mist. It would be a slow death, a death one would have long minutes to struggle against . . . climbing, stalling, diving, whipping, always downward toward the sea."

He wanted to panic, to turn and dive, but he kept himself from moving too precipitately. The *Spirit of St. Louis* was an extraordinarily sensitive airplane that required careful flying every minute; it wasn't an old Standard that could be kicked around in the sky. He maneuvered his way out of the ice clouds and back into clear air. The ice was not so thick on the plane's wires now.

Lindbergh had had removable glass windows built for the plane, windows he could insert from inside the cockpit. At one point during the flight he considered using them to keep out the cold, and also to add streamlining and extra range to the ship. But they would cut him off from sensory contact with the passing air; they would dull the sound of the engine; they would keep the cabin warm—and that might only make sleep irresistible. He had sacrificed several miles' worth of gasoline for the windows, which weighed about three or four pounds, but he never put them in.

Sleep continued to threaten him. He had never known such a terrible urgency to close his eyes, to drift off. He began to doubt that he could stay awake to complete the flight; sleep and ice seemed determined to kill him. He shook himself. He stuck his mittened hand out the window to deflect cold air into his face. He slapped himself, hard, and didn't feel a thing. He noticed his head was hurting; his altitude, still over 10,000 feet, had allowed the air cushion on which he was sitting to expand just enough to force his helmet against the top of the cockpit.

By fighting every second—and probably by occasionally falling asleep for a few seconds, or nearly—Lindbergh thrashed his way in the twilight zone of sleep. The air became clearer, then warmer. He could see the moon. Below, he knew, must be the Gulf Stream; if he was forced down into that body of water, he could live for a long time.

No Sense in Turning Back Now

And then, during the seventeenth hour of flight, he passed the third of his three checkpoints, the point of no return. Before he had been flying away from safety; now he was moving toward it with every passing second.

He had now gone about forty-eight hours without sleep, and the need to close his eyes became the most demanding thing in his life. He actually pried his eyes open with his fingers, but they closed anyhow. His body was in revolt. "Every cell of my being is on strike, sulking in protest, claiming that nothing, nothing in the world, could be worth such effort; that man's tissue was never made for such abuse." He had to stay awake to live; he knew that, and he kept telling himself that basic truth over and over. He was still filling out his log, hour by hour. At the end of eighteen hours he knew he was approximately halfway to Paris. He had planned on a private celebration—a sandwich and some water—but he wasn't hungry enough to eat, and he didn't want any more water. (He had taken a couple of sips since the start of the flight.) He just kept flying like an automaton, dull, spiritless, yet always sensitive to danger. If his turn indicator or his air-speed indicator showed a change, he reacted instantly.

For the next five hours he battled sleep and fog; he was so tired and so often socked in that he couldn't take proper readings, and so neglected his log. Now he kept a record only of the hours of fuel consumed from the various tanks. The sun rose, but the usual morning arousal failed to take place within him. He was flying in a stupor, wasting fuel by not properly setting his mixture and by allowing the engine to turn over faster than necessary. After some hours he saw the sea and could tell from the direction of the spume that a strong wind was blowing, a wind that was helping him— a tail wind. But sleep still threatened. How could he keep on flying for another ten hours? How could he navigate to find his landfalls? "But the alternative is death and failure," he thought. "Death! For the first time in my life, I doubt my ability to endure."

His body was suffering from lack of oxygen. He thrust his head out of the window and took great gulps of air. That helped, but he still wanted sleep. He fought the fog in his brain, he fought the plane; he was fighting to stay alive. And then, as though he were getting over an acute illness, for no discernible reason he began to feel alert again. His strength returned. His eyes stayed open without an effort. He could see and feel and smell. He looked at his watch. It was just about twenty-four hours since he had started out and he was well into his third sleepless day. Somehow he had flown past the need for sleep, just as he had slipped through clouds. The world was suddenly new and bright.

With his head clear, he began planning ahead. He was totally unsure of his position. He might have drifted hundreds of miles off course during his hours of drowsiness; if he had, and his error was to the south, he might have to fly an additional thousand miles over ocean to reach land. Should he, then, throttle down to save fuel? On the other hand, if he was headed toward Ireland, as he thought, and he slowed down, he might not get there before dark. Once again it was his philosophy of risk that made the choice. "If security were my prime motive," he thought, "I'd never have begun this flight at all." Security demanded that he slow down and conserve fuel; instead, he speeded up the engine, gave it a richer mixture, and saw the air-speed indicator rise, by seven miles an hour, to an even hundred.

During his battle with sleep, he had been the prey of hallucinatory visions. He recalled his childhood, his youth; he thought he saw dragons; he thought he saw islands in the middle of the sea. Now he did see something and it was real—porpoises. He wasn't knowledgeable enough about sea life to know whether this meant he was close to land or not.

Ireland Beckons

But when during the twenty-sixth hour of flight he sighted a sea bird, he was reasonably sure he was approaching land. Birds could rest on waves, but they nested on shore. Then supposition merged into certainty when he saw some fishing boats down below. This was the most exciting moment of the flight, he said later.

In the past, Lindbergh had been able to talk to people on the ground by flying low and throttling back on his engine. He tried this with a fishing boat. But when he circled, shouting, "Which way is Ireland?" nobody even came out on deck. He had no idea of how far off course he might be; he had only his compasses to guide him, and they had not been reliable during the night. He circled another boat, shouting. This time a man stuck his head out of a porthole, but he only gawked; he never answered. He didn't even point.

At last Lindbergh gave up in disgust. He had wasted precious minutes of fuel and daylight trying to get the uncommunicative fishermen on deck. He headed eastward.

Within the hour (the twenty-seventh of the flight) he thought he saw land. It had to be Ireland, even though it was much too early to be this close. As he drew nearer, he could see the high mountains, too high for Brittany or Cornwall, and the fields; they were much greener than one would find in Scotland. It *had* to be Ireland. It was. He was more than two hours ahead of schedule; that tail wind had pushed him a couple of hundred miles nearer. He flew over a village. It was beautiful. Everything was beautiful. People streamed into the streets, waving, waving. He felt he had returned to life, to earth.

He arrived over the Irish coast at a point only three miles off his course—Valentia and Dingle Bay. He had figured he might make it within fifty miles. That would have been extremely good dead reckoning. But three miles! "Before I made this flight I would have said carelessly that it was luck. Now, luck seems far too trivial a word, a term to be used only by those who've never seen the curtain drawn or looked on life from far away."

He had kept his watch—his grandfather's nickel-cased watch—set at New York time. It was now 11:52 A.M. in New York—of May 21, the day after he took off. In a few hours he would be in Paris, if all went well. And all was going well. He tried out his switches; both sets of spark plugs were firing. He decided to use up all the fuel in the nose tank to give the plane a heavier tail; this would lessen chances of nosing over on landing.

Paris in Sight

Four hours from Paris, he again revved his engine and got up to an air speed of 110 m.p.h. At this speed he would reach the shore of France while it was still daylight and give himself an edge in the event of a forced landing.

For a while he wondered if he shouldn't fly farther than

Paris. He had plenty of gasoline left. Without gauges, but by calculating time, speed, and distance, he assumed that there was at least enough gasoline in the plane to fly on to Rome. That would be a feat! Another seven hundred miles beyond the impossible goal of Paris!

But then he remembered how it had been over Cleveland one night, when his plane wasn't expected. He had circled and circled, not finding the lights of the airport, and had just about given up hope and decided to search for a field on the outskirts of town when the airport lights went on. The man on the ground said that of course they turned the lights off at night when they didn't expect a plane. Why should they waste all that electricity? Lindbergh was afraid the same thing might happen to him if he pushed on beyond Paris to cities where no one expected him.

It was still daylight when he saw the coast of France. Now Paris was only a little more than an hour away. He was three hours ahead of schedule. That would surprise the people, all right! He thought of what he would do after he arrived. He had no visa; that might be a problem. He had to buy a suit; he had only the flying clothes he was wearing. Maybe he could take his plane on a tour of Europe— even fly on around the world. At the very least, he expected to fly it home. It would demean the *Spirit of St. Louis* to return to the United States on board a ship.

As he passed the 3,500-mile mark, he knew he had broken the world's record for nonstop airplane flight. In a kind of celebration he ate a sandwich—his first food in more than thirty-five hours. It didn't taste very good, but he chewed it down, following each mouthful with a swig of water. He certainly didn't have to conserve his supply of water any longer. He crumpled the paper wrapping and started to throw it out the window. Instead, he stuffed it into the bag. He didn't want his first contact with France to be litter.

As he angled in toward Paris at 4,000 feet, he thought how wonderful a plane the *Spirit of St. Louis* was—"Like a living creature, gliding along smoothly, happily, as though a successful flight means as much to it as to me. . . . *We* have made this flight across the ocean, not *I* or *it*.

Soon he picked up the patterned lights of the Paris streets, the Eiffel Tower—he circled it, naturally—then headed northeast toward Le Bourget. He thought he saw the airport, but it seemed terribly close to the city, so he flew past to make sure there wasn't another field farther along. He returned to Le Bourget—it was Le Bourget, all right—and wondered why they had all those floodlights lit, but no beacons, no approach lights, no warning lights. He banked over the field to get an idea what he was landing in, then circled lower. The wind sock showed a gentle wind.

He came in lower. He could see what seemed like a lot of automobiles on a road nearby. What were they doing there? The plane felt funny; he was coming in as slowly as he dared, almost stalling, yet he might very well overshoot the field. He was flying out of the lighted area into unknown, unseen hazards. He side-slipped, held the nose up, finally felt his wheels touch. Should he stay on the ground and possibly run into a building? Or should he gun the engine and take off again for another landing? He chose the earth; the plane rolled more slowly, but it was rolling into darkness. He couldn't see a thing. At last he could turn, and began to taxi over toward the hangars. It was 10:22 P.M. Paris time, thirty-three and a half hours after he had left Roosevelt Field.

Le Bourget had been empty a moment before. Now, suddenly, out of the darkness burst an avalanche, a flood, a torrent of running figures. People. They were spreading all over the field; they would engulf the plane; they might get hurt by the propeller. He cut the engine, hoping the propeller would not be turning over when they reached him. The *Spirit of St. Louis* was resting in the center of Le Bourget Airport.

CHAPTER 6

Legacy

AMERICA'S DECADES

The Nation Plummets into the Abyss of Depression

Robert Goldston

The disastrous stock market crash of 1929 helped plunge the nation into the Great Depression, which dominated the 1930s. President Herbert Hoover, a decent man who organized humanitarian efforts to stabilize European countries earlier in his career, was unable to find a solution to assist his own. It would take another leader, Franklin D. Roosevelt, and a second world war to lift the country from the clutches of the depression.

In his history of the 1930s, *The Great Depression*, historian Robert Goldston clarifies Hoover's efforts to improve the nation's dissolving economy and explains the impact the Great Depression had upon the next decade.

Herbert Hoover was not, either by temperament or conviction, the man who could cope with a severe depression. His personality was a cold one. Josephus Daniels recalled that Hoover "seemed to regard human beings as so many numbers." William Allen White said he was "constitutionally gloomy, a congenital pessimist." Ike Hoover (a long-time White House usher) observed that the White House staff was "glad when they [the Hoovers] were gone." Secretary of State Henry L. Stimson was impressed by Hoover's austerity and lack of humor. During one and a half years of Cabinet meetings, Stimson could recall no occasion on which a joke had been cracked. Private sessions with the President were, he said, "like sitting in a bath of ink."

While the President's personality struck no sparks of human warmth, his convictions were inadequate for the task that faced him. Hoover's was a philosophy of individualism born of the loneliness of Midwestern life before the turn of the century and of his own individualistic struggle for wealth and power. But, it must be emphasized, Hoover's individualism was not the irresponsible brand represented by either Harding corruption or Coolidge indifference. Hoover saw himself as the prophet of a "New Era" (his own campaign phrase) in which businessmen, financiers, and industrialists would voluntarily undertake the responsibility of keeping the economic ship of state afloat, would maintain employment and wages, production and credit in such a way that the entire people would benefit. Government's role was to aid business in every possible way to achieve these voluntary goals, not to interfere by anti-trust suits, directives, taxes, and regulations. Technological efficiency would eventually establish permanent prosperity. And only the nation's business leaders and corporate technicians could bring about this efficiency. Government support for labor, farmers, the poor, or the unemployed would only undermine that individual "get-up-and-go" instinct which was the most valuable part of the American character. Of course, in times of disaster, some people would need help. But this help ought to come from voluntary local relief activities; people's needs ought to arouse generosity in the hearts of their more fortunate fellow citizens—for this, too, was an essential part of the American character. And governmental activity (or labor union activity) which threatened the freedom of businessmen to operate "for the public good" smacked of socialism, which was to Hoover the worst of all evils. Help the top layers of society and you help (even if indirectly) the lowest layers. As for the masses of people, "The crowd only feels," Hoover wrote; "it has no mind of its own which can plan. The crowd is credulous, it destroys, it consumes, it hates, and it dreams—but it never builds."

By the spring of 1930—six months after the Crash—over 4 million Americans were out of work. And the businessmen who were to operate voluntarily for "the public good" were still responding with idiotic incantations to prosperity.

"Things are better today," [November 4, 1929] said Henry Ford, "than they were yesterday." "Never before has American business been as firmly entrenched for prosperity as it is today" [December 10, 1929], said Charles M. Schwab of Bethlehem Steel. "Conditions are more favorable for permanent prosperity than they have been in the past year," added George E. Roberts of the National City Bank. When Hoover asked Andrew Mellon, Secretary of the Treasury, what he would do about the spreading depression, that multimillionaire tax evader responded, "Liquidate labor, liquidate stocks, liquidate the farmers, liquidate real estate." But Hoover did not feel he could adopt this "final solution" to the problem of the poor. Instead he called conferences. Conferences of businessmen, conferences of industrialists, conferences of financiers and bankers. Upon them he tried to urge the necessity of maintaining wages and jobs, and from them he wrung promises to maintain business as usual, as long as possible. Furthermore, Hoover asked the Federal Reserve Board to lower discount rates so as to make credit available to businessmen, and ordered the Farm Board to investigate the possibility of artificially maintaining prices for farm products. And early in 1930 Hoover backed the Smoot-Hawley Tariff Bill in Congress. This bill, which was promptly passed, raised American tariffs on foreign goods so high that it virtually ensured that foreign nations would never

President Herbert Hoover

again be able to buy in the American market (they could not earn the dollars to do so). It also would bring about retaliatory tariffs against American exports. On March 7, 1930, Hoover proclaimed: "All evidences indicate that the worst effects of the crash upon unemployment will have been passed during the next sixty days." On May 1, 1930, the President said: "I am convinced we have now passed the worst." Will Rogers [humorist and political commentator] commented, "There has been more 'optimism' talked and less practiced than at any time during our history."

And his comment was accurate. Despite pledges to the government, the nation's business leaders saw no way to save themselves but to cut production. Some tried by cutting the work week to spread out available work among more laborers; others tried to keep their employees on by reducing wages. But the truth was that consumption had slumped tremendously. No one was buying, and more and more factories and businesses were closing their doors. During the spring of 1930 breadlines began to appear in New York, Chicago, and other American cities: long lines of patient, hopeless, humiliated men shuffling forward slowly to receive a bowl of watery soup and a crust of bread from charity kitchens, Salvation Army halls, and local relief agencies. In New York the number of families on relief was 200 per cent greater in March, 1930, than it had been in October, 1929.

Throughout the country, depression and the fear of it slowly but surely entwined icy tentacles around American society. William Green, President of the American Federation of Labor, reported that in Detroit "the men are sitting in the parks all day long and all night long, hundreds and thousands of them, muttering to themselves, out of work, seeking work." Sometimes it came abruptly—the dismissal notice in the pay envelope. Often it came slowly. First there would be a slowdown—perhaps only three days of work every week; then, sometimes, a wage cut; then, inevitably, the lay-off. . . .

In Philadelphia, in 1930, children starved. In Chicago,

bands of homeless men slept on the lower level of Wacker Drive, huddled together around camp fires built of straw and scraps, against the cold. In New York, thousands of men, some with families, some without, began building little huts for themselves out of cardboard cartons or scraps of tin and wood along the Hudson River, below Riverside Drive. Gangs of desperate men were seen in towns and cities across the nation, fighting over choice morsels at municipal garbage dumps.

During the autumn of 1930, the Northwest apple growers had an inspiration. Since they had a large crop of apples, and no one to buy them, they organized their distribution among the jobless for resale on street corners. Thus appeared the shivering, ragged apple sellers in American cities. Standing over pitiful wooden crates of apples, they silently beseeched the more fortunate passerby to buy an apple—for a nickel, but perhaps for more, if the buyer was charitable. The Bureau of the Census classified these half-begging apple sellers as "employed." President Hoover later insisted: "Many persons left their jobs for the more profitable one of selling apples." So desperate were conditions in New York City that from faraway Africa, the natives of the Cameroons collected $3.77 which they sent to the city authorities for "the relief of the starving." By midwinter (a harsh and severe winter) of 1931, over eight million Americans were unemployed. By December, 1931, unemployment reached 13.5 million—almost one third of the American labor force. What were these people to do?

Many of them hit the road. Accompanied by families, in broken-down old cars or, increasingly, alone, jobless workers roamed from town to town, city to city, state to state, seeking work that was unavailable. The transient knew in his bones that things were no better ahead than they had been behind, but somehow the movement itself seemed positive. It was something, however hopeless a thing, to do.

These migrants were not traditional hobos. The old-time hobo, following the sun, did as little work as possible. His object was to reduce his needs so that he would not have to work. But Depression migrants were desperately seeking work. No one ever knew how many transients appeared during the Depression, but estimates run to one million. The Southern Pacific Railroad, for example, reported that it had ejected nearly 700,000 vagrants from its trains (box-cars) in 1932. . . .

In some respects it was the children who suffered most. Millions of them dropped out of school, hundreds of thousands lost their families. And while parents starved themselves to see that their children got what little food was available, often this was not enough. A Chicago social worker, distressed by a report from Chicago's Children's Memorial Hospital that a child had just died there of starvation, reported in 1932 that children in that city were "cold and hungry and lacking security and developing physical conditions sure to bring on tuberculosis, and other maladies, and mental attitudes sure to bring on delinquency." Child labor, under appalling sweat-shop conditions, reappeared even in the few areas where it was illegal.

And as despair settled like a dark pall over workers in and from the cities, so, too, during 1930 and 1931, it deepened among the nation's farmers. The Wall Street Crash had worsened the plight of farmers who had already been through a decade of diminishing income. Farm prices fell 30 per cent during the first two years of the Depression. Corn sold for 15 cents a bushel, cotton and wool went for 5 cents a pound, hogs brought 3 cents, and beef 2.5 cents a pound. And farmers didn't know what to do about it—except keep production up, or actually increase it, thereby adding to the slide in prices. Industry could always cut back production to maintain prices, but in 1929 and 1930 farmers feared to cut back production: it required every scrap of produce they could raise just to keep them going at those prices. Farm income, nationwide, fell by 33 per cent from 1929 to 1931.

But the farmer's debts did not fall. Both his taxes and his mortgages had been figured and assumed during the twenties, when farm prices were higher. A farmer who had borrowed, for example, $1,000 on a mortgage when his cotton sold for 15 cents a pound owed, in effect, 6,666 pounds of cotton, but when suddenly the bottom fell out and cotton was worth 5 cents a pound he owed almost 20,000 pounds of cotton. Furthermore, many of the banks which ultimately owned farm mortgages had taken heavy losses either through loans or speculation on the stock market. They could afford less and less to postpone foreclosures.

The countryside showed it. Fences sagging in disrepair, fields unplowed, worn-out farm machinery, unpainted buildings, starving animals. Some farmers found it cheaper to burn crops than to pay to have them hauled to market. William Allen White wrote, "Every farmer, whether his farm is under mortgage or not, knows that with farm products priced as they are today, sooner or later he must go down."

When he did go down—when the sheriff arrived with the dispossess notice, when the auctioneer arrived to sell off the homestead that had taken generations to build—the farmer joined the flow of aimless vagrants heading down roads leading nowhere. He didn't know what had hit him. Something had gone wrong among the money men back East, and he'd never trusted them anyhow. But this time it looked as if they meant to finish him off. The American farmer during 1930 and 1931 must have been grimly amused to see Red Cross food centers sprouting across some of the richest agricultural land in the world to pass out food to starving farmers and their families.

As the second winter of depression deepened, the local relief organizations in cities and towns began to run out of money. Most cities had no regular relief organization. Private charities and public poorhouses had generally been competent to care for those who were out of work. During normal times the unemployed were, by and large, the unemployable. And they were treated as charity cases. But private charity could not cope with the flood of starving people which engulfed the nation during 1931. Many towns and cities had organized public relief programs in 1930, but local taxes and other financial resources were not enough to provide more than a bare subsistence for the masses who were now in need. It seemed that only the federal government could provide the necessary help if thousands of people were not to starve.

But President Hoover remained firmly wedded to his conviction that federal aid was federal interference, that federal relief funds for the states would somehow undermine local initiative. Therefore Hoover inaugurated an advertising campaign carried out by his Organization on Unemployment Relief, to promote private and local charity. The new organization was headed by Walter S. Gifford, President of the American Telephone and Telegraph Company. So slight were the Organization's efforts on behalf of the unemployed that when, in January, 1932, Gifford was questioned by a Senate investigating committee, he had to admit that he did not even know how many people were unemployed, or what the resources were with which local agencies could meet the problem. Nobody had informed Mr. Gifford that New York City, the richest in the country, could now afford to give only $2.39 per week for relief to an entire family. He seemed unaware that huge areas of the country had no relief agencies whatsoever. But he remained convinced of one thing: federal aid would be a positive disservice to the needy.

American businessmen generally agreed with Gifford, although some were beginning to have doubts. Most continued to issue ridiculous statements about imminent prosperity. Most thought that this depression, like so many before it, would soon blow over. Most echoed the sentiments expressed by the United States Chamber of Commerce, which attempted to reassure the country by pointing out that after all, "we have had at least seventeen of these cycles of depression in the last 120 years." Charles Mitchell of the National City Bank remarked, "So long as we live under a system of individual liberty, we are bound to have fluctuations in business." And Albert Wiggin of the Chase National Bank, when asked by Senator Robert La Follette whether there was no way to prevent depressions, replied: "There is no commission or any brain in the world that can prevent it." Shocked, La Follette demanded to know if Wiggin thought the capacity for human suffering was unlimited. "I think so," the banker answered.

Businessmen also opposed relief for the needy. To them it smacked of England's infamous "dole." If government, whether local, state, or federal, undertook to keep people from starving, then those people would grow lazy and, presumably flourishing on their bowl of cabbage soup every day, refuse to work for wages. But this was only in theory. In practice, businessmen were not heartless ogres. They were usually the heaviest contributors to community relief projects. And many attempted to come up with schemes by which private enterprise could help the unemployed.

For example, John B. Nichols, President of the Oklahoma Gas Utilities Company, suggested in a letter to his friend Patrick J. Hurley, Hoover's Secretary of War, that restaurants be asked to dump food left on plates into five-gallon containers. The local unemployed could then earn these five-gallon containers of garbage by chopping wood for local farmers. Hurley was very much impressed by this scheme and urged it upon the government. But not even Hoover would go that far.

Businessmen were confused, to say the least. Nothing in either their personal or corporate past experience had equipped them to understand what was happening to the nation, much less to suggest remedies for it. Feeling uneasily that they ought to appear optimistic, they kept uttering clichés. Charles M. Schwab of Bethlehem Steel advised, "Just grin, keep on working." Walter Gifford offered this thought: "What we must have is faith, hope and charity." Myron C. Taylor of United States Steel thought: "We shall have learned something of high importance [out of the Depression]. It is too soon to say just what we are learning." Sewell Avery of Montgomery Ward and Company admitted sadly: "To describe the causes of this situation is rather beyond my capacity. I am unfortunate in having no friends that seem to be able to explain it clearly to me." On the other hand, Daniel Willard, of the Baltimore and Ohio Railroad, was clear about one thing; "I would steal before I would starve," he announced.

Some businessmen and their friends, however, were beginning to wonder about the system which had made them wealthy. President Nicholas Murray Butler of Columbia University, an arch conservative, warned in 1931 that planning in industry was now essential. "Gentlemen," he pointed out, "if we wait too long, somebody will come forward with a solution that we may not like." Paul Mazur of Lehman Brothers agreed. "The tragic lack of planning that characterizes the capitalistic system," he wrote, "is a reflection upon the intelligence of everyone. . . ."

The nation's intellectuals agreed with that conclusion. Long disowned by a society they had detested when it was wealthy, American intellectuals saw the crash and the onslaught of depression as a judgment on years of greed and a proof that the American system was basically rotten. It seemed that H.L. Mencken [newspaper reporter] had been right about democracy, that it "consists almost wholly of the discovery, chase and scotching of bugaboos. The statesman becomes, in the last analysis, a mere witch-hunter, a glorified smeller and snooper, eternally chanting 'Fe, Fi, Fo, Fum.'" As for Congressmen, Mencken dismissed the typical people's representative as "A knavish and preposterous nonentity, half way between a kleagle of the Ku Klux Klan and a grand worthy of the Knights of Zoroaster. It is such vermin who make the laws of the United States." And democracy itself was meaningless; "All the known facts lie flatly against it," Mencken proclaimed. Mencken was not speaking for himself alone; he expertly voiced the unspoken opinions of many intellectuals. And their opinions were an advance barometric warning of public opinion in general.

As time went on and depression worsened and the federal government continued to sit on its hands, people were growing angry, dangerously angry. Incidents were multiplying across the nation. On March 19, 1930, 1,100 men standing in a breadline in New York seized two truckloads of bread and rolls as they were being delivered to a nearby hotel. In Henryetta, Oklahoma, in July, 1931, three hundred jobless men threatened to beat up and kill local storekeepers unless they were given food; they got their food. In Detroit, in 1932, it was a common occurrence for unemployed men to smash shop windows at night and loot stores. In that same city, two families who resisted eviction by shooting and killing a landlord were later acquitted of murder by sympathetic jurors.

Revolution was not imminent, except in the imaginations of a few hopeful radicals, in 1931. But as humorist Will Rogers warned, "You let this country go hungry, and they are going to eat no matter what happens to Budgets, Income Taxes or Wall Street values. Washington mustn't forget who rules when it comes to a showdown." Lillian Wald, founder and director of New York City's famed Henry Street Settlement House, demanded: "Have you ever heard a hungry child cry? Have you seen the uncontrollable trembling of parents who have gone half starved for weeks so that the children may have food?" But Herbert Hoover had not, in fact, heard or seen such things in America. "Nobody," he told newspaper reporters, "is actually starving. The hobos, for example, are better fed than they have ever been. One hobo in New York got ten meals in one day." Remarks like that have been, historically, in other countries, the building blocks of revolution. Could it happen in America? Will Rogers was a perceptive observer; it could. As 1931 drew to its disastrous end, the atmosphere of America was thick with despair and anger, heavy with muttered threats.

A Merciful End to a Failed Experiment

Herbert Asbury

Prohibition was doomed because from the beginning most Americans refused to obey the law. Their neighborhood bar and glass of beer, or their glass of wine with meals were too much a part of the American social fabric to be eliminated through legislation. The nation's leaders gradually recognized that Prohibition's time had passed and let it slide out of sight in the early 1930s.

One of the top historians of the Prohibition era, Herbert Asbury, explains how the opponents of Prohibition gained support as the 1920s evolved.

D uring the struggle over the ratification of the Eighteenth Amendment and the passage of the Volstead Act, the liquor interests of the country fought alone except for sporadic and ineffectual assistance from a few hotelkeepers' associations and real-estate boards, and the American Federation of Labor, which demanded modification of the act to permit the manufacture and sale of beer. Millions of Americans were opposed to prohibition but were unorganized and lacked spokesmen to present their side of the question. . . .

It was not until the summer of 1919, after forty-five states had ratified the Eighteenth Amendment and so made it a part of the Constitution, that any sort of public protest was heard. Then a few mass meetings were held in New York and elsewhere; twenty thousand people marched through the streets of Baltimore clamoring for beer; ten thousand union men demonstrated for three hours before the Capitol at Washington; resolutions demanding beer were adopted by the American Federation of Labor and the Confederated Labor Union of New York; and a small group of anti-prohibitionists tried to promote a national "Daisy Day," when everyone opposed to prohibition should wear a daisy in his buttonhole. Nothing came of any of these outbursts. They quickly subsided, and were soon forgotten.

Organized opposition to prohibition was slow getting under way. The Association Against the Prohibition Amendment was founded in 1918 by Captain William H. Stayton, who had been active in the affairs of the Navy League, and was incorporated in the District of Columbia in December 1920. Captain Stayton headed the association until 1928, when he became chairman of the Board of Directors and was succeeded as president by Henry H. Curran, who had held many public offices, among them that of Commissioner of Immigration at the Port of New York. The Crusaders, composed of young men, appeared early in 1922, and in 1923 the Moderation League and the Constitutional Liberty League of Massachusetts took the field. Most of the initial financing of these and other groups of lesser importance was provided by the brewers and distillers. None accomplished much until 1926, when they combined with the American Federation of Labor to present evidence to a congressional committee which held hearings on the problems of enforcement.

Between 1927 and 1930 the American Legion came out for repeal and the labor unions abandoned their long-standing demand for beer and urged that the Eighteenth Amendment be wiped out. The Voluntary Committee of Lawyers, incorporated in New York in 1927, opposed the amendment on the ground that it violated the Bill of Rights and was "inconsistent with the spirit and purpose of the

Constitution." The Bar Association of New York adopted resolutions in 1928 calling for the repeal of the amendment and the return of the whole liquor question to the states. Similar action was taken by the bar associations of New Jersey, Detroit, St. Louis, San Francisco, and Portland. The American Bar Association in 1930 adopted a repeal resolution by a vote of 13,779 to 6,340. The last of the important organizations which fought for repeal was the Women's Organization for National Prohibition Reform, which was founded in May 1929 by Mrs. Charles H. Sabin, wife of a New York banker. Mrs. Sabin, who was the first woman member of the Republican National Committee, resigned to become president of the W.O.N.P.R., the membership of which increased from seventeen in 1929 to 1,326,862 in 1932.

The appearance of Mrs. Sabin and her crusading ladies in the prohibition arena was particularly shocking to the drys, because it violated the ancient tradition that women were always on the side of the Lord, and the prohibitionists were as firmly convinced as ever that their cause was the cause of God. Prominent dry leaders assailed the Sabin cohorts in characteristic terms. Dr. Mary Armour, president of the Georgia W.C.T.U., and widely known as "The Georgia Cyclone," was quoted in the New York *American* of May 30, 1929, as saying, "As to Mrs. Sabin and her cocktail-drinking women, we will out-live them, out-fight them, out-love them, out-talk them, out-pray them, and out-vote them." Dr. D. Leigh Colvin, prominent in the councils of the Prohibition party and later its candidate for President, described the members of the W.O.N.P.R. in the New York *Times* of May 23, 1932, as "Bacchantian maidens, parching for wine—wet women who, like the drunkards whom their program will produce, would take pennies off the eyes of the dead for the sake of legalizing booze."

All of the anti-prohibition organizations which entered the fight during the first half dozen years of the dry era advocated modification of the Volstead Act, and not repeal of the Eighteenth Amendment. A vast majority of both wets and drys were inclined to agree with Senator Morris Sheppard of Texas, author of the dry amendment, that "there is as much chance of repealing the Eighteenth Amendment as there is for a hummingbird to fly to the planet Mars with the Washington Monument tied to its tail." And with Clarence Darrow, a famous Chicago lawyer and prominent wet, who said, "The repeal of the Eighteenth Amendment is pure nonsense. One might as well talk about taking his summer vacation on Mars." Very few, if any, wet leaders had anything good to say about that old devil whiskey, but they talked a lot of pious nonsense about the glories of beer and light wines, predicting that if unlimited quantities of these could be made available, the American people would forget their appetite for hard liquors. And all the wets who could make themselves heard above the tumult of propaganda reacted with horror at every suggestion that the saloon might eventually return; they pledged their very souls to prevent such a calamity. However, many thought it should be possible for the people, especially the workingman who was perishing without his legal beer, to buy liquor by the drink. Nobody ever figured out how this could be accomplished except through the medium of something very similar to the saloon.

The first organization to abandon the double talk about modification and revision of the Volstead Act and demand outright destruction of the Eighteenth Amendment seems to have been the Women's Committee for Repeal of the Eighteenth Amendment, which in 1927, "tired of taking a halfway position," changed its name from the Women's Committee for Modification of the Volstead Act. The idea of repeal, however, had been advanced before. In 1924 Edward A. Alexander, a New York lawyer, began urging Democratic leaders to ask Congress to submit a repeal amendment to state conventions elected by popular vote, a method of amending the Constitution which had not been used for more than a hundred years. The New York Democratic organization, shuddering at the political perils involved, refused to have anything to do with Alexander's suggestion, but a resolution embodying his proposal was introduced in Congress in 1926 by Senator Edward I. Edwards of New Jersey. A somewhat similar measure, providing for a nation-wide referendum on the liquor question, was introduced by Senator Walter E. Edge, also of New Jersey. Neither got out of committee and, except for a few newspaper stories, attracted little attention, although Senator Edge's resolution was approved, with amendments, by Senator William E. Borah of Idaho, a powerful dry leader.

By the middle 1920s prohibition had become almost a national obsession; it overshadowed all other questions. The people talked of little else. Books and pamphlets about it rolled off the presses by the thousands. It was a rare magazine which didn't publish at least one article about it in every issue. The newspapers were filled with it; one New York paper alone printed almost seventeen thousand prohibition items in eight years, and a large proportion were on the front pages. As we have seen, the federal courts and prosecution agencies devoted a disproportionate amount of time to it. As William Howard Taft had predicted, it was the principal issue in every election campaign. To state and municipal officials it was a continuing headache. Mayor William E. Dever of Chicago spoke for many when he told a congressional committee in 1926, "It is an everyday—yes, an hourly—difficulty with us in Chicago . . . our attention is engrossed from morning until night with this particular subject. It is almost impossible to give anything like good government along general lines, this one subject presses so strongly upon our attention. . . . I find myself immersed in it, to the very great damage of the city, from morning until night.". . .

Secure in their Panglossian dreamworld, the drys ignored the plain fact that a nation-wide shift of public sentiment was in progress. It was clearly shown in official referendums, of which nineteen were held in eleven states between 1920 and 1929; and in numerous unofficial polls conducted by magazines, newspapers, labor unions, and other organizations. The largest of the latter were those of the *Literary Digest* in 1922 and the Newspaper Enterprise Association in 1926. In the *Digest* poll 922,382 ballots were counted, and 61.4 per cent were for modification of the Volstead Act. The N.E.A. was assisted by 326 newspapers in forty-seven states, and 1,747,630 votes were received. Of these, 81.1 per cent favored repeal or modification. In both polls a large majority were for modification. Ten of the official referendums were on the repeal or enactment of state laws, and six were won by the drys. Nine dealt with the Eighteenth Amendment and the Volstead Act— eight with modification and one with outright repeal—and the wets won seven, some by large majorities. In New York the vote was 1,763,070 to 598,484 in favor of an appeal to Congress for modification of the Volstead Act, and in Illinois a similar proposition carried by a majority of 284,039. Eight states, with one fourth of the country's population, voted on various aspects of the liquor problem in 1926, and 59.4 per cent of the ballots cast were wet.

The Association Against the Prohibition Amendment and other wet organizations made a great to-do about these polls and referendums in their propaganda, but the dry leaders insisted that they were worthless, since they were not binding upon Congress, where the final decisions were made. The Anti-Saloon League accused the newspapers and magazines of rigging their polls, of permitting thousands to vote two or three times, and of manipulating the final figures. The drys declared that they had boycotted all of the referendums except the ones in which they were victorious, and called attention to the fact that despite the growth of wet sentiment, the people continued to elect dry congressmen. Wayne B. Wheeler, general counsel of the Anti-Saloon League, said that each of the four Congresses chosen after the ratification of the Eighteenth Amendment had been drier than its predecessor. Even in the "wet year" of 1926, while the wets gained about twenty-five seats in the House of Representatives, the drys elected twenty-nine out of thirty-five senators. The drys maintained large majorities in both houses until 1932; the wet strength never exceeded 30 per cent, and most of the time was less than 20 per cent. The wets attributed their failure to gain more of a foothold in Washington to the refusal of Congress to reapportion the country after the 1920 census, as required by law. A more probable reason, however, was that the people were not yet ready to vote nationally as they talked and voted locally, a political phenomenon not uncommon in this country. There can be no doubt, however, that millions of Americans were getting very tired of the dry paradise.

The most important development of the mid-twenties was the radical change in the character of the wet leadership. The brewers and the distillers had faded into the background, and were replaced by railroad presidents, bankers, industrialists, businessmen, lawyers, educators, and authors. To read the names of the directors of the Moderation League, the Association Against the Prohibition Amendment, and similar organizations was almost to call the roll of American financial, industrial, and business power. The annual report of the Association Against the Prohibition Amendment for 1929 listed 227 members of its national board of directors, almost every one of whom was a rich man and a prominent figure in American life. Among them were fifteen of the twenty-eight directors of General Motors Corporation, and such nationally known tycoons as General W.W. Atterbury, president of the Pennsylvania Railroad; Pierre, Lammot, and Irénée du Pont; John J. Raskob, a Du Pont vice-president and chairman of the Democratic National Committee; Edward S. Harkness, a director of the New York Central Railroad and of the Southern Pacific; Arthur Curtiss James, capitalist and a director of a dozen corporations; Nicholas F. Brady, capitalist; Henry B. Joy, former president of the Packard Motor Car Company; Charles H. Sabin, of the Guaranty Trust Company; Newcomb Carlton, president of Western Union; Haley Fiske, president of the Metropolitan Life Insurance Company; Elihu Root, noted lawyer and former Secretary of State; and Percy S. Straus, president of R.H. Macy & Company.

On the other hand, the dry leadership had deteriorated.

The Rev. Earl L. Douglass, in his *Prohibition and Common Sense,* published in 1931, described it as "limping, to say the least. There are many able leaders among the drys," he continued, "but there is also a great lack of unity. . . . There has not existed among them that spirit of unity and co-operation which victory requires. There has been too much talk and too little action. Conferences of dry workers have too often resulted in nothing but the passage of resolutions." The drys suffered an irreparable loss when Wayne B. Wheeler died in 1927; they were never able to replace him, and his sagacious counsel and unusual qualities of leadership were sorely missed. Bishop James Cannon, Jr., who as chairman of the legislative committee of the national Anti-Saloon League was already an important figure, became the recognized leader of the drys, but he was no Wheeler. . . .

Moreover, once the Eighteenth Amendment had been safely tucked away in the Constitution, the drys had considerable difficulty collecting money. For this there were three main reasons—the decline of their organizations in hustle and efficiency, the apathy of prominent drys who still thought that the battle for a boozeless America had been won in 1920, and the defection of wealthy contributors who had gone over to the wet side. Pierre du Pont, for example, had been an ardent prohibitionist until about 1925, when he became active in the work of the Association Against the Prohibition Amendment. Thanks to du Pont and many other rich men who gave freely, the wets had plenty of money, and their astute leaders eventually built up a propaganda machine which was at least as powerful as the steam roller which the Anti-Saloon League had used to force the Eighteenth Amendment through Congress and the state legislatures. The drys professed to be terribly shocked at the huge sums spent by the wets, and were horror-stricken when an annual report of the association showed expenditures of $818,723.41 in a single year. As a matter of fact, this was less than half as much as the Anti-Saloon League annually poured into propaganda and political activity in the days when the drys were sweeping everything before them.

In other respects, also, the drys were at a disadvantage. Since it was impossible for them to admit that anything could be wrong with either the Eighteenth Amendment or the Volstead Act, they were compelled to defend the status quo; and, by inference, the bootlegger, the speakeasy, the rumrunner, and all the other evils with which the country had been afflicted since the ratification of the amendment. When the wet propagandists published official government reports and figures showing the extent of the illicit liquor traffic and the crime and corruption which made it possible, the drys could only scream that the booze hounds were lying, or take refuge in the feeble argument that prohibition was a great social experiment and deserved a fair trial. When the drys produced famous economists who proved that the prosperity of the 1920s was due entirely to prohibition, the wets trotted out even more renowned calculators who proved that the drys didn't know what they were talking about and were possibly a little insane. None of these flights of economic fancy were much more reliable than the estimates on liquor consumption. . . .

It was the depression which finally broke the back of the dry camel. The wets exploited this national disaster to the utmost. Their trained economists shouted that it was altogether due to prohibition, and who was to prove that it wasn't? In every conceivable medium of propaganda the wets belabored the obvious facts that legalizing liquor would create thousands of much-needed jobs and greatly increase dwindling federal revenues. These arguments helped to convert many politicians who had hitherto been true to their dry principles; they held the belief, later shown to be somewhat naïve, that what the government didn't have the government couldn't spend. It was clear within six months after the Wickersham Commission had made its report that the Eighteenth Amendment was surely headed for oblivion; the only question was, when? The end came considerably quicker than almost anyone had anticipated. The

Democrats were so confident that early in March 1931 Alfred E. Smith and John J. Raskob tried to compel the party's national committee to make a public announcement demanding the immediate repeal of the amendment. They were stopped by Franklin D. Roosevelt, who contended that it was too early for the party to commit itself. Nobody doubted, however, that when the Democratic convention met in 1932 it would adopt a repeal plank. And so it did, unanimously and amid great disorder, with boos and hisses for the few dry delegates who tried to protest. The plank said, "We favor repeal of the Eighteenth Amendment," and demanded that Congress immediately submit a repeal amendment to state conventions elected by popular vote. Safeguards were urged to prevent the return of the saloon, and to enable the dry states to protect their territories from the inroads of the liquor traffic. The Republican convention wasn't quite so bold; it didn't specifically commit the party or its candidate to repeal. Otherwise the Republican plank was the same as that of the Democrats. What most of the voters seemed to remember, however, was what Roosevelt said when he made his dramatic appearance at the Democratic convention to accept the nomination. "I say to you," he shouted, "that from this date on, the Eighteenth Amendment is doomed!"

President Roosevelt took the ax to prohibition as soon as he entered the White House, issuing an executive order which reduced the appropriation of the Prohibition Bureau from $8,440,000 to $3,600,000 and that of the Bureau of Industrial Alcohol from $4,000,000 to $2,500,000. Nine days after his inauguration the President asked Congress to modify the Volstead Act to permit the manufacture and sale of beer with an alcoholic content of not more than 3.2 per cent. Congress immediately did so, and the new law became effective on April 7, 1933. Once more beer trucks rumbled through the streets without gangster escorts, and thousands of speakeasies flung their doors wide and became legal beer saloons. Meanwhile Congress had passed a resolution submitting a repeal amendment to state conventions, the Senate on February 17 and the House on February 20, 1933. The fight for delegates to these conventions began at once, although the dry forces were so demoralized that they didn't put up much of a fight. A great deal of the credit for hurrying things along, and for getting out the vote, was given to the "Bacchantian maidens" of the Women's Organization for National Prohibition Reform, who scurried about the country by the hundreds of thousands. On April 10 the first state convention was held in Michigan, and the repeal amendment was ratified unanimously. Utah, the thirty-sixth state, voted for ratification by three to two on November 7, and on December 5 the convention made it official. The Twenty-first Amendment thus became a part of the Constitution, and the noble experiment was at an end.

When President Roosevelt signed the proclamation notifying the country that repeal had been ratified, he said, "I ask the wholehearted co-operation of all our citizens to the end that this return of individual freedom shall not be accompanied by the repugnant conditions that obtained prior to the adoption of the Eighteenth Amendment, and those that have existed since its adoption. . . . I ask especially that no state shall by law or otherwise authorize the return of the saloon either in its old form or in some modern guise."

Well, of course, there are now no "saloons" in the United States. Instead there are bars, taverns, grills, and cocktail lounges. But by and large it is the same old rose with the same old smell. Anyone who will walk along Bourbon Street in New Orleans, North Clark and South State streets in Chicago, and any of several streets in New York, and observe what the seller of liquor-by-the-drink is doing with his second chance, is almost bound to recall one of Will Rogers's famous sayings:

"The poor dumb clucks. They ain't learned a thing!"

Chronology

1920

January 16—The Eighteenth Amendment goes into effect and brings in Prohibition.

March 28—Movie stars Douglas Fairbanks and Mary Pickford are married in Los Angeles.

May 5—Nicola Sacco and Bartolomeo Vanzetti are arrested for murder in Massachusetts.

August 26—Ratification of the Nineteenth Amendment gives women the right to vote.

September 28—A Chicago grand jury indicts eight players of the Chicago White Sox baseball team for purposely throwing the 1919 World Series.

November 2—Radio station KDKA makes the industry's first radio broadcast; Warren G. Harding is elected president.

1921

March 4—Harding is inaugurated as president.

July 14—Sacco and Vanzetti are found guilty by a Massachusetts jury.

July 21—Aviation promoter Billy Mitchell's aircraft sink a battleship in a demonstration that proves the effectiveness of air power.

August 2—Famed Italian tenor Enrico Caruso dies in Italy.

September 7–8—The first Miss America Pageant is held in Atlantic City, New Jersey.

November 11—President Harding's speech on Veteran's Day, delivered at Arlington National Cemetery in Washington, D.C., is carried by radio to huge crowds in New York and San Francisco.

1922

May 30—The Lincoln Memorial in Washington, D.C., is dedicated.

June 24—More than one thousand members are initiated into the Ku Klux Klan at a rally in Tulsa, Oklahoma.

August 2—Alexander Graham Bell, inventor of the telephone, dies at age seventy-six.

December 1—American archaeologist Howard Carter unearths the tomb of Egyptian ruler King Tutankhamen.

1923
March 3—Henry R. Luce and Briton Hadden publish the first issue of *Time* magazine.

August 2—Harding dies in San Francisco; Vice President Calvin Coolidge is sworn in the following day.

1924
June 15—The Ford Motor Company produces its 10-millionth automobile.

November 4—Coolidge wins election as president.

1925
July 21—John T. Scopes is found guilty of teaching the theory of evolution by a Dayton, Tennessee, jury.

August 8—Forty thousand members of the Ku Klux Klan march by the White House.

September 8—Dr. Ossian Sweet is arrested in Detroit, Michigan, for the murder of Leon Breiner; famed attorney Clarence Darrow, fresh from his work in Tennessee in the Scopes case, travels to Detroit to defend Sweet.

October 28—Billy Mitchell, tireless promoter of American air power, is court-martialed and eventually found guilty of insubordination.

1926
March 16—Scientist Robert H. Goddard launches his first liquid-fueled rocket in Massachusetts.

May 9—Admiral Richard Byrd flies to the North Pole.

August 6—Gertrude Ederle becomes the first woman to swim the English Channel.

August 23—Silent film idol Rudolph Valentino dies.

1927

May 21—Charles A. Lindbergh lands at Le Bourget airfield in Paris to complete his crossing of the Atlantic Ocean.

August 23—Sacco and Vanzetti are executed in Massachusetts's Dedham Prison.

October 6—The first sound motion picture, *The Jazz Singer*, opens.

1928

August 27—The Kellogg-Briand Pact, which outlawed war as an instrument of national policy, is signed in Paris.

November 6—Herbert Hoover wins election as president.

November 18—Walt Disney's *Steamboat Willie*, the first cartoon with sound, opens in New York.

1929

February 14—Seven Chicago criminals are slaughtered in the infamous St. Valentine's Day Massacre, most likely orchestrated by Al Capone to eliminate his rivals.

October 29—The stock market collapses on a day known as Black Tuesday; the event starts the downward path to the Great Depression.

For Further Reading

Frederick Lewis Allen, *Only Yesterday: An Informal History of the Nineteen-Twenties*. New York: Harper & Row, 1931.

Kenneth Allsop, *The Bootleggers*. London: Arlington House, 1968.

Herbert Asbury, *The Great Illusion: An Informal History of Prohibition*. Garden City, NY: Doubleday, 1950.

Judith S. Baughman, ed., *American Decades, 1920–1929*. Detroit: Gale Research, 1996.

David M. Chalmers, *Hooded Americanism: The History of the Ku Klux Klan*. Durham, NC: Duke University Press, 1987.

Jonathan Daniels, *The Time Between the Wars*. Garden City, NY: Doubleday, 1966.

Burke Davis, *The Billy Mitchell Affair*. New York: Random House, 1967.

Editors of Time-Life Books, *This Fabulous Century: Volume III, 1920–1930*. New York: Time-Life Books, 1969.

Philip S. Foner, *History of the Labor Movement in the United States*. Volume IV. New York: International Publishers, 1965.

John Hope Franklin, *From Slavery to Freedom: A History of Negro Americans*. New York: Alfred A. Knopf, 1974.

Elizabeth Frost and Kathryn Cullen-DuPont, *Women's Suffrage in America: An Eyewitness History*. New York: Facts On File, 1992.

John Kenneth Galbraith, *The Great Crash, 1929*. Boston: Houghton Mifflin, 1961.

Ray Ginger, *Six Days or Forever?: Tennessee v. John Thomas Scopes*. Chicago: Quadrangle Books, 1958.

Erica Hanson, *A Cultural History of the United States Through the Decades: The 1920s*. San Diego: Lucent Books, 1999.

Isabel Leighton, ed., *The Aspirin Age, 1919–1941*. New York: Simon and Schuster, 1949.

William E. Leuchtenburg, *The Perils of Prosperity, 1914–1932*.

Chicago: University of Chicago Press, 1958.

George E. Mowry, ed., *The Twenties: Fords, Flappers, and Fanatics*. Gloucester, MA: Prentice-Hall, 1963.

David Nevin, *Architects of Air Power*. Alexandria, VA: Time-Life Books, 1981.

William Preston Jr., *Aliens and Dissenters: Federal Suppression of Radicals, 1903–1933*. Cambridge, MA: Harvard University Press, 1963.

Francis Russell, *The Shadow of Blooming Grove: Warren G. Harding in His Times*. New York: McGraw-Hill, 1968.

Arthur M. Schlesinger Jr., *The Crisis of the Old Order, 1919–1933*. Boston: Houghton Mifflin, 1957.

Irving Settel, *A Pictorial History of Radio*. New York: Grosset & Dunlap, 1960.

David A. Shannon, *Between the Wars: America, 1919–1941*. Boston: Houghton Mifflin, 1965.

Andrew Sinclair, *The Available Man: The Life Behind the Masks of Warren Gamaliel Harding*. New York: Macmillan, 1965.

———, *Prohibition: The Era of Excess*. Boston: Atlantic, 1962.

Edmund Stillman, *The American Heritage History of the 1920s and 1930s*. New York: American Heritage, 1970.

Mark Sullivan, *Our Times: The Twenties*. New York: Charles Scribner's Sons, 1935.

Studs Terkel, *Hard Times*. New York: Pantheon Books, 1970.

Index

Abyssinians, 154
Act 590, 94–95
Adler, Philip A., 76
African Americans
  black pride movement by, 154–55
  cultural and intellectual renaissance of, 159–60
  in Harlem, 157–59
  in labor force, 160–62, 163
  labor unions of, 162–63
  music by, 191–92, 194, 195–96
  northern migration, 70
  progress made by, 14
  on West Indians, 153
  white hostility, toward dignity of, 61
  see also Sweet, Ossian
Air Commerce Act of 1926, 204
airlines, commercial, 203, 204
  see also aviation
air mail, 204
alcoholism, 113, 117
Alexander, Edward A., 236–37
Allen, C.B., 208
Allen, Frederick Lewis, 141
American Bar Association, 235
American Civil Liberties Union (ACLU), 84, 95
American Communist Party, 13
American Federation of Labor, 234
American Metal Bank, 44
anarchists, 100, 101, 108
Anthony, Susan B., 112
Anti-Saloon League, 10, 238, 240–41
Armour, Mary, 235
Armstrong, Louis, 14, 196
Arthur, Urlic, 75
Asbury, Herbert, 118, 233
Association Against the Prohibition Amendment, 234, 238, 239
automobile, 17
  color/horsepower, 201–202
  Ford, 201
  influence on
    railways, 198
    road construction, 202–203
    sexual revolution, 150
    tourism, 202
  manufacturing, 200–201
  as necessity, 199–200
  as status symbol, 202
  tunnel and bridge construction from, 204
aviation, 17–18, 203–205
  see also Lindbergh, Charles A.

Babson, Roger, 49
Bailey, Pearl, 195
Baker, Josephine, 195
Bane, A.C., 117
Bara, Theda, 15–16
Bar Association of New York, 235
Barrett, Clarabelle, 180
baseball, 16, 182, 183
Battling Butler (movie), 177
Beckett, Samuel, 172
Behr, Edward, 131
Benchley, Robert, 138
Berardelli, Alessandro
  murder of, 97–99
  revolver of, 99, 100
Beringer, Bertha, 137
Billingsley, Sherman, 137
Black Renaissance. *See* Harlem
Black Star Line, 155–56
Black Thursday, 53
Black Tuesday, 18
Blake, Eubie, 191–92
Blue Ridge Corporation, 27
blues music, 194–95
Boardman, Fon W., Jr., 197
Boda, Mike, 100
Boedecker, Ken, 208, 209, 210
Borah, William E., 33, 237
Bow, Clara, 15–16
Breiner, Leon, 72, 79
bridges, 203
Brisbane, Arthur, 28
Britton, Nan, 33, 39
Broadway Melody (movie), 171
Broadway musicals, 192
Bronx River Parkway, 203
Brotherhood of Railroad Car Porters, 162
Bruno, Harry, 208, 210–11
Bryan, William Jennings, 73, 112
  death of, 91
  on evolution, 82–83
  on witness stand, 85–89
Buchanan, Pat, 95
Burns, James, 102, 104
Butler Act, 91–92
Byrd, Richard E., 204
Cagney, James, 171
Cane (Toomer), 160
Cannon, Bishop James, Jr., 240
Capone, Al, 9, 11
Carlton, Newcomb, 239
Catholics
  and Klu Klux Klan, 59, 63, 65
Chaplin, Charlie, 16, 164, 166, 172–75

contrasted with Buster Keaton, 172
in talking pictures, 171
children
  during Great Depression, 227
  labor by, 162
  see also youth
Churchill, Winston, 50–51
City Lights (movie), 171
Coacci, Ferruccio, 100
College (movie), 177
Collett, Glenna, 180, 182
Colvin, D. Leigh, 235
commercial airlines, 203, 204
Committee of Fifty, 113
Confederated Labor Union of New
  York, 234
Constitutional Liberty League of
  Massachusetts, 234
Coolidge, Calvin
  on economy, 10
  on Gertrude Ederle, 185
  hands-off approach of, 45–46
  as Harding's running mate, 33
  presidential election of, 44–45
Cops (movie), 169
country music, 194
Cox, James M., 30
Cramer, Charles, 36, 38
Crawford, Joan, 15–16
creationism, 93–95
crime, 11–12
Cullen, Countee, 14
Curb Exchange, 53, 55
Curran, Henry H., 234

Daisy Day, 234
dancing, 143, 145
Daniels, Filmore Watt, 68
Darrow, Clarence
  defending
    African Americans, 72–73
    John Scopes, 83–84
      closing argument, 89–90
      examining Bryan, 85–89
      life after, 92
      reasons for, 83–84
    Ossian Sweet, 73, 75–77
      closing argument, 77–78
      on judge and jury, 73–74
      on not guilty verdict, 80
      on prosecutor's argument, 73–74
      in second trial, 78–80
  on repealing eighteenth amendment,
    236
Darwin, Charles, 96
  see also evolution, teaching
Daugherty, Harry
  corruption by, 34–35, 44

and Harding's presidential nomination,
  31, 33
  resignation, 39
Davis, John W., 45
Day Dreams (movie), 169
Democrats
  on Eighteenth Amendment, 241–42
Dempsey, Jack, 17, 182
Denby, Edwin, 40, 44
dirigibles, 204–205
Disney, Walt, 16
Doheny, Edward L., 40, 41, 43
Don Juan (movie), 170
Dorsey brothers, 196
drugstores, 135
Duffus, Robert L., 59–60
du Pont, Irénée, 239
du Pont, Lammot, 239
du Pont, Pierre, 239, 240

Earhart, Amelia, 204
Eastman, Max, 108
economy, 9–10
  see also stock market
Ederle, Gertrude, 17
  as celebrity, 178–79
  commercial backing of, 185
  emergence of, 181–82
  life after heroic status, 188–89
  physical characteristics, 184
  swimming English Channel, 185–88
  as victory for women, 179–80
  as wholesome, 184–85
Ederle, Margaret, 181
Edison, Thomas Alva, 168
Edwards, Edward I., 133, 237
Eighteenth Amendment, 116, 233–34
  repealing of, 234–37, 241–42
Einstein, Isadore. *See* Izzy
Ellington, Duke, 14, 196
English Channel. *See* Ederle, Gertrude
Europe, James Reese, 192
evolution, teaching
  as constitutional, 92–93
  reconciling concept of God with, 96
  vs. teaching creationism, 93–94
  see also John Scopes trial

Fairbanks, Douglas, 16, 166, 171
Fall, Albert B., 43, 44
  corruptness of, 35
  and Teapot Dome scandal, 40–41
Falzini, Luigi, 101–102
farming
  and African Americans, 161
  and Great Depression, 23, 227–28
  stock market, 50
fashion, 142–43, 145–46

Federal Farm Board, 19
Federal Home Loan Bank Act, 19
Federal Reserve Board
  and Great Depression, 224
  lack of action by, 52, 55
  stock market warning by, 28
film. *See* movies
Film (movie), 172
Fiske, Haley, 239
Fitzgerald, F. Scott, 143–45
flappers, 142–43
football, 16–17
Forbes, Charles, 36, 37–38
Ford, Henry, 224
  and African American migration, 70
  on alcohol use, 113
  auto manufacturing by, 201
Freud, Sigmund, 149–50
Frogge, Johnny, 207
Frost, Stanley, 58–59, 61

Gabourie, Fred, 168
Gallico, Paul, 179, 182, 184
Garrison, William Lloyd, 111
Garvey, Marcus, 14
  black pride movement by, 154–55
  and Black Star Line, 156–57
  and Klu Klux Klan, 155–56
  newspaper of, 159
  prison sentence of, 157
  as West Indian, 153
General, The (movie), 175–77
George Washington Bridge, 203
Gifford, Walter S., 229, 230
Giles, Frank, 105–106
Goddard, Calvin, 103, 104
Goguen, J. Henry, 105
Goldman, Sachs, and Company, 27
Goldman Sachs Trading Corporation, 27
Gold Rush, The (movie), 172–73, 174, 176, 177
Goldston, Robert, 222
Goodman, Benny, 196
gospel music, 194
Graf Zeppelin, 205
Great Depression, the, 19
  American businessmen on, 229–31
  children during, 227
  dating from stock market crash, 23–24
  farming during, 23, 227–28
  Hoover on, 224–25, 232
  influence of, on Prohibition, 241
  intellectuals on, 231
  in midst of prosperity, 22–23
  migrants of, 192–93
  public's reaction against, 231–32
  relief programs during, 228–29
  threat of, 21

movement of people during, 226–27
  unemployment during, 225–26
Great Dictator, The (movie), 171
Guinan, Mary Louise, 138

Hale, Georgia, 174
Hantaman, Nathan, 67–68
Harding, Florence Kling, 31, 33
Harding, Warren Gamaliel
  Alaska trip, 38–39
  Cabinet and administration of, 33–36
  contrasted with Woodrow Wilson, 29–30
  death of, 39
  inadequacy of, 36–37
  Negro blood in, 31
  Ohio origins of, 30–31
  presidential nomination of, 31, 33
  scandals in administration of, 37–38
  as senator, 31
  Teapot Dome scandal under, 39–41, 42–44
Hardy, Oliver. *See* Laurel and Hardy
Harkness, Edward S., 239
Harlem
  African Americans in, 14, 157–59
  intellectualism and culture in, 159–60
Hays, Arthur Garfield, 73
Hays, Will, 43–44
Headwaiters and Sidewaiters Society of Greater New York, 162
Herman, Woody, 196
High and Dizzy (movie), 166–67
highways, 198, 202, 203
Holiday, Billie, 195
Holland Tunnel, 203
Holm, Eleanor, 181
Home to Harlem (McKay), 159, 160
Hoover, Herbert, 33, 204
  gloomy personality of, 222–23
  on Great Crash, 54
  on Great Depression, 224–25, 229, 232
  in Harding's Cabinet, 34
  philosophy of individualism of, 223–24
  on stock market crash, 18–19, 27–28
Hoover, Irwin (Ike), 45, 222
housing segregation. *See* Sweet, Ossian
Hoyt, Edwin P., 47
Hubbard, Dwight, 75
Hudson autos, 201
Hughes, Charles Evans, 33, 34, 37
Hughes, Langston, 14, 159
Hurley, Patrick J., 230

immigrants
  post-WWI feelings on, 61
  see also Sacco, Nicola; Vanzetti, Bartolomeo

Inherit the Wind (movie), 92
Interstate Commerce Commission, 198
investment trusts, 26–27, 49
Iver Johnson Company, 99
Izzy
  accomplishments of, 128
  disguises of, 125–28
  end of enforcement career, 130
  first assignments of, 119–21
  hired as enforcement agent, 119
  ingenuity of, 123–25
  media on, 129
  physical characteristics, 119
  as postal clerk, 118
  teaming with Moe, 121–22
  timing of raids by, 122
  on use of guns, 128, 129
  see also Moe

James, Arthur Curtiss, 239
James, Harry, 196
James, Hilda, 181
jazz music, 193–94, 195–96
Jazz Singer, The (movie), 16, 170
Joachim, Joseph, 191
John Scopes trial
  appeal after, 91–92
  arrest of John Scopes, 84
  Clarence Darrow on, 83–84
  immediate aftermath of, 91
  legacy of, 92–93
  and literal interpretation of Bible, 85–88
  verdict, 89–91
  William Jennings Bryan
    on witness stand in, 88–89
    view of, 82–83
Johnson, Charles S., 157
Johnson, Hiram, 33
Johnson, Robert, 194
Jolson, Al, 16
Jones, Bobby, 17, 182
Jones-White Act, 199
Joplin, Scott, 191
journals. *See* media
Joy, Henry B., 239
J.P. Morgan and Company, 26–27
Jury, Frank, 106

Katzmann, Frederick, 101
Kawin, Bruce F., 164
Keaton, Buster, 164, 168–72
  antiheroism in, 177
  contrasted with Chaplin, 172
  in *The General*, 175–77
Kellerman, Annette, 183–84
Kellogg-Briand Pact of 1928, 12
Keystone Kops, 16
Kieran, John, 182, 183

Klu Klux Klan, 13–14
  beliefs of, 63–65
  corporal punishment by, 67–68
  costume, 63
  growth of, 58–59
  and Marcus Garvey, 155–56
  members, 59–61
  in North, 70
  regulating conduct in community, 65–66
  rise of, 61–63
  use of ostracism, 66–67

labor
  African Americans in, 160–63
  auto industry, 200–201
  during Great Depression, 225, 226
  women in, 14–15, 148–49
LaFollette, Robert M., 44–45, 229–30
Lamont, Thomas, 51
Langdon, Harry, 164
Lardner, Ring, 182
Laurel, Stan. *See* Laurel and Hardy
Laurel and Hardy, 164–66, 171
Lawrence, David, 37
League of Nations, 117
League of Women Voters, 148
Legge, Alexander, 50
legislation, on
  academic freedom, 92
  African American labor, 160–61
  commercial aviation, 204
  Prohibition, 115
    see also Volstead Act
  railways, 198
  ships, 199
  tariffs, 224–25
  teaching creationism, 94–95
  women's fashions, 145–46
Limelight (movie), 172
Lindbergh, Charles A., 18, 204
  arrival in Ireland, 218
  arrival in Paris, 218–20
  arriving at airfield for take-off, 207–208
  arriving in Canada, 212
  communicating with fishermen, 217–18
  decision to leave for flight, 208–10
  flying in an icy cloud, 214–15
  on flying in the night, 214
  flying over St. John's, 213–14
  night before flight of, 206–207
  sleepiness during flight, 211, 212–13, 215–17
  take-off for flight, 210–11
Literary Digest poll, 237–38
Livingstone, Belle, 138
Lloyd, Harold, 164, 166–67

Locke, Alain, 160
Lomax, Alan, 195
London, 56
Lowden, Frank, 33
Lowell, A. Lawrence, 103
Lunceford, Jimmie, 196
Lyman, Deac, 207, 208

Mack, Connie, 113
Mack, Julian, 157
Mack, Marion, 177
magazines
  sex, 151–52
Magrath, George Burgess, 98–99
Malone, Dudley Field, 86–87, 88
Mammoth Oil Company, 40, 43
March, Fredric, 171
Mast, Gerald, 164
Mazur, Paul, 231
McAdoo, William G., 45, 197–98
McCahill, Frank, 208
McCullum, Peter, 100
McGeehan, W.O., 183
media
  African American, 159
  on dangers of alcohol, 113–14
  on Gertrude Ederle, 184–85, 186–87
  on Izzy and Moe, 122, 129, 130
  on John Scopes trial, 89
  polls on Prohibition by, 237–38
  on Prohibition, 237
Mellon, Andrew, 18, 34, 52, 224
Mencken, H.L., 46, 182, 231
Merchant Marine Act of 1920, 199
Merrill, Charles, 53
Metallgesellschaft and Metall Bank, 36, 44
Mickey Mouse, 16
migrants, 226–27
Miller, Glenn, 196
Miller, Thomas W., 36
Mills, Florence, 192
Miss America pageant, 184
Mitchell, Billy, 18
Mitchell, Charles, 49, 229
Mitchell, Gladys, 70
Moberly, Mabs, 195
Model A auto, 201
Model T auto, 201
Moderation League, 234
Modern Times (movie), 171
Moe
  accomplishments of, 128
  disguises of, 125–28
  end of enforcement career, 130
  hired as enforcement agent, 121–22
  ingenuity of raids, 123, 124
  media on, 129

timing of raids, 122
use of guns by, 128–29
Moll, Lester S., 73, 76
movies, 16, 164–65
  Buster Keaton, 168–72
  Harold Lloyd, 166–67
  Laurel and Hardy, 165–66
  sex in, 152
  silent taken over by sound, 170, 171
Mulligan, Ed, 208, 209, 210
Muni, Paul, 171
Murphy, Frank, 73–74, 76, 79, 80, 81
music, 143
  blues, 194–95
  Broadway musicals, 192
  jazz, 193–94

NAACP (National Association for the Advancement of Colored People), 14, 72, 80, 154
Nardo, Don, 82
Nash autos, 201
National Broadcasting Corporation, 17
Negro Factories Corporation, 156
New Negro, The (Locke), 160
Newspaper Enterprise poll, 238
newspapers. *See* media
New York Stock Exchange, 24, 47, 48, 53
Nichols, John B., 230
nineteen twenties. *See* twenties

Orciani, Ricardo, 100, 102
Organization on Unemployment Relief, 229
Origin of Species, The (Darwin), 93
Our Hospitality (movie), 177

Packard autos, 201
Palmer, A. Mitchell, 13
Palmer, Robert, 194
Pan-American Petroleum and Transport Company, 41, 43
Paris
  Lindbergh's arrival in, 218–20
Parmenter, Frederick, 97–98
  murder of, 97–98
Patton, Charley, 194
Pawnshop, The (movie), 173
Pegler, Westbrook, 182
Perrett, Geoffrey, 153
Phillips, Cabell, 21
Pickford, Mary, 15–16, 171
Pins and Needles (musical), 193
Playhouse, The (movie), 168
Porter, Andrew, 133
Proctor, William, 102
Prohibition, 10–11
  becoming law, 132–33

breaking law on, 133–35
 by drugstores, 135
 and manufacturing liquor, 135–36
 speakeasies, 137–39
 vineyards, 136–37
Calvin Coolidge on, 45
and crime, 11–12
defections from movement, 116
end of, 242–43
enforcement of. *See* Izzy; Moe
Great Depression's influence on, 241
history of, 111–12
influence of sexual revolution on, 150
laws implementing, 115
as national obsession, 237
organizations opposing, 234–36
origin, 131–32
power of "wets" vs. "drys," 238–41
public protest against, 233–34
referendums and polls on, 237–38
repealing Eighteenth Amendment,
 235–36, 241–42
support from
 journals, 113–14
 religious reformers, 112
 research and science, 112–13
 socialists, 114–15
triumph of, 116–17
Protestantism
 and Klu Klux Klan, 63, 65
Pullman Company, 162–63

R–34, 205
radio, 17
ragtime music, 191
Railroad Labor Board, 198
railroads, 197–98
Railway Labor Act, 198
raisin cakes, 136–37
Ramsey, H.K., 60
Randolph, Philip, 162
Rascoe, Burton, 51
Raskob, John J., 242
Raulston, Judge, 87, 88, 89
Reconstruction Finance Corporation, 19
Redding, Grover Cleveland, 154
Red Scare, 13
referendums on Prohibition, 237, 238
rent party, 158
Republican National Committee, 43–44
Republican Party
 on Prohibition, 111–12, 242
Rice, Arnold S., 58
Rice, Grantland, 182
Richards, Thomas F., 68
Roach, Hal, 165
Roberts, George E., 224
Robeson, Paul, 14

Robinson, Edward G., 171
Robinson, Tom, 183
Rockne, Knute, 17
Rogers, Will, 225, 232
 on Gertrude Ederle, 179–80
 on John Scopes trial, 89
 on Prohibition, 11
Roosevelt, Franklin D., 19
 on Great Crash, 54, 55
 on Prohibition, 242–43
Root, Elihu, 239
Ross, Ishbel, 189
Ross, Walter S., 206
Rounders, The (movie), 167
Runyon, Damon, 182
Ruse, Michael, 94
Rushing, Jimmy, 196
Russell, Francis, 97
Ruth, Babe, 16, 182

Sabin, Charles H., 235, 239
Sacco, Nicola, 13
 arrest of, 100
 ballistic tests for guns used by, 103–105
 bullet identification for trial of, 102–103
 as guilty, 107
 murders accused of, 97–100
  anarchist motives, 108–109
 pistol found on, 100–101, 106, 107
Sacco-Vanzetti murder case. *See* Sacco,
 Nicola; Vanzetti, Bartolomeo
Safety Last (movie), 167
Sann, Paul, 42
Sawyer, "Doc" Charles, 37
Schulman, Sam, 206
Schwab, Charles M., 224, 230
science, 149
 see also evolution, teaching
Scopes, John T. *See* John Scopes trial
Sennett, Mack, 164
sex, 143–44, 145
 magazines, 151–52
 in movies, 152
 Prohibition revolutionizing, 150
 Sigmund Freud revolutionizing, 149–50
Shaw, George Bernard, 182, 183
Shearer, Norma, 171
Shenandoah (dirigible), 205
Shenandoah Corporation, 27
Shephard, Morris, 235–36
Sherlock Jr. (movie), 169, 170
Shevlin, James, 119
shipbuilding, 199
Shuffle Along (Broadway show), 159,
 191–92
silent film. *See* movies
silos, 136
Sinclair, Harry, 40, 41, 43

Sissle, Noble, 191
Skidmore, Abram, 208, 210–11
Slater, Rexford, 102
Sloan, Alfred P., 54
Smith, Alfred E., 45, 242
Smith, Bessie, 14, 195
Smith, Jess, 35, 36, 38, 44
Smith, Moe. *See* Moe
Smith, Page, 111, 191
smoking, 143
Smoot-Hawley Tariff Bill, 224–25
socialists
  on alcohol use, 114–15
Sons of the Desert (movie), 166
speakeasies, 11, 12, 137–39
Spirit of St. Louis. See Lindbergh,
  Charles A.
sports, 16–17
  and alcohol, 112–13
  Babe Ruth, 182, 183
  women in, 179–80, 181–82
  see also Ederle, Gertrude
Stayton, William H., 234
Steamboat Bill, Jr. (movie), 177
Steamboat Willie (cartoon), 16
Stillman, Edmund, 29
Stimson, Henry L.
  on Herbert Hoover, 222–23
stock market, 10
  brokerage offices for, 26
  buying on margin, 24–25
  Great Crash, 18, 55
    approaching of, 48–50
    deaths over, 54–55
    Hoover's response to, 18–19, 27–28
    London on, 56
    optimism before, 53–54
    plummeting stocks before, 50–51
    restoring investor confidence before,
      51–53
    understanding of, 55–56
  Great Depression, dating from crash
    of, 23–24
  and investment trusts, 26–27
  national mania on, 25
  sensing doom in, 27–28
  volume of trading, 24
Stolley, Richard B., 183
Stone, Irving, 46
Stork Club, 137–38
Straton, John Roach, 122
Strauss, Percy S., 239
Studebaker autos, 201
Swain, Mack, 175
Sweet, Henry, 80, 81
Sweet, Ossian
  after acquittal, 81
  arrest of, 72

found not guilty, 80
move to new home, 71–72
protests against, buying house, 69,
  70–72
trial of
  Clarence Darrow defending, 72–73
  closing arguments for, 77–78
  judge/jury for, 73–74
  prosecution's argument in, 74–75
  second, 78–80
  as witness, 76
  witnesses supporting, 75–76
swimming. *See* Ederle, Gertrude
swing music, 195–96

Taft, William Howard, 31, 237
Taylor, Myron C., 230
Teapot Dome scandal, 39–41, 42–44
This Side of Paradise (Fitzgerald), 143–45
Thompson, William, 103, 104
Tilden, Bill, 17, 182
Tin Pan Alley music, 191–93
Toms, Robert M., 73, 75, 76
Toomer, Jean, 160
transportation
  automobile, 17, 199–203
  aviation, 17–18, 203–204
    see also Lindbergh, Charles A.
  dirigibles, 204–205
  railroads, 197–98
  shipbuilding, 199
Transportation Act of 1920, 198
Tresca, Carlo, 108
trials. *See* John Scopes trial; Sacco,
  Nicola; Sweet, Ossian; Vanzetti,
  Bartolomeo
tunnels, 203
Turner, A.L., 71
twenties
  economy during, 9–10
    see also stock market
  impact of WWI on, 146–47
  influence of WWI on, 61–62
  intolerance during, 13–14
    see also African Americans; Ku Klux
      Klan
  isolationism during, 12–13
  moral codes during, 141–42
  radio during, 17
  trials during. *See* John Scopes trial;
    Sacco, Nicola; Sweet, Ossian;
    Vanzetti, Bartolomeo
  see also music; Prohibition; sports;
    transportation; women
Twenty-First Amendment, 12, 243

unemployment. *See* Great Depression, the
unions, 162

African American, 162
  on Prohibition, 234
United Corporation, 26–27
Universal Negro Improvement
  Association (UNIA), 14, 154–55, 156
U.S. Congress
  "wets" vs. "drys" in, 238–40
U.S. Navy, 12, 40, 199
U.S. Post Office Department, 204
U.S. Steel, 49

Valentino, Rudolph, 16
Van Amburgh, Charles, 102, 104–105
Vanzetti, Bartolomeo, 13
  arrest of, 100
  ballistic tests for guns used by, 103–105
  bullet identification for trial of, 102–103
  as innocent, 107–108
  murders accused of, 97–100
  pistol found on, 101–102
Veteran's Bureau, 37–38
vineyards, 136–37
Volstead, Andrew J., 131–32
Volstead Act, 116
  becoming law, 132–33
  modifying, 235–36, 238, 242
  origin, 131–32
Voluntary Committee of Lawyers, 234
voting, 148

Wadsworth, Lincoln, 99
Wainwright, Helen, 181
Waiting for Godot (play), 172
Wald, Lillian, 232
Walker, James, 55
Wallace, Henry, 34
Wall Street. See stock market
Wall Street Journal (newspaper), 48
Walsh, Tom, 43
Ware, Susan, 178
Warner Brothers, 170
Washington Naval Conference, 12
Waters, Ethel, 195
Waters, Muddy, 195
Waterworks Improvement Association,
  70–71
Watson, Thomas B., 139
Way Out West (movie), 166
Weller, Jac, 106
Welliver, Judson C., 37
West Indians, 153–54
  in Harlem, 159
  see also Garvey, Marcus
Whalen, Grover, 187
Wheeler, Wayne B., 238, 240
White, Frank J., 94
White, Walter, 73
White, William Allen, 37, 222

whites
  and African American labor, 161
  Garveyites on, 155
  in Harlem, 159, 160
  hostility toward African American
    dignity, 61
  protests against Ossian Sweet, 69,
    70–72
Whitney, Richard, 49, 51, 52
Wiggin, Albert, 229
Willard, Daniel, 231
Willard, Frances, 112
Williams, Esther, 181
Williams, Henry Smith, 114
Willis, Helen, 17
Wills, Helen, 17, 182
Wilson, Woodrow
  contrasted with Warren Harding, 29–30
  on Prohibition, 132
Winchell, Walter, 137–38
wine production, 136–37
Woman's Christian Temperance Union,
  113
women
  blues singers, 195
  changing standards of behavior, 143–46
  fashion, 142–43, 145–46
  freedom from household, 148
  in labor force, 148–49, 162
  in politics, 148
  progress made by, 14–16
  on Prohibition, 112, 235
  and sex revolution, 149–52
  in sports, 179–80, 181–82
  swim suits for, 182–84
  war's impact on, 146–47
Women's Committee for Modification of
  the Volstead Act, 236
Women's Committee for the Repeal of
  the Eighteenth Amendment, 236
Women's Organization for National
  Prohibition Reform, 243, 235
Women's Swimming Association (WSA),
  181, 185
Wood, Leonard, 33
Woodhull, Victoria, 112
World War I
  influence on 1920s, 61–62, 146–47
  public opinion on, 12
Wukovits, John F., 69

youth
  changing moral standards for, 142–46
  moral codes of, 141–42
  sexual revolution of, 149–52
  war's impact on, 146–47
  see also children